D0912938

THE GREAT COMPOSERS AND THEIR WORKS

VOLUME I

NICOLAS SLONIMSKY

Edited by Electra Yourke

SCHIRMER BOOKS
AN IMPRINT OF THE GALE GROUP
NEW YORK

For permission to reprint some of the material in this collection, the author gratefully acknowledges the Los Angeles Philharmonic Association and *The Christian Science Monitor.*

Schirmer Books
An Imprint of the Gale Group
1633 Broadway
New York, NY 10019

Library of Congress Catalog Card Number: 99-42808

Set ISBN: 0-02-864955-9
Volume 1: 0-02-865474-9
Volume 2: 0-02-865475-7

Printed in the United States of America

Printing Number

1 2 3 4 5 6 7 8 9 10

Library of Congress Cataloging-in-Publication Data

Slonimsky, Nicolas, 1894–1995
    The great composers and their works / Nicolas Slonimsky ; edited by Electra Yourke.
        p.   cm.
        ISBN 0-02-864955-9 (set). — ISBN 0-02-865474-9 (v. 1). — ISBN 0-02-865475-7 (v. 2)
        1. Music—History and criticism. 2. Music appreciation.
    I. Yourke, Electra.   II. Title.
    ML160.S48   2000
    780'.9—dc21   99-42808
                                                                              CIP

This paper meets the requirements of ANSI/NISO Z.39.48–1992 (Permanence of Paper).

TO DAVID R
—*è ben trovato*

CONTENTS

VOLUME II

XVIII SERGEI PROKOFIEV: His Signature—SRG PRKFV (1891–1953) 563

FOREWORD

THE FOUNDATIONS OF MY FATHER'S LEGACY are the rock-solid volumes found in every music library, the indispensable *Baker's Biographical Dictionary of Musicians* and *Music Since 1900*. Compiling and updating successive editions of these works occupied much of his later life, along with writing his autobiography, *Perfect Pitch*, and a more idiosyncratic "reading dictionary," the *Lectionary of Music*. The *Lexicon of Musical Invective*, vituperative reviews of composers' works since Beethoven was, and is, a classic; in a very different way, so is the *Thesaurus of Scales and Melodic Patterns*, a dizzying musical sourcebook greatly valued by composers, arrangers, and performers.

In addition to these and other volumes, he produced a huge number of short pieces over his entire adult life in the United States, appearing first in the *Boston Evening Transcript* and in musical publications in the 1920s. In succeeding decades, his short writings appeared as program notes, reviews, record liner notes, and newspaper and magazine articles on every conceivable musical topic, especially composers, performers, individual works, musical form and technique, national styles, as well as innumerable musical oddities, anecdotes, and minihistories. Each was written for a single specific purpose and publication—he never wrote on spec.

The Great Composers and Their Works includes a small portion of these miscellaneous writings. With few exceptions, these entries have not previously appeared in book form. Most of the biographies were written for the *Christian Science Monitor* during the 1950s and 1960s, and a substantial number of the entries on individual pieces were written as program notes for the Los Angeles Philharmonic and the Little Orchestra Society. The rest were culled from accumulated clippings and carbon copies dating from the 1920s into the 1980s. This considerable time span, and the publications' differing readerships, accounts for interesting variations in perspective, writing style, and level of musical analysis.

In selecting these composers and these works, I was obviously constrained first of all by what exists and, within that, by what groupings might constitute a relatively balanced and complete "chapter" on a major composer and his (alas, there are no women covered in this volume) works. Considering that these writings were individual and unrelated in origin, the coverage turns out to be remarkably broad, though regrettably missing important composers and compositions. I hope that readers will find the book no less valuable for not being all-inclusive.

This volume is all Slonimsky. Nothing inauthentic has been added, written, rewritten, inserted, substituted, elongated, or otherwise corrupted. Nevertheless, these materials could not always be presented together in full exactly as they originally appeared in a newspaper, concert program, or record liner. Editing consisted primarily of cutting repetitive biographical or analytic material. Present-tense references to composers alive at the time of writing have been changed to the past tense and mention of contemporaneous events deleted.

Although he was relatively diligent about retaining manuscript copies and clippings, my father never reworked them for later use. Indeed, I doubt he ever looked at them again. Every piece was written afresh. In compiling this volume, I often found myself comparing two or even three articles on the same piece of music, all different, all differently interesting, with not so much as a phrase repeated. In some such instances I retained and inserted valuable or especially well-written segments from versions not selected.

My father took delight in dropping indigestible words into his writings, little verbal nuts that must be cracked before being swallowed. I have been merciless in retaining all that appeared in my selections. Accordingly, you are warned that, if the meaning of, for instance, "colubrine," "gemmation," "purfling," "Canossa," or "fanfaronade" has slipped your mind, a dictionary—the larger the better—should be kept close at hand.

It is not intended that this book or even its chapters be read straight through in their entirety. The book is conceived as an extended set of program notes anchored in a biographical base, a volume to consult in association with listening to a live or recorded performance, a companion and guide to brief you on the event, designed to expand your musical experience. And if you like a guide/raconteur with humorous anecdotes and spicy stories, you've got the right guy—albeit the risqué parts are sometimes a bit quaint.

This book comes into being as, I hope, a credible addition to the Slonimsky "canon." If it is successful in that regard, thanks are due to a number of musical types who provided valuable guidance to this nonmusician editor. Richard Carlin of

Schirmer Books showed the first gleam of the eye, spending days with me in the bowels of the Library of Congress digging the raw materials out of acres of boxes housing the then-uncatalogued Slonimsky collection. When I had sorted and created a preliminary assembly, Dr. Malena Kuss provided an incisive qualitative scan that helped me cook the materials down to a provisional table of contents. Robert Beckhard found some additional articles and reviews in his addictive archival pokings. Styra Avins and Terry Eisinger, the ultimate Brahms mavens, reviewed that chapter for factual and linguistic accuracy. Randy Schoenberg and the entire Schoenberg family responded to my request for permission to quote their eminent relative, and Sabine Feisst provided many specifics as well, plus overnight translation service. Finally, Richard Kassel vetted the entire manuscript, plowing undaunted through the words and the works and the centuries. He pointed out issues resolved by subsequent scholarship, advised on the relative importance of musical works, established the order of entries in each chapter, and proposed cuts and revisions.

The project was animated by my belief that musicians and music-lovers would welcome more Slonimsky writings. No longer can there be new ones, but the trove of which this is part enjoyed only ephemeral exposure at publication and deserves to be explored. In a lifetime that actually exceeded a century, my father was witness, participant, and chronicler of the transformation of his art. Educated in the traditional, he championed the revolutionary. In his first career, as a conductor, he challenged a reluctant public to open its ears and reconsider its assumptions. When he took up the cause with words, he found a second and perhaps less risky career as a musicologist, in which his commitment to the new could be expressed alongside his mastery of the great musical tradition.

For me, compiling this volume has, in a way, extended that long life. In the process, I have reexperienced the flavor of the sixty-two years of our joint existence, and tried to assure that he continues to be heard.

Electra Slonimsky Yourke
New York City
September 1999

PRELUDE: Interview with Myself

MY VISITOR CAME IN WITHOUT RINGING the bell—the door was ajar—and surveyed the rows of bookshelves lining the walls and the orchestral scores lying in artistic disarray on top of the piano with an air of intimate acquaintance with every object in the room.

"L. O. Symkins is my name," he declared, and his voice sounded strangely familiar, like a phonograph recording of one's own words. "I came to ask you how you happened to select musicology as your vocation."

"I did not select musicology," I replied. "Musicology selected or, rather, annexed me."

"I am sure," my visitor observed, "that the annexation was not against your will. You've been called the Scourge of Music Dictionaries, and no one becomes a scourge unwillingly."

"Perhaps you are right. Musicology came to me by way of general lexicography," I said. "Ever since childhood I was fascinated by encyclopedias. I memorized the alphabetical indications on the bindings: 'A to Anno'; 'Annu to Balt'; 'Balt to Brai'; 'Brai to Cast'; 'Cast to Cole'; 'Cole to Dama...'"

My visitor nodded: "Yes, yes! The *Encyclopedia Britannica*." He seemed well versed in lexicographical matters.

"My interest in encyclopedias," I continued, "made me aware of their inadequacies. Some information found in these impressive volumes lacked precision. That annoyed me. Particularly unsatisfactory were the articles about music and musicians. And since I am a professional musician, I naturally began to think of ways and means to secure documentary data from unimpeachable sources, such as birth registers, old programs, and similar documents that would confirm or refute the information in music dictionaries."

"So I suppose you were delighted when you found that musicians were born on wrong dates, that opera stars sang Wagner at the putative age of ten, that Lully was appointed court orchestra leader at thirteen. . ."

"How do you know all this?" I exclaimed. "This is exactly the sort of thing I have been extirpating from the dictionaries. Take the Lully case. According to a highly reputable encyclopedia, he was born in 1639 and was appointed music director of the court orchestra in 1652; that is, at the age of thirteen. But he was really born in 1632 and got his job at twenty, which is precocious enough for anybody. Incidentally, Lully's tercentenary was celebrated on the wrong day all over France. He was born on November 28, 1632, and not on November 29, as most music dictionaries say."

"I suppose you have obtained Lully's birth certificate to prove the date. Undoubtedly you got the exact hour of his birth as well."

"Four-thirty in the afternoon," I replied modestly.

My visitor was silent for a moment. "This . . . chronomusicology is not the only thing that interests you in music, I hope," he said.

"Certainly not. Musicology, as I understand it, covers a lot of ground: musical analysis, musical theory, even musical geography."

"By musical geography you probably mean the mapping of musical regions, particularly those yet unexplored," remarked the visitor.

"Quite so. For instance, I became intrigued by the fact that so few Latin American composers were represented in music dictionaries. So I made a grand tour south of the border, and when I returned, I had two hundred and ninety composers in my musicological bag. I figured out that there is one composer per four hundred forty-three thousand square miles of territory in South America, Central America, and the West Indies. I also drew a map of Latin American dances. The national dance of Chile is the *zamacueca*, and the name fitted very nicely into the elongated strip of Chilean territory on the map."

"How about purely theoretical investigations?"

There was a knowing look in my visitor's eyes. I had a definite feeling that he knew the answers to his questions in advance. Still I decided to go along. I admitted that I was the author of a huge book of newfangled melodic patterns, very serpentine in outward appearance on music paper, complete with master chords that would enable anyone to produce as dissonant a harmony as the heart desires.

"One more question," my guest insisted. "Did you ever invent a word that got into a dictionary?"

"Yes, I did. 'Pandiatonicism.'"

"Pan . . . what?"

"'Pandiatonicism,'" I repeated firmly. "It is the modern technique of free combinatory usage, melodically, contrapuntally, and harmonically, of the seven different tones of the diatonic scale." I was convinced that he could readily supply the definition himself. Anticipating his further importunities, I told him that my polysyllabic creation has been duly incorporated into several American and European music dictionaries.

"Didn't you invent 'invecticon,' too?" he asked.

"No," I replied. "I did not. A friend of mine did, but I used the word for the index in my anthology of criticism entitled *Lexicon of Musical Invective.*"

I could not bear the knowing look in my visitor's eyes. "It is now my turn to ask you a question," I said. "Is L. O. Symkins your real name?"

"Why, of course! In fact, it is my surreal name. I am your anagram." He quickly looked at his wristwatch, and I noticed that it was not a wristwatch at all, but a word-counter. "I must really be going," he said. "It is already 861 words o'clock."

The word-counter on my own wrist gave the same number of words in our interview.

JOHANN SEBASTIAN BACH
(1685–1750)
Musical Fountainhead

THE WORD *BACH* MEANS "BROOK, stream." It is symbolic that the greatest man of music, Johann Sebastian Bach (1685–1750), should bear such a meaningful name. For Johann Sebastian Bach, music is the fountainhead of crystal waters. The stream divides itself into **contrapuntal** branches; the speed of the stream varies; the tributaries of intricate counterpoint reach a confluence of **harmony**; but this confluence is often stirred by turbulent undercurrents, creating a suspended **dissonance**; it is only after further progress that the final equilibrium is reached, resolving into a final chord, serene and triumphant.

Contrapuntal. Pertaining to composition with two or more simultaneous melodies.
Harmony. A musical combination of tones or chords; a composition's texture, as two-part or three-part harmony.
Dissonance. A combination of two or more tones requiring resolution.

Polyphonic. Consisting of two or more independently treated melodies; contrapuntal; capable of producing two or more tones at the same time, as the piano, harp, violin, xylophone.

Johann Sebastian Bach came from a remarkable family of musicians. Long before his time, musicians named Bach were famous throughout Thuringia as municipal players, the *Stadtpfeifer*, so that even musicians of different names were commonly described as "the Bachs." The family was clan-conscious and often arranged meetings in the towns of Eisenach (where Johann Sebastian was born), Arnstadt, or Erfurt. At one of these meetings, 120 Bachs made their appearance. They amused themselves by performing popular songs with improvised vocal and instrumental parts in a fine **polyphonic** manner. These Bachs were expert artisans, but they also possessed jollity. Johann Sebastian himself was greatly interested in his family, and in his later years started a detailed genealogy, which is preserved under the title *The Origin of the Family of Musical Bachs*.

With such a musical background, Bach as a boy was destined to become a professional musician. He was lodged with his elder brother, who held him in strict discipline, never allowing him to go beyond prescribed exercises. But Bach's musical curiosity could not be stifled. In a latticed cabinet in his brother's house there was an alluring object; not a sweet pie, not a sugary confection, but something much more precious to young Bach: a volume of pieces for the harpsichord by various German composers. His brother would not permit him to use the music, but Bach managed to extract the rolled sheets through the lattice openings and copy the music at night by moonlight. An old story relates that he completed his task in six months, a few days each month when the moon was shining. This was the only surreptitious act in Bach's entire life, for it is difficult to find in the annals of music a master more forthright and less tempted by guile than Johann Sebastian Bach.

Intellectual curiosity and a reverence for older masters were the great driving forces of Bach's character as a musician. As a boy of fifteen he started out on his life's career, first as a choirboy, then as an organ player. When he served as an apprentice in North Germany, he undertook a walk of thirty miles to Hamburg, to hear the great organist Johann Adam Reinken. He stopped at a roadside inn, and had two small fish for his meal. To his surprise, he found a coin in each and so was able to provide for the next meal.

Bach's first important position was as an organist in Arnstadt. Only eighteen, he was already well qualified to perform, to compose, and to improvise. But his artistry drove him farther than the requirements of this modest post. He let his musical fancy roam, and was strongly reprimanded by his superiors for using "strange variations" in playing the hymns, which in this unusual form confused the congregation. There was another reason for this reprimand; drawn by the fame of the organist Dietrich Buxtehude (1637–1701), Bach took a leave of absence to make a journey to Lübeck, where Buxtehude held his famous evening concerts. Legend has it that Bach made the entire long journey on foot.

There are indications that Bach hoped to inherit Buxtehude's job in Lübeck after his retirement, but encountered an insurmountable obstacle in the person of the eldest of Buxtehude's five daughters, who was offered to him in marriage as a *conditio sine qua non* for getting the job. (Buxtehude himself had to marry his predecessor's daughter to obtain his Lübeck position.) At another time, Handel also made a trip to Lübeck, and he, too, was deterred from seeking the post by the confrontation with Fräulein Buxtehude.

Bach returned to Arnstadt with renewed zeal for music. At the age of twenty-three he went to Weimar, leaving his cousin, one of the innumerable musical Bachs, in charge of his post at Arnstadt. In Weimar, he wrote most of his great organ works, and in his next place of employment, Cöthen, the greatest of his **chamber music** works. He conducted the orchestra for Prince Leopold, who himself took part as the player on the viola da gamba. It was in Cöthen that Bach wrote

Chamber music. Vocal or instrumental music suitable for performance in a room or small hall.

Concerto (It.). An extended multi-movement composition for a solo instrument, usually with orchestra accompaniment and using (modified) sonata form.

his famous Brandenburg **concertos**, dedicated to Duke Christian Ludwig of Brandenburg.

Bach learned the art of composition through a diligent study of the vocal and instrumental works of German and Italian composers of the seventeenth century. Sometimes he copied works by contemporary masters; manuscripts extant in Bach's own handwriting without further identification have plagued generations of Bach editors and have at times led to the erroneous attribution of these copies to Bach himself. The chronology of his works is not always easy to establish. Not many original manuscripts have come to us, and very few bear the date of composition.

The circumstances of Bach's life and his teaching in Leipzig are well known, and the records of his pedagogic activities are plentiful. The Thomasschule (St. Thomas School) was an ancient and venerable institution founded in the year 1212 "to uphold and expand Christianity and German culture on a pagan frontier." Bach arrived in Leipzig in 1723, with a family of five children. Charles Sanford Terry, in his biography of Bach, gives a complete account, from the archives of the Thomasschule, of the small things in Bach's domestic routine. Thus we know just what repairs were made in Bach's house, the exact dates when the walls were whitewashed, and even the name of the scrubwoman. We know that Bach's kitchen got a new oven. From the birth records we also know that children were born into Bach's family annually. The mortality was high. There was a little girl Bach born in 1723, who died shortly thereafter; there was an imbecile child born to the Bachs in 1724. There was another one who died in infancy in 1725. Finally, in 1726, a daughter was born who not only survived infancy, but eventually got married. There were four more children after her.

Bach's appointment at the Thomasschule did not come without difficulties. The senate of Leipzig, in whose hands the appointment of teachers was placed, first turned to Georg Philipp Telemann (1681–1767), then to Christoph Graupner (1683–1760). Telemann had declined the offer, and Graupner could not accept it because his patron, the landgrave of Hesse, would not release him from his contract. When finally the senate invited Bach, a member of that august body declared: "Since it is impossible to get the best, we will have to be satisfied with second best."

Bach's duties were manifold. He was a cantor, director of a chorus of fifty-five boys. The school played a great role in the community, and one of its important civic duties was attending the funerals in town. It was also profitable: the school charged a definite fee, so many groschen for attendance by the entire school, correspondingly less if only part of the school attended. The cantor was to receive fifteen groschen for each funeral when the entire choir attended. The town authorities cooperated by arranging funerals in the afternoon, so that lessons would not be missed. Weddings were also profitable: Bach's fee as choir director was one thaler for each wedding.

Discipline at the Thomasschule, as in all German schools of the time, was very severe. The scholars were punished both by fines and by whipping. The use of impertinent language, in Latin or German, was punished by a fine of six pfennigs, and vomiting, even if involuntary, and not as a consequence of drinking, called for a fine of two groschen. Musical faults were punishable, too, and a mistake in singing called for the application of the birch. The rods and birches were in the charge of older boys who were called "purgers" (*Purganten*).

Bach was fortunately relieved of some of the duties of a cantor. To escape the association with extramusical tasks, he preferred to be styled *director musices*. The comparative leisure allowed Bach to compose prodigiously, but there is no evidence that Bach himself or his immediate colleagues ever

Bach Timeline

1685	Born in Eisenach, Germany
1703	First professional job, as church organist in Arnstadt
1705	Takes leave of absence to study organ with Dietrich Buxtehude in Lubeck
1707	Hired as church organist in Muhlhausen; weds his cousin, Maria Barbara Bach
1708	First published work, cantata "Gott ist mein König" ("God Is My King")
1709-17	Court organist to duke of Weimar
1717-23	Kapellmeister and music director to Prince Leopold of Anhalt in Cöthen
1720	First wife dies
1721	Completes the Brandenburg concertos
1722	Marries Anna Magdalena Wilcken; composes *The Well-Tempered Clavier*
1723-49	Cantor of Thomasschule, Leipzig where he directs church choirs and choir school
1727-29	*St. Matthew Passion* composed and performed
1729	Organizes the Collegium Musicum, giving weekly concerts of secular music
1747	*The Musical Offering* composed after a visit to Frederick the Great of Prussia
1747-49	Mass in B Minor assembled from several earlier choral works
1750	Dies following failed cataract surgery, leaving unfinished *The Art of the Fugue*

Pianoforte (It.). A stringed keyboard instrument with tones produced by hammers; a piano.

Fugue. Contrapuntal imitation wherein a theme proposed by one part is taken up equally and successively by all participating parts.

Canon. Musical imitation in which two or more parts take up, in succession, the given subject note for note; the strictest form of musical imitation.

Prelude. A musical introduction to a composition or drama.

Atonality. The absence of tonality; music in which the traditional tonal structures are abandoned and there is no key signature.

Polytonality. Simultaneous use of two or more different tonalities found in modern music.

Dodecaphonic. Technique of modern composition in which the basic theme contains twelve different notes.

realized the greatness of the music written by the cantor of the Thomasschule. An early French dictionary sets Bach down as a "skillful composer of polyphonic music," nothing more.

Frederick the Great of Prussia, who was a flute player and a composer himself, wished to see Bach at his Potsdam Palace. When Bach was finally able to accept the invitation, Frederick himself led him through the palace. At the king's request, Bach tested the harpsichords and **pianofortes** installed in the palace rooms, and improvised a **fugue** in six parts for the king. Frederick then gave him a theme, which Bach elaborated in the form of a trio for flute, violin, and harpsichord. The final version of the work was in the form of a "puzzle **canon**." Bach presented it to Frederick with a flattering dedication, in conformity with the custom, to "a sovereign admirable in his music as in all other arts of war and peace."

Bach's works were intended in most part for the practical purpose of instructing young musicians. The technical achievement of Bach's forty-eight **preludes** and fugues is an unexcelled marvel of creative music. Bach's inventions for keyboard instrument are no less wonderful from the structural point of view. And yet these studies, designed to instruct, possess a beauty of expression that is apparent even to the untutored. In some passages of these works, Bach transcends the limits of harmonic combinations permissible in his time; such moments presage the development of modern music.

With the exception of opera, Bach left the mark of his genius in every musical form. For a modern musician, his music is a treasure trove of fantastically bold contrapuntal and melodic devices; his use of unrelated diminished seventh chords and modulating excursions into the tonality of the Neapolitan sixth comes very close to the techniques of **atonality** and **polytonality**. It is even possible, by selecting appropriate passages in Bach's works, to find quasi-**dodecaphonic** usages.

INSTRUMENTAL WORKS

Chaconne in D Minor for Unaccompanied Violin, from Partita No. 2, BWV 1004 (1720)

Bach's sonatas and partitas for unaccompanied violin present an unexampled challenge. In these works Bach achieved the extraordinary feat of writing **counterpoint** in two, three, and four **voices**, and even fugues, on a single stringed instrument. This he achieved by double, triple, and arpeggiated quadruple stops; by dint of harmonic and melodic figurations a rich pattern of modulation is contrived, all this without sacrificing the fluency of the melodic line and the clarity of harmonic progressions.

Bach wrote a group of three **sonatas** and three partitas for unaccompanied violin in the period between 1718 and 1723, when he was in his middle thirties. In Bach's time, the term "sonata" still retained its etymological meaning "sounded"—that is, to be played on an instrument, without further specification as to form, as distinct from a **cantata**, meaning "sung." An instrumental sonata was usually in the form of a suite in four movements, alternately slow and fast. A partita (*partita* in Italian means "divided") was an instrumental suite of dance forms, known as "classical suite." It includes an **allemande** (which means "German" in French, but the reason for this attribution is obscure) in fast 4/4 time; **courante** (literally, "running"), a rapid dance in 3/4 time; **sarabande** (the origin of the word is dubious, but the form developed in Spain), a stately dance in measured triple time; bourrée (French for "brushwood"), a rapid dance in 2/2 time; and gigue, a fast movement in 12/8 time.

Bach's Second Partita for Unaccompanied Violin includes the most famous movement ever written for violin solo, the D-Minor **Chaconne**. A mystery surrounds the etymology and

Counterpoint. Polyphonic composition; the combination of two or more simultaneous melodies.

Voice. The singing voice; used as synonym for "part."

Sonata (It.). An instrumental composition usually for a solo instrument or chamber ensemble, in three or four movements, connected by key, contrasted in theme, tempo, meter, and mood.

Cantata (It.). A vocal work with instrumental accompaniment.

Allemande (Fr.), allemanda (It.). A lively German dance.

Courante (Fr.), **coranto** (It.). An old French dance in 3/2 time.

Sarabande (Fr., Ger.). A dance of Spanish or Oriental origin; the slowest movement in the suite.

Chaconne (Fr.). A Spanish dance; an instrumental set of variations over a ground bass, not over 8 measures long and in slow 3/4 time.

Musikalisches Opfer

Sr. Königlichen Majestät in Preußen ꝛc.

allerunterthänigst gewidmet

von

Johann Sebastian Bach.

Allergnädigster König,

Ew. Majestät weyhe hiermit in tiefster Unterthänigkeit ein Musicalisches Opfer, dessen edelster Theil von Deroselben hoher Hand selbst herrühret. Mit einem ehrfurchtsvollen Vergnügen erinnere ich mich annoch der ganz besondern Königlichen Gnade, da vor einiger Zeit, bey meiner Anwesenheit in Potsdam, Ew. Majestät selbst, ein Thema zu einer Fuge auf dem Clavier mir vorzuspielen geruheten, und zugleich allergnädigst auferlegten, solches alsobald in Deroselben höchsten Gegenwart auszuführen. Ew. Majestät Befehl zu gehorsamen, war meine unterthänigste Schuldigkeit. Ich bemerkte aber gar bald, daß wegen Mangels nöthiger Vorbereitung, die Ausführung nicht also gerathen wollte, als es ein so treffliches Thema erforderte. Ich faßte demnach den Entschluß, und machte mich sogleich anheischig, dieses recht Königliche Thema vollkommener auszuarbeiten, und sodann der Welt bekannt zu machen. Dieser Vorsatz ist nunmehro nach Vermögen bewerkstelliget worden, und er hat keine andere als nur diese untadelhafte Absicht, den Ruhm eines Monarchen, ob gleich nur in einem kleinen Puncte, zu verherrlichen, dessen Größe und Stärke, gleich wie in allen Kriegs- und Friedens-Wissenschaften, also auch besonders in der Musik, jedermann bewundern und verehren muß. Ich erkühne mich dieses unterthänigste Bitten hinzuzufügen: Ew. Majestät geruhen gegenwärtige wenige Arbeit mit einer gnädigen Aufnahme zu würdigen, und Deroselben allerhöchste Königliche Gnade noch fernerweit zu gönnen

Ew. Majestät

Leipzig den 7. Julii
1747.

allerunterthänigst gehorsamsten Knechte,
dem Verfasser.

Musical Offering

to His Royal Majesty in Prussia and

most humbly dedicated
by

Johann Sebastian Bach

Most gracious King,

To Your Majesty is dedicated herewith in deepest humility a Musical Offering, whose most excellent part itself proceeds from your own lofty hand. With a respectful delight I remember still the quite singular royal grace when, some time ago, during my stay in Potsdam, Your Majesty condescended to play for me on the clavier a theme for a fugue, and at the same time most graciously obliged me to enlarge on the same forthwith in your own highest presence. To obey Your Majesty's command was my most humble duty. However, I noticed quite soon that, because of the lack of necessary preparation, the performance did not succeed as well as such a superb theme required. I consequently resolved and undertook immediately to work out completely this truly royal theme and then publish it to the world. This project has now been completed to the best of my ability, and it has no other purpose than this sole irreproachable one: to exalt, although only in one small aspect, the glory of a monarch whose greatness and might, just as in all the sciences of peace and war so also especially in music, everyone must admire and venerate. I make bold to add this most humble request: that Your Majesty deign to honor the present small work with a gracious reception, and that you further extend the highest royal favor to

Your Majesty's

Leipzig, 7 July
1747

most humbly obedient servant,
the composer

the origin of the chaconne. There is a theory that it was imported from Mexico in the sixteenth century and was originally an unrestrained and orgiastic mestizo dance. If so, then the chaconne lost all its wildness during the passage from Mexico to Europe. The Baroque form of the chaconne is one of the most concentrated and unified movements, further restrained by a thematic bass line that governs the harmony.

This particular unaccompanied Chaconne is a marvel of melodic, harmonic, and contrapuntal organization. Beginning in deliberate 3/4 time, in the key of D minor, it maintains a stately movement with a quarter note as the principal unit. It is then "doubled" twice, and proceeds in animated motion in sixteenth notes, with several passages in thirty-second notes. There follows a section in D major. The illusion of full harmonies is sustained by the rapid alternation of the lower and upper pedal points on the dominant. Then the original statement in D minor returns with ingenious variations in sixteenth notes, thirty-second notes, and triplet passages. The **coda** simply recapitulates the original statement.

Coda (It.). A "tail"; hence, a passage ending a movement.

Orchestral Suite No. 3 in D Major, BWV 1068 (c. 1729–31)

The suite is a collection of dances, with a prelude or an **overture** to open the series. The number of dances and their nature varies. Usually the first dance is in common time (4/4), and in quick movement. The second dance is slow and stately. The third dance may be a spirited **allegro**. Then comes a group known under the comprehensive name "gallant dances." These may include a minuet or a gavotte, or any of the French dances current in the sixteenth and the seventeenth centuries. The concluding movement is usually a **gigue**. In Bach's time, not much significance was attached to titles. A suite might have been called an overture, a **partita**, or even a **sinfonia**. It is only later in history that the titles have assumed the significance of a definite form.

Overture. A musical introduction to an opera, oratorio, etc.

Allegro (It.). Lively, brisk, rapid.

Gigue (Fr.), **giga** (It.). A jig.
Partita (It.). A suite.
Sinfonia (It.). A symphony; an opera overture.

Inversion. The transposition of one of the notes of an interval by an octave; chord position with lowest note other than root.

Bourrée (Fr.). A dance of French or Spanish origin in rapid tempo in 2/4 or 4/4 time.

The Overture of Bach's Suite No. 3 in D Major is in common time (4/4), which is the usual time signature for the opening movement in most suites. There are three themes in the Overture, and the one in dotted rhythm serves as background for the entire Overture. The counterpoint is not as complex as it is in Bach's fugues, and even the Bachian device of **inversion** is free, so that only the direction of the melody is reversed. The Overture consists of two contrasting sections. The first is of a symphonic nature; the second section is based on the imitation of a characteristic rhythmic figure.

The melody of the second movement has become popular under the title Air on the G String, in a violin arrangement by the German violinist August Wilhelmj (1845–1908), who transposed Bach's original melody a ninth lower in order to exploit the rich sonorities of the lowest string on the violin. In Bach's original, the violin part does not require the G string at all. The late Donald Francis Tovey called it a "devastating derangement." Derangement or not, it is effective, and the temptation to use it in place of the movement as written by Bach is great.

The third movement of the suite is a twin Gavotte, each gavotte consisting of two sections. The first Gavotte is repeated after the second. A **Bourrée** follows the Gavotte. Both the gavotte and the bourrée are dances of French peasant origin, but it would be risky to try to establish the etymological derivation of these dances. The final movement of the suite is a Gigue, which is a frenchified version of the old English jig. It is in 6/8 time, and, like all the dances of the suite, is in two sections.

Concerto No. 1 in C Minor for Two Harpsichords, BWV 1060 (1729)

The solo parts in Bach's concertos were often interchangeable. A concerto for harpsichord could have been originally a violin concerto. Double and triple concertos were often

Concerto for Two Harpsichords in C Minor

BWV 1060

arranged by Bach for different groups of solo instruments. The Concerto for Two Harpsichords in C Minor was probably written not for keyboard instruments but for violin and oboe with orchestral accompaniment. At least, traces of typical oboe or violin passages are detectable in the two harpsichord parts.

The concerto must have been written in 1729 in Leipzig, at the time when Bach took over the direction of the Collegium Musicum there. The meetings were held weekly, and Bach was expected to provide the music. It is probable that there were good pianists (or rather, harpsichord players) among the members of the Collegium Musicum. It is possible also that Bach had in mind two of his sons as soloists in the concerto.

Adagio (It.). Slow, leisurely; a slow movement.

The C-Minor Concerto is in three movements, Allegro, **Adagio**, and Allegro. The opening movement, in 4/4 time, is distinguished by the characteristically Bachian persistence of musical motion. The solo instruments and the accompanying orchestra echo one another in free imitation. The thematic material is expressive and rhythmic. The succeeding slow movement, Adagio, is in 12/8, in the key of E-flat major. The rhythmic design contributes to a feeling of sustained energy, with even division of twelve or twenty-four notes to a bar. A **modulation** leads to the **dominant** (fifth step, G) of the principal key of C minor. The final Allegro, in 2/4 time, proceeds along a brisk pattern. The rhythmic drive is determined, leading to a conclusive ending.

Modulation. Passage from one key into another.
Dominant. The fifth tone in the major or minor scales; a chord based on that tone.

Ricercare à Six, from The Musical Offering, BWV 1079 (1747), orchestration by Anton Webern

We hear from Potsdam that last Sunday, May 7, 1747, the famous Capellmeister from Leipzig, Bach, arrived with the intention of hearing the excellent Royal music. In the evening, at about the time when the regular chamber music in the royal apartments usually begins, His Majesty was informed that Capellmeister Bach had arrived at Potsdam and was waiting in His Majesty's antechamber for His Majesty's most gracious permission to listen to the music. His August Self immediately gave orders that Bach be admitted, and went, at his entrance to the so-called Forte-and-Piano, condescending also to play, in person and without any preparation, a theme to be executed by Capellmeister Bach in a fugue. This was done so happily by the aforementioned Capellmeister, that not only His Majesty was pleased to show his satisfaction, but also all those present were seized with astonishment. Bach has found the subject propounded to him so exceedingly beautiful that he intends to set it down on paper in a regular fugue and have it engraved on copper.

In these words, the *Spenersche Zeitung* of Berlin, in its issue of May 11, 1747, apprised its readers of the visit of Johann Sebastian Bach at the palace of Frederick the Great of Prussia. On that famous occasion the king, who was an excellent musician, played for Bach on the harpsichord a fine tune of his own invention, containing both **diatonic** and **chromatic** elements, and asked him to improvise a fugue on it.

Diatonic. Employing the tones of the standard major or minor scale.

Chromatic. Relating to tones foreign to a given key (scale) or chord; opposed to diatonic.

Bach's response is history. Upon his return to Leipzig, he expanded his improvisation by writing a magnificent "musical offering" (*Das musikalische Opfer*), a cornucopia of learned devices comprising a mirror canon, imitation in contrary motion, a crab canon (with the royal theme played backward), and culminating in a magnificent "**ricercare**" in six voices. His offering was entitled "Regis Iussu Cantio Et Reliqua Canonica Arte Resoluta" ("At the King's Command, Theme and Additions Resolved by Canonic Art").

Ricercare (It.). Instrumental composition of the sixteenth and seventeenth centuries generally characterized by imitative treatment of the theme.

The term *ricercare* or *ricercar* (literally, "to research") was originally applied to the "searching" of correct intonation on a string instrument, in other words, tuning. By a semantical extension it came to signify the seeking of the tonality of

Ricercare.

the principal part of the work, a preamble or a prologue. Through further differentiation, the ricercare developed into a full-fledged fugal exposition, and the terms "ricercare" and "fuga" became interchangeable. Bach's *Musical Offering* is indeed a manifestation of the highest art of the fugue.

Bach's marginal remarks in the manuscript are most revealing of the traditional obsequiousness to ruling sovereigns of the time. To illustrate the augmentation, in which the thematic notes assume double value, Bach writes: "As the notes augment, so may the King's fortune grow." At the change of the key, Bach submits, "As the modulation rises, so may rise the glory of the King." There is also a riddle canon, with the Latin motto "Quaerendo invenietis" ("By seeking you shall find out"), in which the performer must find the proper place and form of the entries. The quest is not simple, since the imitation is to be made in inversion.

Anton Webern (1883–1945), who adapted his great polyphonic skill mainly to dodecaphonic techniques, had profound reverence for the great masters of the Baroque art, and particularly for Bach, and approached the task of orchestrating the concluding portion of Bach's ricercare with great fidelity to the spirit of the music. But he believed, as did his revered teacher Arnold Schoenberg, that Classical music must be arranged in terms of modern instrumental ideas. In his orchestration, Webern used a flute, oboe, English horn, clarinet, bass clarinet, bassoon, horn, trumpet, trombone, harp, and **string quartet**. The opening notes of the "Royal Theme" are given to the muted trombone, and the rest of the subject is allotted to muted horn and muted trumpet. This overlapping of instruments is fashioned after the medieval ***hocketus*** (literally, "hiccup"), an effect created by a deliberate discontinuity of a melody. Expression marks and tempo indications in Webern's score are noteworthy: *zart fliessend, fliessender, sehr fliessend, rubato*. Who would think that an ultramodernist like Webern, arranging the music of Bach, would ask the play-

String quartet. A composition for first and second violin, viola, and cello.

Hocket, hoquet. Texture in which one voice stops and another comes in, sometimes in the middle of a word; a hiccup.

ers to perform tenderly, flowingly, more flowingly, and in free measure? In this instance, classicism and modernism suddenly turn romantic.

ORGAN WORKS

Toccata, Adagio, and Fugue in C Major, BWV 564 (c. 1708–17)

In 1703, when Bach was only eighteen years old, he received his first position as organist, at the New Church in Arnstadt. His duties were set forth as follows:

> Whereas our right honorable and gracious Count and Lord, Count of Schwarzburg, has been pleased to appoint you, Johann Sebastian Bach, to be organist of the New Church, you shall in particular be faithful, loyal, and useful to his lordship, and in general show yourself apt and adroit in your calling, eschewing other tasks and occupations, and on Sundays, feast days, and other seasons appointed for public worship in the said New Church, shall attend at the organ committed to you and perform thereon as shall be required of you. In your conduct and behavior you shall be God-fearing, temperate, well disposed to all, shunning ill company, and in every way show yourself an honorable servant and organist before God and your worshipful masters. In return, you shall receive for annual pay and entertainment 50 florins, and for board and lodging 30 thalers, drawn as follows: from the tax on beer taverns, 25 florins, from church funds, 25 florins, and the rest from the hospital.

This was the beginning of Bach's career as a virtuoso of the organ. But apparently his extemporaneous embellishments of church **chorales** were not always welcomed by the congregation. In the minutes of the New Church of Arnstadt there is found the transcript of Bach's questioning by the Superintendent Olearius, in which the latter admonished Bach to abandon his ways of playing: "Complaints have been made that you accompany the hymns with strange variations, and mix the chorale with many ornaments alien to the melody, which confuses the congregation. If you desire to introduce a countertheme, you must keep it, and not change it to yet another."

A more serious and less answerable complaint voiced at the same meeting was that Bach took four months for his leave of absence, instead of the allotted time of four weeks. Bach explained, rather weakly, that he thought his assistant could attend to the needs of the congregation during his absence. The true explanation is that Bach used the time for a journey to Lübeck to hear the great Buxtehude play. The pretty story to the effect that he made that journey on foot is not borne out by existing evidence.

The great **Toccata**, Adagio, and Fugue in C Major must have been written during Bach's Weimar period, between 1708 and 1717. It is not improbable that Bach played this work in the presence of the hereditary prince of Hesse, who was so impressed with Bach's playing that he took a ring off his finger and gave it to Bach as a token of appreciation. Constantin Bellermann, rector of the Minden Lyceum, recorded his impression of Bach's prodigious technique of the pedals: "His feet, flying over the pedals as though they had wings, made the notes reverberate like thunder." Referring to the prince's gift of a ring, Bellermann asks rhetorically: "Now, if Bach's feet deserved so rich a gift, what reward would be worthy of his hands?" There is an extended pedal solo in the Toccata, which requires "flying feet" for adequate performance.

The word "toccata" comes from the Italian *toccare*, "to touch"; it is a piece for a keyboard instrument, in the form of a free **fantasia**, or a prelude. The first part, a prelude, is es-

Chorale. A hymn tune of the German Protestant Church, or one similar in style.

Toccata (It.). A composition for organ or harpsichord (piano), free and bold in style.

Fantasia (It.), **fantasie** (Ger.). An improvisation; a piece with free imitation in the seventeenth to eighteenth centuries; a piece free in form and character.

sentially in unison structure, in rapid movement, with frequent pauses between well-marked phrases. The second part is an adagio, in which an ornamented melody is projected onto an even-measured bass figure. The third part is a lively fugue, in which the subject has a so-called tonal answer, obtained, as in any fugue, by transposing the subject a fifth higher or a fourth lower, and then replacing the first supertonic to occur in the answer by the tonic.

Passacaglia in C Minor, BWV 582 ### (c. 1708–17)

The problem of modern arrangements of Baroque music, particularly Bach, is a vexatious one. In their Calvinistic fanaticism, musical fundamentalists regard any attempt to transcribe Bach's music for a medium other than the one Bach intended it for as a cardinal sin. Paraphrasing the Italian dictum "Tradutore—traditore" ("To translate is to betray") they say, in effect, "Trascritore—traditore."

Yet Bach himself was an industrious arranger of instrumental works by his Baroque contemporaries, among them Antonio Vivaldi (1678–1741). The protean capacity of Bach's own arrangements is demonstrated by two of his keyboard concertos which are arrangements of his violin concertos— surely the most extraordinary case of transplantation of unrelated instrumental species. The title of Bach's *Das Wohltemperierte Klavier* (*The Well-Tempered Clavier*) indicates merely that the work (which was written primarily for didactic purposes) is designed for a keyboard instrument.

The piano virtuoso Ferruccio Busoni (1866–1924), who was second to none in his dedication to Bach, did not flinch from his intention of making a piano arrangement of Bach's Chaconne, originally for unaccompanied violin, lavishing on it all the gothic splendor of pianistic sonorities. To purists, Busoni's modus operandi was an abomination of desecration, and they invoked the strongest Baroque anathema on his head. Incidentally, in his own performances of Bach, Busoni allowed himself surprising dynamic and agogic liberties, even to the point of using **rubato**. It is doubtful that a pianist who today tried to emulate Busoni's free interpretation could pass muster even at a conservatory recital. The musical morality of today is much more severe.

The harpsichordist Wanda Landowska suggested that the proper rule of comportment in playing Bach should be the same as in society: one should feel free, but not to the extent of putting one's feet on the table or trampling the drawing-room carpet in mud-covered boots. Schoenberg stated his own attitude toward modern arrangements of Bach with great definitude in connection with his transcriptions of two organ chorales of Bach for a modern orchestra. "Our present musical concepts," he wrote, "demand clarity in the motivic procedure, in both the horizontal and vertical dimensions. We must achieve this transparency of design in order to build a musical structure in a proper manner. I therefore regard my transcriptions of Bach's works not only as my right, but also as my duty." And Schoenberg did not hesitate to include in his orchestration such un-Bachian instruments as the triangle and the **celesta**.

Even liberal musicians object to tampering with the actual notes in Bach's music. The German-American composer Lukas Foss (b. 1922) was roundly castigated for his irreverent treatment of Bach's pieces, which he decomposed and re-assembled according to the precepts of the stochastic method of composition. And then there is that great Baroque composer P. D.Q. Bach, the author of such works as a Toot Suite for Organ (three grinders), Concerto for Piano vs. Orchestra, and various MADrigals.

Bach's **Passacaglia** and Fugue in C Minor is peculiarly suitable for orchestral transcriptions. The grand sonorities of the original, written for organ or **cembalo**, make the transfer-

Rubato (It.). Prolonging prominent melody tones or chords.

Celesta. Percussion instrument consisting of tuned steel bars connected to a keyboard.

Passacaglia (It.). An old Italian dance in stately movement on a ground base of four measures.

Cembalo (It.). Harpsichord, pianoforte; in old times, a dulcimer.

ence to string and brass choirs seem natural. The Baroque passacaglia reflects the spirit of *Zopfmusik*—"pigtail," or old-fashioned, music—to perfection. The "pigtail" is the cantus firmus
placed in the bass, which determines the harmonic progressions, while the upper voices engage in ornamental variations.
Bach took the subject for his C-Minor Passacaglia and Fugue
from a Passacaglia by André Raison, a French organist active in
Paris early in the eighteenth century. The fugue in this instance is a modern misnomer; Bach indicates his fugal sequel
to the passacaglia as "thema fugatum," a canonic development
of the theme rather than the classical type of fugal structure.
Bach elevates this "fugation" to a glorious edifice of florid
counterpoint.

RELIGIOUS VOCAL WORKS

Cantata No. 51, "Jauchzet Gott in allen Landen" (date unknown)

The figure of Bach looms so immense on the musical horizon
that we are often reluctant to enter Bach's technical labora-
tory, to examine his tools and pry into his methods, for fear
that by watching his modus operandi we might lose grasp of
his inspiration. Yet Bach's own attitude toward his works was
that of an expert craftsman who has achieved his mastery over
the material by repeated use of well-tried formulas, musical
punches, and clichés. Bach took the florid singing line from
the **Gregorian chant**, and developed it into a fine art. There
is no essential difference between Bach's use of such florid figures in his vocal and his instrumental pieces, except for the
natural limitations of the medium. In his capacity as a practic-
ing church organist, Bach was duty-bound to produce a given
number of organ pieces and various arrangements of hymns
and other religious songs.

Gregorian chant. A system
of liturgical plainchant in the
Christian Church, revised by
Pope Gregory I for the Roman
Catholic ritual.

One of the most remarkable practices in Bach's time was the literal illustration of the text. Numerous examples of such illustrations are found in the fascinating book of André Pirro, *L'Esthétique de Jean Sebastien Bach*. In it the author examines the relationship between certain words in the text and certain **intervals** in Bach's music. The vividness and consistency in the employment of identical intervals for identical concepts are striking. For instance, the word "far" is invariably translated by the interval of a minor ninth; the concept of firmness and steadfastness is illustrated by a repeated note; anguish is expressed by narrow chromatic intervals; upward movement is transcribed in the form of an upward **arpeggio**; downward movement is depicted by a downward progression along the diminished seventh chord; descent to hell and reference to Satan are also expressed in the intervals of the diminished seventh chord. The opening phrase of the chorale "Oh, Difficult Step" is represented by three whole tones in an ascending row, a usage forbidden in vocal music. The phrase "Lead on" is illustrated by a continuous upward scale covering more than three octaves.

The score of Bach's cantata "Jauchzet Gott" is marked "For the fifteenth Sunday after Trinity and at any other time." Obviously, then, the text and the meaning of the cantata were adaptable for different periods of the church calendar. The feeling of jubilation that pervades the music makes it particularly suitable for a festive occasion, New Year's Day, Michaelmas Day, or an election of the council. There is evidence that the words of several arias were rewritten to suit such diverse occasions. The author of the text may have been Bach himself.

The cantata consists of five sections, **aria**, **recitative**, aria, chorale, and **alleluja**. The music is set in the key of C major, which was often associated with rejoicing and thanksgiving. The form is that of a solo cantata without chorus. The part of the soloist, a soprano voice, abounds in ornamental passages and figurations that require exceptional virtuosity. Various guesses have been made as to the identity of the

Interval. The difference in pitch between two tones.

Arpeggio (It.). Playing the tones of a chord in rapid, even succession.

Aria (It.). An air, song, tune, melody.
Recitative. Declamatory singing, free in tempo and rhythm.
Alleluia. The Latin form of *Hallelujah* (Praise the Lord!) as used in the Roman Catholic service.

Falsetto. The highest of the vocal registers.

singer for whom Bach wrote the work. Almost certainly it must have been a boy singing **falsetto**, possibly Bach's son Philipp Emanuel.

Cantata No. 53, "Schlage doch" (date unknown)

Bach was a composer of "utilitarian" music (*Gebrauchs-musik*), designed for special purposes, church services, weddings, as pedagogical aids. A remarkable feature of Bach's vocal music is its melodic symbolism, the illustrative use of musical phrases. In one extraordinary instance, the words "Lead me" are illustrated by an ascending scale of twenty-four steps, followed by relays from the bass to high soprano. This illustrativeness of the vocal line was highly useful in practice, for it enabled the listener to form an association between the melody and the verbal phrase, and incidentally helped in understanding the words, even in perfect enunciation.

Bach was equally literal whenever the text contained references to sounds and instruments. When the words spoke of "thundering drum rolls," there were drums expressly included in the score. And when the voice invokes "the flutes' melodious choir," three flutes respond in the orchestra. When the voice enjoins the flutes to stop—"Flutes be silent!"—they instantly comply.

Bach's church Cantata No. 53, "Schlage doch," speaks of the last stroke of the clock; the campanella is included in the score to illustrate the clock chime. This cantata was probably written for a funeral service, but the date and the occasion are uncertain. The words may be translated thus:

Strike then, oh desired hour!
Strike, announce the desired day!
Come, ye angels, near to me.
Open to me Heaven's eyes,

That I might see soon my Jesus,
In my soul's serene repose.
I await in my inner heart
Only the last stroke of the clock.
Strike then, oh desired hour,
Strike, announce the desired day!

Cantata No. 158, "Der Friede sei mit Dir" (date unknown)

On June 25, 1708, Bach wrote "a submissive memo to the honorable and distinguished parochial councilors of St. Blaise's, the church at Mühlhausen where he was employed as organist:

> Your Magnificence, noble and learned gentlemen, my gracious patrons and masters, God has been pleased to open to me an unexpected situation, a more adequate subsistence and the opportunity to pursue the object which concerns me most, the betterment of church music. . . . His serene Highness, the Duke of Saxe-Weimar, has been graciously pleased to give me the entrée to his Capelle as one of his chamber musicians.

His Magnificence, the burgomaster, and the noble gentlemen of the council of St. Blaise's let Bach go not without regret, and Bach became the court organist and *camer musicus* at Weimar, the celebrated town of old German culture, which has been described as "something between a capital and a village," where Goethe and Schiller later lived in greatness, where Liszt shone, and where young Richard Strauss made his spectacular beginning. Goethe apostrophized Weimar in a distich which, freely translated, reads:

> O, Weimar, you have an uncommon fate:
> Like Bethlehem in Israel, little and great!

Among Bach's duties at Weimar, as previously at Mühlhausen, was the composition of "agreeable and harmonious cantatas." He had a very small choir at his disposal, probably not more than twelve singers in all. The number of instrumentalists was also very limited, but by the provisions of the contract every *musicus vocalis*, that is, singer, could be used in the orchestra as *musicus instrumentalis*. The cantatas were to be sung each Sunday, and there were also special festivals, for which special cantatas were to be written. According to Neumeister, a Lutheran clergyman who published a collection of biblical poems in 1700, with which Bach must have been thoroughly familiar, "A cantata seems to be nothing else than a portion of an opera composed of recitativo and aria together." A cantata could be very long or very short, depending upon the number and arrangement of separate parts. It could also be scored for any number of vocalists and instrumentalists, according to needs and available performers. Bach wrote nearly two hundred cantatas in all, but the authorship of some has not been authenticated. The dates of composition of these cantatas are established with great difficulty.

The Passion of Our Lord According to St. Matthew, *BWV 244 (1727)*

The Bach family represents the most cogent argument in favor of the heredity of acquired characteristics. At least twenty Bachs who were musicians are cited in music dictionaries for their accomplishments. Moreover, Bachs were exceptionally fertile. The greatest Bach of them all, Johann Sebastian, was married twice and had twenty children, four of whom became important musicians in their own right. So many Bachs in the generation preceding Johann Sebastian had been organists, choir masters, vocalists, and town pipers that the name Bach was sometimes used as a synonym for a musician. The very letters of Bach's name, B-A-C-H, in German nomenclature (B flat, A, C, B natural in English usage) form an interesting chromatic

Opening of Bach's *The Passion of Our Lord According to St. Matthew*, BWV 244

theme which has been used as a subject in a number of works by many composers; Bach himself intended to use it in the last fugue of his work *The Art of the Fugue*, but it remained unfinished at his death.

The year of Bach's birth, 1685, was annus mirabilis in music history, for it was also the year of the birth of George Frideric Handel. (Domenico Scarlatti was born in the same year, too.) The birthplaces of the two great German musicians were a short distance from each other, but they never met. Handel went to London, where he rose to fame as a composer of great **oratorios**. Bach remained a modest organist, music master, and composer of religious music for his church. Another strange coincidence in the lives of Bach and Handel: both were operated on for cataracts by the same English surgeon. Handel's operation was successful, but not Bach's. Mercifully, Bach died before blindness lowered its veil. He was buried in a churchyard in Leipzig, but the location of his grave was not properly marked, and it was not until nearly a century and a half after his death that the coffin with his remains was found and identified. A famous physiologist of the day had a set of striking photographs taken of Bach's skull and bones. The photos were published in a deluxe edition as an awesome souvenir of human greatness.

Bach's life was deficient in spectacular events. After the death of his father, he was trained in music by his older brother, a methodical pedant, who played the same chorales in the same church for forty years. When he allowed himself to add a **grace note** or a **trill,** the congregation would comment on it as an extraordinary occasion: "Our Bach got quite excited today!" Johann Sebastian did not follow his brother's example in pedantry. During his employment as organist at the age of nineteen in Arnstadt, he was once summoned to the consistory and reprimanded for "introducing into the music many strange variations, with the admixture of numerous alien tones, thus bringing about confusion in the congregation." An even more

Oratorio (It.). An extended multi-movement composition for vocal solos and chorus accompanied by orchestra or organ.

Grace note. A note of embellishment, usually written small.

Trill. The even and rapid alternation of two tones which are a major or minor second apart.

serious reprimand was administered to Bach for leaving church during a sermon and going into the wine cellar.

Bach's duties at his posts in the Lutheran churches consisted of composing religious services for performance on holidays and training young scholars in music. His instrumental works were mostly didactic in nature. Even the epoch-making *Well-Tempered Clavier* was designed by Bach, according to the explicit description on the title page, to instruct music lovers in the art of playing on keyboard instruments in all twenty-four major and minor keys, and to enlighten them in the technique of counterpoint. Before Bach, usable keys were limited to those with a few sharps or flats in the key signature. Bach democratized the practice by extending composition to all keys in the circle of scales.

From his predecessors, Bach learned to interpret melodic intervals and chords symbolically. Early in the Baroque period, major keys became associated with positive and happy conditions and events, while minor keys were used to express sadness and death. Ascending intervals portrayed the spirit of determination and firm volition; descending **progressions** reflected indecision and hesitancy. Chromatic convolutions denoted suffering and distress; diatonic and triadic progressions indicated energy and healthy endeavor. Sometimes, intervals illustrated the text literally. The throwing of dice for Christ's garments is represented by trill-like figures; the dividing of the lot among the soldiers, by **syncopation**; the Cross, by an involuted **melisma**; and the silence of Christ during the questioning, by rests between chords in the accompaniment. Chords, other than major and minor, possess peculiar connotations in the musical vocabulary of the Baroque period. The most important among them is the chord of the diminished seventh, because of its protean capacity of fitting into any key, major or minor, by enharmonic change. This chord invariably makes its appearance whenever sin, disaster, or hell are mentioned in the text.

Progression. The advance from one tone to another (melodic) or one chord to another (harmonic).

Syncopation. Shifting of accents from strong beat to weak beat or between beats.
Melisma. A melodic ornament with more than one note to a syllable.

The adoption of such associative devices is easily explained. They facilitate the understanding of the text when it is not intelligible in performance, as is often the case. A passage like "In Adam's Fall, sinned we all," illustrated by a series of falling intervals and harmonized by diminished-seventh chords, immediately conveys the substance and the sentiment of the phrase, a feeling of distress, sorrowful realization, and acknowledgement of guilt. This intervallic vocabulary becomes in Baroque music the lingua franca of musical expression.

The foundation of Bach's sacred music is the Lutheran chorale. Heinrich Heine said that Luther's chorale "Ein' feste Burg" is the Marseillaise of the Reformation. The melodic materials of Protestant church music are rooted in German national songs. Bach's contemporary, the Hamburg music critic Johann Mattheson (1681–1764), deplored the "malady of melody" in German music. Bach remedied this condition by bringing the German chorale to the melodic apogee of expressiveness. But Bach also used the accumulated musical experience of other nations. The French writer Romain Rolland said: "Bach absorbed French and Italian art of composition, but his music remains echt deutsch." The peak of German sacred music is reached in Bach's great Passions.

Passion plays, with recitation and singing, date back to the early centuries of Christianity. Gradually, a standard order of scenes was established, and all four Gospels were often performed during Holy Week. The cast included the Evangelist, who narrated the course of events (usually a tenor), Christ (usually a bass), and a chorus representing the crowd. After the Reformation, Passions were performed to German texts in Protestant countries; the Latin text continued to be used in Roman Catholic districts.

The emergence of opera in the seventeenth century influenced the character of Passions, often imparting dramatic characteristics to the performance. As a theatrical spectacle of an operatic nature, Passion plays survive in the open-air productions in Oberammergau, in Bavaria, with a cast recruited among the common people of the countryside. The powerful attraction of the subject, even in modern times, is demonstrated by the extraordinary success of the setting of the St. Luke Passion by the Polish composer Krzysztof Penderecki (b. 1933).

Bach wrote two Passions, one based on the gospel according to St. John and one on the gospel according to St. Matthew. Some portions of Bach's music for the *St. Mark Passion* are also extant. Disparate numbers for the *St. Luke Passion*, in Bach's handwriting, have long been known, but stylistic analysis seems to indicate that the work is by a lesser composer, copied by Bach for use in church services. The text of the *St. Matthew Passion* was supplied to Bach by a local postal official in Leipzig, who had a knack for turning out striking devotional prose. He collaborated with Bach in other works; many of his texts became famous thanks to Bach's music.

The *St. Matthew Passion* is in two parts, containing arias, recitatives, chorales, duets, choruses, and instrumental interludes. Several chorales in the score are derived from secular songs by other composers, among them "Innsbrück, ich muss Dich lassen," in the harmonization of the Flemish composer Heinrich Isaac. As if to prove the unlimited magic of musical transliteration, Bach uses—in place of the genial words of the original, bidding farewell to the gemütlich Alpine town—the tragic query addressed to Christ: "Who has struck you so?" Five chorales in the *St. Matthew Passion* are derived from "Mein Gemuth ist mir verwirret" by Hans Leo Hassler (1564–1612). The music of another chorale comes from a surprising source, a French love song, "Il me suffit de tous mes maux," which Bach found in a sixteenth-century anthology. Such derivations from popular songs by no means degrade the religious sentiment of the music. The practice is not new; the frivolous medieval folk melody, "L'Homme armé," served as the cantus firmus of many sacred works by Renaissance composers.

Bach brought out the *Passion According to St. Matthew* on Good Friday, April 15, 1729, at the Thomaskirche in Leipzig. It is unlikely that the performance was at all adequate. Bach consistently complained about the inferior quality of choristers and instrumentalists at the school. They drank habitually and often begged in the streets. Besides, Bach experienced difficulties with his church superiors. According to his contract, Bach was required "to extend due respect and obedience to the eminent council, sustain its honor and reputation, and obey the inspectors and the rector of the school." Bach also had to sign a pledge to write the kind of music that "would not be too long or operatic in character, and would contribute to the piety of the congregation." On occasion he was reprimanded for contravening these instructions.

Despairing of his prospects in Leipzig, he began looking elsewhere for employment opportunities. In a typically humble letter to a former schoolmate who occupied an influential post at the Russian consulate in Danzig, he asked him for a recommendation to secure another position. He candidly detailed his distressing financial situation at the Thomaskirche, where he had to depend on wedding and funeral services to eke out his meager allowance. "My present employment," he wrote, "pays me about 700 thalers. If there are more funerals than usual, my income increases proportionately; but when the air is salubrious, these extra earnings fall off. For example, I lost more than 100 thalers last year because the number of funerals was only average." The letter was never answered, and Bach remained in Leipzig.

The *Passion of Our Lord According to St. Matthew*, unquestionably the greatest work of its kind, had to wait a hundred years for another complete performance after its original presentation at the Thomaskirche. On March 11, 1829, the twenty-year-old Felix Mendelssohn conducted it in Berlin. The event was tantamount to a rediscovery of Bach's greatness. Great impetus was given for further performances of Bach's works and to wide publication of his music. In 1850, on the hundredth anniversary of Bach's death, a complete edition of Bach's collected works was undertaken in Germany. By this act Bach had finally received full recognition as the fountainhead of Classical music.

GEORGE FRIDERIC HANDEL
(1685–1759)
The Magnificent

FOR SHEER SPLENDOR OF SOUND there is no other composer whose music can match that of George Frideric Handel. It is a flowing river of tones that seems to be following its predestined course without intervention of a human hand. There is in it dignity and beauty and a sort of impersonal greatness that makes the word "genius" least appropriate to Handel. For men of genius are in a constant state of turmoil; they are often victims of moods and passing fancies; they work under an inner compulsion that drives them to accomplishment almost against their will.

Handel was not an ordinary genius. His creative impulse was strong and dependable; he could compose music under any circumstances, and the speed of his production was astounding. He wrote one of his operas in two weeks, and he completed his greatest score, *Messiah*, in twenty-four days.

Handel was a supreme master of the musical craft. His fugal **counterpoint** is a thing of wonder. Yet despite the greatness of his knowledge, his music is distinguished by a fundamental simplicity of melodic line and harmonic sequence. This simplicity is explained by the fact that to Handel the singing voice was the supreme criterion of natural excellence. His instrumental writing was a reflection of the vocal line. His music breathed at a measured pace; his rhythmic design was steady despite the artful **syncopation** of his **fugues** and **canons**.

Handel was born in Halle, Germany, in 1685—a great year in music, for Bach and Domenico Scarlatti were also born in that year. In seventeenth-century Germany, music was regarded as little more than a menial occupation, and Handel's father had greater ambitions for the boy. But musical talent is a stubborn thing, and early in life Handel found himself irresistibly drawn to keyboard instruments. He taught himself to play the notes on a dumb **spinet** in which the strings were covered with heavy cloth. Then he met a friendly organist who let him practice on a real instrument. Soon Handel learned the elements of composition. An opportunity was presented to him to go to Hamburg, where he wrote his first opera. Then he traveled in Italy. He became an accomplished professional composer.

That was the time when the English court and English society were eager to secure the services of foreign composers for the London opera houses. Like many other Germans and Italians, Handel found himself in London, with promises of a fine career and rich material rewards.

Handel's first London production was an opera, *Rinaldo*, in Italian, which was sumptuously staged. In the garden scene there were real birds in huge cages, and natural flowers. Han-

Counterpoint. Polyphonic composition; the combination of two or more simultaneous melodies.

Syncopation. Shifting of accents from strong beat to weak beat or between beats.
Fugue. Contrapuntal imitation wherein a theme proposed by one part is taken up equally and successively by all participating parts.
Canon. Musical imitation in which two or more parts take up, in succession, the given subject note for note; the strictest form of musical imitation.
Spinet. An obsolete harpsichordlike instrument; a small modern piano.

del's music was rewarded by enthusiastic applause. The court looked on him favorably, and he was asked to write music for a grand festival to be held on the Thames. It was an extraordinary spectacle. Handel conducted an orchestra in a large flat barge which followed the king's boat. The suite of instrumental pieces he composed for the occasion came to be known as *Water Music*.

But Handel was not the only lord of music in London. An Italian composer named Giovanni Battista Bononcini (1670–1747) was also writing operas for London's theaters at the time, and he was favored above Handel by the aristocratic Queensberry, Rutland, and Marlborough families. The adherents of the rival factions decided to test the relative merits of the two composers by asking them to contribute one act each to an opera dealing with the Roman hero Muzio Scaevola (the man who put his right arm into the fire to prove his courage).

The combined opera was not a success, but it inspired an epigram by the Lancashire poet John Byrom that created a phrase that became a part of the English language: tweedle-dum and tweedle-dee. Here is the complete text:

> Some say, compar'd to Bononcini
> That Mynheer Handel's but a Ninny;
> Others aver, that he to Handel
> Is scarcely fit to hold a Candle:
> Strange all this Difference should be,
> Twixt Tweedle-dum and Tweedle-dee.

It should be explained that *mynheer* is Dutch for "Mr." or "Sir," and that in eighteenth-century parlance this title was equivalent to "Dutchman," and "Dutchman" was equivalent to "German," the word "Dutch" being a variation of "deutsch," which is the German word meaning German.

History showed that Tweedle-dum Handel proved to be much greater than Tweedle-dee Bononcini. Still, Handel had to face strong competition from the Italian-loving section of the English public. He produced one opera after another, without much success.

Providentially, this failure proved to be a great boon to music. Disillusioned in his career as an opera composer, Handel decided to turn to **oratorio**, and wrote his greatest masterpieces in this genre, culminating in the *Messiah*. His last oratorio, *The Triumph of Time and Truth*, was given at Covent Garden in London in 1757; as usual, Handel presided at the organ and directed the performance.

A few years before his death, Handel began to lose his eyesight. He had an affliction that was incurable; an operation was attempted but it brought no relief. The news of his illness was even published in a London theatrical journal. But still Handel continued to play in public, performing on the organ. Money was coming in from performances of his old works, and Handel was able to pay off all his debts. He had enough strength to lead a performance of *Messiah* at the keyboard a week before his death. He was buried in Westminster Abbey.

The famous British musical historian Charles Burney (1726–1814) gives his impression of Handel, whom he knew personally, in these words:

> The figure of Handel was large, and he was somewhat unwieldy in his actions; but his countenance was full of fire and dignity. His general look was somewhat heavy and sour, but when he did smile, it was the sun bursting out of a black cloud. There was a sudden flash of intelligence, wit, and good humour, beaming in his countenance which I hardly ever saw in any other.

Handel's greatness lies primarily in his oratorios and operas. His instrumental music, though of very fine quality, does not impose as Bach's instrumental music does. His suites for harpsichord are brilliant without being inspired.

Oratorio (It.). An extended multi-movement composition for vocal solos and chorus accompanied by orchestra or organ.

Of much greater importance are his instrumental **concertos**. Some of his organ concertos may have been composed as interludes for his oratorios. But the most glorious of Handel's instrumental compositions are his twelve grand concertos, written in the style of a **concerto grosso**. There are usually three instrumentalists forming the section known as **concertino**, and four sections known as **ripieno**. *Concertino*, of course, means "little concerto," and *ripieno* is the same word as the English "replenish," so that these string parts are designed to provide the support rather than the essential substance. In all these works there is a part for the figured bass, to be executed on the harpsichord.

Handel cast his mighty shadow on English music for a century after his death. English composers of oratorios were mesmerized by Handel's art so that they could do no more than produce mediocre facsimiles. It was not until the advent of Mendelssohn that a new great influence swung the British nation. In America, too, Handel was the musical god. His works were among the first Classical compositions heard in colonial America. Boston's Handel and Haydn Society has much more Handel than Haydn in it, and *Messiah* still traditionally opens its season. Long before Bach became widely known, Handel was acknowledged as the greatest of the greatest.

Concerto (It.). An extended multi-movement composition for a solo instrument, usually with orchestra accompaniment and using (modified) sonata form.

Concerto grosso (It.). An instrumental composition employing a small group of solo instruments against a larger group.

Concertino (It.). The group of soloists in a concerto grosso.

Ripieno (It.). A part that reinforces the leading orchestral parts by doubling them or by filling in the harmony.

Overture to Agrippina *(1709)*

A revival of Handel's operas began to materialize in Germany in the 1920s. It gathered momentum quickly, and soon was followed by a similar revival in England and elsewhere in Europe. A true reconstruction of the ambience of Handel's day in opera appears impossible, however, mainly because of the present unavailability of castrated singers, whose parts have to be replaced by women or **countertenors**, which latter are also rare. And the wanton supremacy of celebrated singers which allowed them to strut on the stage like so many roost-

Countertenor. A male singer with an alto range.

ers crowing their cockle-doodle-doo's in the high register of their voices in complete disregard of the written notes, could not be tolerated today. In Handel's time, Baroque opera was indeed baroque in the primary sense of the word—bizarre, strange, ungainly.

Although virtually all of Handel's operas were written to Italian librettos, few of them were produced in Italy in Handel's lifetime. A signal exception was *Agrippina*, which was staged in Venice on December 26, 1709, during Handel's stay there. It deals with the murderous mother of Nero, who was herself murdered by Nero's hired killers, after an attempt to scuttle the boat in which she was returning from her visit to her son failed. (She swam ashore.) The scenario, by an Italian nobleman, is much less bloody than the historic events, and includes no murders. In the final chorus, the Emperor Claudius, his wife Agrippina, her son and his stepson Nero, Nero's future successor, the Emperor Otho, Otho's wife Poppaea, who subsequently became the second wife of Nero himself, and for whose sake Nero killed his mother, all sing together in perfect Baroque harmony.

Aria da capo (It.). Three-part form of operatic aria: principal section with main theme; contrasting section with second theme and key change; elaborated repeat of principal section.

The overture, in G minor, is a typical Italian sinfonia, with thematic materials independent of the contents of the opera itself. The Neapolitan influence, particularly that of Alessandro Scarlatti (1660–1725), is much in evidence in the score, with its **da capo arias** and formal divisions, but Handel scholars seem to descry in it signs of an incipient dramatic style in the new manner of "the Great Saxon."

The Faithful Shepherd: *Suite (1712; revised 1734)*

Handel was the first of the three great German composers (the other two were Haydn and Mendelssohn) whose second country was England. He was the only one who became naturalized as an English citizen. Perhaps his name should have an umlaut on the a, but during his life in England, he signed his name without one. He also changed the German form of his name Georg Friedrich to the half-English, half-Gallic form George Fréderic. But he spoke in a heavy German accent to the end of his days. De Quincey gives a description of Handel in England. "A Polyphemus as to enormity of appetite," he used to order a dinner for seven. "He rang furiously for the dinner to be served, upon which the waiter would timidly suggest that perhaps his honor might choose to wait for the six commensals who had not yet arrived. "De who, de what?" would Handel exclaim. "The company, sir," was the waiter's reply. "De gombany!" ejaculated Handel. "I am de gombany!"

Handel died in England, and was buried in the Westminster Abbey, at the feet of the coffin of the duke of Argyle. One hundred eleven year later, Charles Dickens was to become Handel's "silent neighbor," in the words of Hugo Leichtentritt, in his great Handel biography.

By a curious twist of musical politics the German Handel became the greatest protagonist of Italian opera in England. There was a great deal of struggle between the opera in English and the opera in Italian in the early 1700s. The music critic Charles Burney (1726–1814) sets down the year 1705 as the period when the first real opera on an Italian model, though not in the Italian language, was produced on the English stage. The celebrated essayist, poet, and statesman Joseph Addison (1672–1719) rebelled against "the absurdity of going to an opera without understanding the language in which it is performed." The English singers who felt that they were displaced from the English stage by the Italian invaders, and were further handicapped by the fact that many Italian singers preserved their **bel canto** by early castration (a practice that the beef-eating Britons never applied to their own opera singers), joined in the campaign. There is a report that a servant of Katharine Tofts, an English singer, "committed a rudeness of

Bel canto (It.). The art of "beautiful song," as exemplified by 18th and 19th century Italian scripts.

the playhouse by throwing of oranges, and hissing when Mrs. L'Epine, the Italian gentlewoman, sung."

When Handel arrived in England in the autumn of 1710, the Italian opera reigned supreme. He was given the collaboration of an Italian poet, and in 1711 his opera *Rinaldo* was produced. Handel composed forty-six operas, all to Italian texts. He wrote with great facility. Thus, *Rinaldo* was written in fourteen days.

Il Pastor fido (*The Faithful Shepherd*) was the second opera written by Handel for the Italian season in London. The story was conventional, abounding in interlocked love triangles. The shepherd Mirtillo is loved by two shepherdesses, Amarillis and Eurilla. Silvio loves Amarillis, but is loved by Dorinda. Mirtillo, "the faithful shepherd," wins Amarillis through the oracular powers of a priestess of Diana, and Dorinda wins Silvio. A contemporary opera-goer noted in his diary after the performance, "The scenery represented merely an Arcadian landscape. The costumes were old. The opera was short." Apparently Handel thought well of *Il Pastor fido*, for many years later he presented a new version "intermix'd with chorus's" with an added prologue entitled "Terpsichore."

Charles Burney in his celebrated *General History of Music* gives a detailed account of the first performance of *The Faithful Shepherd*, its music and its singers, among whom the **castrato** Valeriano, was the most successful. He calls the overture "one of the most masterly and pleasing of the kind," and comments further, "The first air for a soprano lets us know what kind of voice the Cavalier Valeriano was possessed of; and the pathetic style of the first part of his song, as well as the agility necessary to the execution of the second, seem to imply abilities in that performer of no mean kind."

Burney mentions the "purity and simplicity" of Handel's music, which, "when the melody and the voice are exquisite would be always pleasing to an audience, as a contrast to rich harmony and contrivance." He observes, however, that "some

Castrato (It.). A castrated adult male singer with soprano or alto voice.

of these airs are now too trivial and far advanced in years to support themselves totally without harmony." Burney notes that the ornamental style of Handel's vocal writing,

> so much admired at the beginning of the century, has, however, been long banished from the opera as undramatic for the voice part is so much overpowered and rendered so insignificant by the complicated business of the accompaniments that she loses her sovereignty. Such ingenious contrivances seem best calculated for instruments where narration and poetry are out of the question; but in a drama where instruments are, or ought to be, the humble attendant on the voice, riot and noise should not be encouraged. . . . Handel has been accused of crowding some of his songs with too much harmony; but that is so far from being the case in this opera that he not only often leaves the voice without any other accompaniment than a **violoncello**, but sometimes even silences that.

Violoncello (It.). A four-stringed bow instrument familiarly called the cello.

On the opera in general, Burney says:

> It is inferior in solidity and invention to almost all his other dramatic productions, yet there are in it many proofs of genius and abilities which must strike every real judge of the art, who is acquainted with the state of dramatic music at the time it was composed. In the first place, it was a pastoral drama, in which simplicity was propriety. Besides, Handel had, at this period, no real great singer to write for. Valeriano was only of the second class. . . . Nothing but miraculous powers in the performers can long support an opera, be the composition ever so excellent. Plain sense and good poetry are equally injured by singing unless it is so exquisite as to make us forget everything else. If the performer is of the first class,

and very miraculous and enchanting, an audience seems to care little about the music or the poetry.

Water Music *(1717)*

The 1880 edition of the *Encyclopedia Britannica* contained the following paragraph in its article on Handel: "The system of wholesale plagiarism carried on by him is perhaps unprecedented in the history of music. He pilfered not only single melodies but frequently entire movements from the work of other masters, with few or no alterations, and without a word of acknowledgment."

This severe judgment ignores the permissive ways of the eighteenth century, when musical larceny was common, as was the purloining of verses and even of scientific discoveries, on a par with respectable adultery, provided it was carried out within one's own class. The only imperative was not to get caught. Handel escaped detection, and as a result scholars are still struggling with the monumental task of segregating the "pilfered" portions in Handel's music from the self-borrowed, revised, renamed, and original creations. Bononcini, Handel's hapless Italian rival in the competition for supremacy on the London opera scene, was not so lucky. He was imprudent enough to submit to a stuffy London academy a **madrigal** previously published by another Italian composer. When that composer objected, Bononcini was promptly run out of town. He went to Paris, where he unsuccessfully attempted the transmutation of base metals into gold in collaboration with a local alchemist and lost all his savings. He eventually wound up in Vienna, where he died in misery.

Despite the elimination of his Italian rival, Handel failed to achieve success in the field of opera. It was a felicitous failure for music, for it forced Handel to turn to oratorio, in which he attained the summit of glory, culminating in his crowning masterpiece, *Messiah*. It is as the composer of oratorios in the

Madrigal. A vocal setting of a short lyric poem in three to eight parts.

OVERTURE.

Opening of Handel's *Water Music*

English language that Handel endeared himself to his adoptive country and had the honor of burial in Westminster Abbey. Incidentally, the year of his birth on the marble pedestal is marked 1684 instead of 1685. This is due to the fact that Handel was born in February and the first of the year, according to the Julian calendar in force at the time, was in March. No such calendaric misadventure befell Bach, Handel's great contemporary, who was born a few weeks after Handel, in March, and thus safely within the new year 1685.

The circumstances surrounding the composition of the *Water Music* have been embellished by romantic inventions, but the basic facts seem to be clear. In 1710 Handel was appointed court director of music to the elector of Hannover. While occupying that post he made two visits to England, where he produced some operas. While he was in London, the elector of Hannover became King George I of England, and Handel, with his old patron on the throne, decided to remain in England. In 1727 he became a British subject.

On July 17, 1717, the king arranged a spectacular aquatic festival on the Thames River. The king with his retinue occupied a luxuriously appointed boat, which was followed by a barge with some fifty musicians. Handel was commissioned to write instrumental music to be played on the river, and it was subsequently published under the title *Water Musick*. It is impossible to establish whether this score contained the pieces actually played on the barge.

Concerto Grosso No. 12 in G Major (1739)

What the fugue is to Bach, the concerto grosso is to Handel. Just as Bach established the fugal tradition by perfecting an art that had existed before him, so Handel created an architecturally perfect type of the concerto grosso, which was not his invention. In a concerto grosso the "soloist" is not a single instrumentalist assigned a virtuoso role, but a group of instruments bearing the collective name of concertino—"little concert." This concertino group is accompanied, echoed, and generally aided and abetted by a large group of instruments of less pronounced individuality, which group constitutes the concerto grosso—"big concert." It is from the nonsoloist group that the entire composition takes its name.

Handel wrote twelve compositions for strings entitled concerto grosso in one month, October 1739. There was an advertisement in the *London Daily Post* announcing "Twelve Grand Concertos . . . composed by Mr. Handel." It added that "subscriptions are taken by the author, at his house in Brook Street, Hannover Square." After their publication in April 1740, another advertisement mentioned the fact that the concertos were "played in most public places with the greatest applause."

The Concerto No. 12, Op. 6, is in the key of G major, associated in Handel's music with lively and virile moods. The concertino group consists of two violins and cello. An introductory musical paragraph leads to an **Allegro**, which opens a characteristic Handelian merry-go-round. The increase in the musical momentum is achieved by sequences rising higher and higher. There is a **cadenza** for the violin, and the movement slows up to a conclusion. The second movement is an **Adagio** in a minor key, distinguished by stately eloquence. There follows an Allegro in the form of a full-fledged fugue. The subject of the fugue is based on the three notes of the G-major triad. The first violin of the concertino group opens the fugal festivities. It is fugally imitated by the second violin, and then by the cello, which latter is bolstered up by its colleagues from the nonsoloist group. Another fugal subject, also derived from the G-major triad, is introduced by the cello, and is passed over to the second and the first violin. There is much episodic development, and sequences are

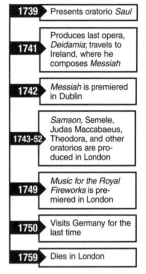

Handel Timeline (cont.)

1739	Presents oratorio *Saul*
1741	Produces last opera, *Deidamia*; travels to Ireland, where he composes *Messiah*
1742	*Messiah* is premiered in Dublin
1743-52	*Samson*, Semele, Judas Maccabaeus, Theodora, and other oratorios are produced in London
1749	*Music for the Royal Fireworks* is premiered in London
1750	Visits Germany for the last time
1759	Dies in London

Allegro (It.). Lively, brisk, rapid.

Cadenza (It.). An elaborate passage played or improvised by the solo instrument at the end of the first or last movements of a concerto.

Adagio (It.). Slow, leisurely; a slow movement.

rampant. At one point, a melodic figure is repeated eight times on different degrees of a descending scale. The movement comes to a close after every development of the two fugal themes appears exhausted. There is the inevitable cadenza before the slow **coda**. The last movement is an Allegro in jig time, typical of the Classical instrumental suite. It is a short movement in brisk motion.

Coda (It.). A "tail"; hence, a passage ending a movement.

FRANZ JOSEPH HAYDN
(1732–1809)
A Genius of Perfection in Music

FRANZ JOSEPH HAYDN EXEMPLIFIED THE SPIRIT of the eighteenth century in the charm, orderliness, and simple poetry that were the virtues of the age. The eighteenth century was the era of mass production in music. A formula was developed, and imitation became easy for minor composers. The sheer quantity of symphonic works of Haydn and Mozart is staggering; in comparison, nineteenth-century symphonists were laggards. The romantic elevation to individual symphonic creation had to wait until the advent of Beethoven. But the level of productivity fell spectacularly in the post-Classical years.

Haydn's life was serene and unperturbed by tragedy. He had a difficult childhood in the little town of Rohrau in Lower Austria, where he was born, but soon he was sent to Vienna, where he applied himself to earnest study under favorable circumstances. Still a young man, he was fortunate in securing a position in 1761 as second Kapellmeister to Prince Paul Anton Esterházy on his estate in Eisenstadt. There he composed some of his greatest symphonies, string quartets, and also a series of pieces for the baryton, a now obsolete bass viol, a string instrument favored by the prince, who played on it himself.

Haydn is popularly known as "the father of the symphony." Cautious musicologists are unwilling to support this designation, for it is seldom possible to establish a priority on any musical form, and there were symphonies written before Haydn. But there is no doubt that Haydn gave the firm outline to the Classical symphony in several movements that became the model for composers of a later day. In **chamber music** as well, Haydn's historical role is great. He created the string quartet, which has the same formal consistency as a symphony. Haydn's string quartets show an amazing development of **counterpoint**; like his symphonies, they became the models emulated by his successors.

In 1791 an enterprising German violinist, Johann Peter Salomon, approached Haydn in Vienna to write a group of symphonies for his concerts in London. Salomon himself was to be the "leader," that is, first violinist at the London concerts, and Haydn was to conduct from the **pianoforte**. Haydn accepted Salomon's persuasive and lucrative offer, and Salomon deposited five thousand gulden in a Vienna bank for Haydn as security. The story is told that before Haydn left Vienna, Mozart asked him how he expected to get along in England without the knowledge of English, and that Haydn replied, "My language is understood all over the world." It was during his first trip to London in 1791 that Haydn learned of Mozart's death.

Chamber music. Vocal or instrumental music suitable for performance in a room or small hall.

Counterpoint. Polyphonic composition; the combination of two or more simultaneous melodies.

Pianoforte (It.). A stringed keyboard instrument with tones produced by hammers; a piano.

Salomon was a master of publicity and advertised his concerts in the London newspapers with fine commercial flair. "The celebrated Haydn's arrival was yesterday announced in the musical circles," read the notice in the *London Oracle* of February 6, 1794. "Mr. Salomon most respectfully acquaints the Nobility and Gentry," it continued,

> that his first concert will be on Monday next, the 10th February. Subscriptions are at 5 Guineas for the 12 concerts. The Ladies' Tickets are blue and the Gentlemen's are red. Dr. Haydn will supply the Concerts with New Compositions, and direct the Execution of them at the Piano Forte. Every nerve is to be exerted to leave an impression deeper than ever of this excellent band. The Doctor has been writing with all his original fancy and fertile combination. Some Italians of fine taste have heard him in private, and they express most liberally their astonishment at his science and power.

Haydn did not limit his London activities to music. His personal journal abounds in references to English matrons and widows who showered their attentions upon him. About each one of them he remarked, "The finest woman I ever saw." He carefully saved a batch of letters from a Mrs. Schroeter, breathing womanly passion, and commented with regard to them that the lady, although sixty years of age, was still very beautiful. In the meantime, an Italian singer with whom Haydn had a liaison of long standing expressed her anxiety about Haydn's long absence. As to Haydn's wife, whom he left in Vienna, she was concerned mainly with the purchase of a new house. But when she died, Haydn avoided further matrimony, despite his written promise to the widowed Italian singer to marry her after "the four eyes" (her husband's and his wife's) were closed for eternity.

Haydn was so prolific that he himself could not remem-

Haydn Timeline

1732	Born in Rohrau, Austria
1740	Becomes soprano singer in chorus of St. Stephen's Cathedral in Vienna
1759	Becomes Kapellmeister to Count Ferdinand Maximilian von Morzin in Lukavec
1760	Marries Maria Anna Keller
1761-1802	Serves as second then first Kapellmeister at Esterhazy estate at Eisenstadt
1790	Takes up permanent residence in Vienna after the Esterházy orchestra is disbanded
1791	First London concert in the Hannover Square Rooms; receives honorary doctor of music degree from Oxford University; first performance of Symphony No. 92, "Oxford"
1792	Travels through Bonn and meets Beethoven
1794	Returns to London, where his twelve "London" symphonies (also known as "Salomon" symphonies) are performed; leads newly revived Esterhazy orchestra
1796	Composes six masses for church at Esterházy, including *Missa in tempore belli* (*Mass in Time of War*), the "Heiligmesse" ("Holy" Mass), and the "Nelsonmesse" ("Nelson" Mass)
1796-98	Composes *Die Schöpfung* (*The Creation*), first performed at Schwarzenberg Palace in Vienna
1797	Composes "Gott erhalte unser Kaiser," the Austrian national anthem

(continued)

Haydn Timeline (cont.)

1801	Oratorio *Die Jahreszeiten* (*The Seasons*) performed at Schwarzenberg Palace
1802	Beset by illness, resigns Eisenstadt post
1808	Last public appearance at a concert in his honor in the Great Hall of the University of Vienna, Antonio Salieri conducting *Die Schöpfung*
1809	Dies in Vienna

ber how many symphonies he wrote, and the catalogue that he compiled is very incomplete. As a result, musicologists until this day cannot agree on the authenticity of numerous works attributed to Haydn. One of the items taken off the Haydn list is the celebrated "Toy" Symphony, the score of which includes a trumpet, a drum, a whistle, a triangle, a quail, and a cuckoo. It now seems certain that the work was written by Mozart's father, possibly in collaboration with Haydn's brother, Michael.

Mastery and supreme professionalism combined in Haydn with gentle humor. When Prince Esterházy made up his mind to disband his private orchestra, Haydn accepted the princely decision with regret and, as a final contribution, composed and performed the "Farewell" Symphony. According to the instructions in the score, the musicians left, one by one, after completing their parts, until only the conductor remained on the stage; he blew out the candle and departed. Prince Esterházy was touched by this little spectacle, and decided to retain the orchestra.

Haydn was an eminently practical man. Like most composers of his day, he wrote music to order. Such was the perfection of his technique that he never had to wait for inspiration to come, and the quality of his music was uniformly high. One of Haydn's commissions was the composition of the Austrian national hymn, "Gott erhalte unser Kaiser" ("God Save Our Emperor"), which remained in force until the fall of the Austro-Hungarian Empire.

In the eyes of awed posterity, Haydn appears as a formidable father spirit, the demiurge of the symphony, the progenitor of the string quartet, the presiding officer of musicians' heaven. However, the life of Haydn, abounding in colorful episodes, shows him as a puckish rather than paternal spirit, given to mischievous moods even on solemn occasions. The jocular implications of the "Farewell" Symphony and the

"Surprise" Symphony are characteristic manifestations. Haydn could write a perpetual **canon** on a dog's death. When he himself felt bodily exhaustion, he had a card printed with the first bars from one of his vocal works, "The Old Man": "Gone forever is my strength—|/|Old and weak am I!" It is ironic that even in death Haydn continued to play poor Yorick. His skull was stolen from the coffin by a deranged admirer; it was later returned anonymously to Prince Esterházy, but proved to be spurious. At one time several Haydn skulls were in circulation in Vienna. In 1932, on the Haydn bicentennial, the authenticity of the skull reposing in the Vienna Academy of Music was accepted with seeming finality.

Canon. Musical imitation in which two or more parts take up, in succession, the given subject note for note; the strictest form of musical imitation.

SYMPHONIES

Symphony No. 88 in G Major (1787)

According to a convenient textbook description, Haydn was "the father of the symphony," even though the symphonic form was first developed earlier in Haydn's century by the musicians of the Mannheim School. But Haydn was undoubtedly the "perfecter of the symphony," whose mastery of **polyphonic** craftsmanship and orchestration enabled him to diversify the symphonic palette with ingenious rhythmic variations and instrumental colors. He added a third dimension to the rather bleak surfaces of the Baroque structures. He became the first Classicist of music, applying the same art of formal excellence in diversity to the composition of string quartets. Here the parental relationship of the creator to the product stands clear. Haydn was certainly the father of the string quartet.

Polyphonic. Consisting of two or more independently treated melodies; contrapuntal; capable of producing two or more tones at the same time, as the piano, harp, violin, xylophone.

The fanciful nicknames attached to many of Haydn's symphonies—the "Surprise" Symphony, the "Military" Symphony—are inventions by publishers to attract performers.

Sinfonia No. 88

I

Some are grouped according to the place of their performance—the "London" symphonies, the "Paris" symphonies.

Symphony No. 88 was a commissioned work, written for the violinist Johann Peter Tost, formerly a member of the Esterházy orchestra led by Haydn. In 1788, Tost went to Paris, carrying with him the scores of two symphonies by Haydn, identifiable as Nos. 88 and 89, which he had arranged to publish in France. For good measure, he also sold for publication a symphony by the young Bohemian composer Adalbert Gyrowetz, and brazenly put Haydn's name on the score. When poor Gyrowetz came to Paris some years later and claimed the symphony as his own, neither publishers nor musicians at large would believe him. Thus another spurious work was added to the Haydn catalogue. Somehow the two genuine symphonies found their way to Haydn's Vienna publisher, and Tost accused Haydn of unfair dealing. Distressed by this imbroglio, Haydn wrote to the Paris publisher asking him to straighten out the situation and to find out whether Tost had sold him some other works of Haydn to which he had no right. "Please, write me quite frankly," Haydn begged the Paris publisher, "and tell me how Tost conducted himself in Paris, and particularly whether he engaged in any Amours." In the meantime, the Bastille fell and, in the revolutionary turmoil, Tost apparently escaped from Paris.

The G-Major Symphony is in four movements. An introductory **adagio** leads to the main body of the movement, **Allegro**, a characteristically energetic piece of music progressing on its own momentum once the creative spark is struck. Remarkably enough, the traditional entry of trumpets and drums is deferred to the second movement, **Largo**, producing a singular impact because of the delay. The next movement, **Minuetto**, follows the Classical formula. The Finale: Allegro con spirito offers a treat to the musical cognoscenti in a magisterial canon with precise imitation between the upper and the lower strings, a locus Classical of polyphonic studies.

Adagio (It.). Slow, leisurely; a slow movement.
Allegro (It.). Lively, brisk, rapid.

Largo (It.). A slow and stately movement.
Minuetto (It.), **minuet**. An early French dance form.

Symphony No. 92 in G Major ("Oxford") (1789)

Of Haydn's 104 symphonies, at least two dozen have acquired descriptive nicknames, most of them unjustified. But the "Oxford" Symphony is quite proper in its designation. Haydn conducted it at the University of Oxford in July 1791, in acknowledgment of an honorary degree of doctor of music conferred on him on that occasion. The work itself was written three years earlier, but the Oxford performance was the first. Haydn received a handsome remuneration for his services, but he had to pay the travel expenses. He noted in his expense book: "One and a half guineas for the bell peals at Oxforth [*sic*]—and half a guinea for the robe." He was greatly pleased with the sumptuous vestment he wore at the ceremony, for according to reports the robe was a resplendent affair of cream-colored silk.

The Oxford doctorate was arranged for Haydn by the famous English music historian Charles Burney. So genuinely elated and patriotically proud was Burney at his part in the undertaking that he burst into verse to celebrate Haydn's landing on the British islands:

> Welcome, great master, to our favorite isle,
> Already partial to thy name and style;
> Long may thy fountain of invention run
> In streams as rapid as it first begun;
> While skill for each fantastic whim provides,
> And certain science ev'ry current guides.

The press reports were as magnificent as any Haydn had received in England. "A more wonderful composition never was heard," wrote the *Morning Chronicle*. "The applause given to Haydn, who conducted this admirable effort of his genius, was enthusiastic; but the merit of the work, in the opinion of all the musicians present, exceeded all praise."

Sinfonia No. 92
"Oxford"

I

Tonic. The keynote of a scale; the triad on the keynote (tonic chord).

Dominant. The fifth tone in the major or minor scales; a chord based on that tone.

Sonata (It.). An instrumental composition usually for a solo instrument or chamber ensemble, in three or four movements, connected by key, contrasted in theme, tempo, meter, and mood.

Coda (It.). A "tail"; hence, a passage ending a movement.

Allegretto (It.). Quite lively; moderately fast.

Finale (It.). The last movement in a sonata or symphony.

The "Oxford" Symphony is typical of his style, both in form and content. The principal key is G major, and there are few modulatory deviations from it. A brief adagio, in 3/4, serves as an introduction to an Allegro spiritoso, with the strings announcing both subjects, the first in the **tonic**, the second in the **dominant**, as decreed by **sonata form**. The development is thorough, and the **coda** is protracted. There follows an Adagio in D major, in 2/4 time, written in simple ternary form. The Minuetto, returning to G major, is marked **allegretto**; it includes a contrasting trio in which the bassoons and the horns create a bucolic atmosphere. The **Finale**: Presto, in 2/4, is full of kinetic energy.

Symphony No. 95 in C Minor (1791)

The task of cataloguing Haydn's symphonies and other instrumental works has been an important branch of musicological industry for some century and a half, and the end is not in sight. In the meantime, bloody polemics rage on the pages of musical periodicals regarding the attribution of this or that Haydn item, with the learned contenders, shoulder deep in the dust of Central European libraries, calling each other names. It has already been proved that the celebrated "Toy" Symphony was not written by Haydn, but by Mozart's father, and that the melody on which Brahms wrote his Variations on a Theme by Haydn was borrowed by Haydn from another source.

Happily, no cloud hangs over the twelve "London" symphonies, which Haydn wrote for the German violinist and manager Johann Peter Salomon, active in England, and which were performed during Haydn's two visits to London, in 1791–92 and 1794–95. The published edition states unequivocally: "Printed for the Proprietor, Mr. Salomon, and to be had at Monzani and Cimador's Music Shop, No. 2 Pall Mall." These "London," or "Salomon," symphonies are Haydn's last, numbering from No. 93 to No. 104. Haydn conducted Symphony

No. 95 himself from the pianoforte, with Salomon leading the violin section.

There are four movements. The first, Allegro, opens with a germinal motive that invites fugal development by an artful arrangement of intervals around the strategic dominant of the key. These potentialities are exploited in due time. The subject proper is an ascending figure rich in kinetic energy. The second important theme is in the relative major key. In the recapitulation it appears in the key of C major.

The second movement, Andante cantabile, is in E-flat major, in 6/8 time. It is an instrumental **aria** with variations. An elegiac episode in the homonymous key of E-flat minor occurs before the return of the theme. There follows a Minuet, in C minor, with a trio in C major. It is a typical Classical movement, in which Haydn shows himself to be a perfect musical courtier.

Aria (It.). An air, song, tune, melody.

The finale, **Vivace**, is in the form of **sonata-rondo**, in **alla breve** (2/2) time. It begins with a lively subject in C major, and develops in the best tradition of Classical musical architecture, of which Haydn was a master.

The symphony is prefixed by the words "In Nomine Domini," and the words "Laus Deo" ("Praise be to God") appear at the end of the manuscript, a lifelong habit. Haydn was deeply religious and believed in the necessity of prayer and gratitude for divine help in his work.

Vivace (It.). Lively, animated, brisk.
Sonata-rondo form. A rondo-form movement in at least seven sections, where the central episode functions as a development section.
Alla breve (It.). In modern music, two beats per measure with the half note carrying the beat; also called "cut time."

Symphony No. 99 in E-flat Major (1793)

Symphony No. 99 was announced by Salomon in the London program as "New Grand Overture." (No distinction was made in common usage at the time between a symphony and an overture.) "The incomparable Haydn produced an Overture of which it is impossible to speak in common terms. It abounds with ideas as new in music as they are grand and impressive; it rouses and affects every emotion of the soul. It was received with rapturous applause," commented the *Morning Chronicle* on the day after the concert. The symphony was repeated the following week, eliciting further enthusiasm from the *Chronicle*:

> The richest part of the banquet, as usual, was due to the wonderful Haydn. The first movement was encored; the effect of the wind instruments in the second movement was enchanting; the hautboy [oboe] and flute were finely in tune, but the bassoon was in every respect more perfect and delightful than we ever remember to have heard a wind instrument before. But indeed the pleasure the whole gave was continual, and the genius of Haydn, astonishingly inexhaustible, and sublime, was the general theme.

The first of the symphony's four movements, opening with an introduction, adagio, erupts in a brilliant Vivace assai, built in a characteristic **binary form**, in which the second half is a mirror image of the first. The movement is built in sonata form that is, however, remarkably free of convention, with the melodic material of the whole related in thematic structure to the principal theme.

Binary form. Movement founded on two principal themes, or divided into two distinct or contrasted sections.

The second movement, Adagio, in G major, in 3/4 time, introduces a songful subject, which develops in a number of ingenious rhythmic variations. Haydn projects the woodwind instruments to great advantage in a graceful interlude, which so enchanted the reviewer of the *Morning Chronicle* of London at the first performance of the symphony.

Piano (It.). Soft, softly.
Forte (It.). Loud, strong.
Modulation. Passage from one key into another.

The third movement, Allegretto, is a minuet, in E-flat major. It is spaciously designed, with fine contrasts of **piano** and **forte**. The trio travels to the remote key of C major, and the **modulation** to the original tonality is bold. The Finale: Vivace, in 2/4 in E-flat major, is a rondo with ingratiating countersubjects. The whole movement, with its leaping

appoggiaturas across large intervals, imparts a rococo sense of coquettish play. After a momentary pause, the principal theme returns in full splendor. The ending is in forte.

Appoggiatura (It.). "Leaning" note; a grace note that takes the accent and part of the time value of the following principal note.

Symphony No. 104 in D Major ("London") (1795)

The key of the 104th Symphony is variously designated as D minor, D major, or simply D, which latter designation, although ambiguous, is more rational, seeing that it accounts for the introduction, which is in D minor, and the exposition of the first movement, which is in D major.

The date of the performance would never have been established had Haydn not identified the new symphony, performed in London on May 4, 1795, as "die 12. und letzte der englischen" ("the twelfth and last of the English ones"). The program of the concert listed a "New Overture" and, in parentheses, "**Sinfonia**"—for in 1795, the concert managers (and composers, for that matter) still allowed the terms "overture" and "sinfonia" to be used interchangeably, although musical science of the period had already differentiated them. The "London" Symphony was given for Haydn's last benefit concert. Haydn wrote in his diary, in his realistic manner: "The hall was filled with a picked audience. The whole company was delighted, and so was I. I took in this evening 4,000 gulden. One can make as much as this only in England." Four thousand gulden was then equivalent to about two thousand dollars.

Sinfonia (It.). A symphony; an opera overture.

The introduction, in D minor, has sixteen bars in slow tempo. It opens with a fanfarelike proclamation by full orchestra which, in this symphony as in most Haydn symphonies, includes strings, woodwinds (two of each), two horns, two trumpets, and kettledrums. This fanfare recurs twice, in F, and in D, contrasted with the intervening passages in piano. There is a pause at the end of the introduction. The principal movement, Allegro, opens with a tuneful theme in

4/4, in the strings. The key is D major, by which the whole symphony is usually designated. The full orchestra bursts in, with some new material, rhythmic and lively. The music soon heads for the dominant, which course, in the tradition of all Classical forms, is as inevitable as the move of the king's knight in a chess opening. In place of a new second subject, the flute and the first violins take up the first theme in the dominant. This is very unusual in sonata form, and a symphony is nothing more than an orchestral sonata. The exposition ends in the key of the dominant, which is as it should be, according to the Classical formula.

The development of a symphony is like speculation about facts. The facts are the original subjects of the **exposition**. In the development section, they are pleasantly distorted, repeated in various keys, raised chromatically to shrieking pitch, or lowered into the gloom of the bass register. Indeed, there is often but a reminiscence of a theme left, a reflection of a vision of a dematerialized soul. The development of the first movement contains allusions to the second half of the principal theme, a four times reiterated note, and a plaintive appoggiatura, first in the strings, then in the flute and the oboe, in canonic imitation with the lower strings. The echoing of the reminiscent figure continues until the usual pause on the dominant, leading to the **recapitulation**, which is, in sonata form, a repetition of the exposition, with such variations as the composer may deem permissible or desirable. The principal theme appears in the strings, as it did in the exposition, and then reappears, obscurely hidden in the second oboe, with **contrapuntal** figures in the flute and the first oboe. The full orchestra comes in. There are imitations in canon between the woodwinds and the strings. The movement ends brilliantly.

On March 10, 1794, the London journal *The Oracle*, commenting on the second movement of a Haydn symphony, remarked rhetorically: "For Grace and Science, what is like it?" In

Exposition. The opening of a sonata movement, in which the principal themes are presented for the first time.

Recapitulation. A return of the initial section of a movement in sonata form.

Contrapuntal. Pertaining to composition with two or more simultaneous melodies.

Symphony No. 104, its science is bold, its modulations whimsical, but the Grace is there, spelled with a capital G. The main theme of the movement appears in variation form, in the original key of G major. Then it modulates upward, in **chromatic** progression. There is a pause after a string passage, and the flute plays a short **cadenza**, accompanied by oboes and bassoons. Another chromatic modulation brings in the dominant key. The theme returns **fortissimo**, embellished with triplet figurations. The flute continues the figure alone. The movement ends **pianissimo**, with a fine passage in the horns.

The Minuet, in D major, opens with a vigorous upbeat. The initial eight-bar period is then echoed in lighter orchestration. The dynamic contrasts of **tutti** and lighter scoring continue throughout the Minuet. There is a two-bar rest, and a two-bar **trill** before the end of the section, which is not repeated. The trio, in B-flat major, follows immediately. Only the first period of the trio is repeated. After the trio, the Minuet is resumed **da capo**, as all minuets must, to bring them back to the original key.

The fourth movement opens with a spirited dancelike tune, against the background of sustained horns and cellos. The time is alla breve (2/2), as in the first movement. The key is D major. The first violins carry the theme, in the low register, then an octave higher, joined by the oboe. The full orchestra is then brought into play, and the theme appears in various guises.

Haydn here uses once more the modification of sonata form that he applied in the first movement, and the principal theme in the dominant key serves in place of a new subject. There is a display of technique in the first and second violins, in converging and diverging scales. A quiet interlude follows with a dreamy melody in the relative minor key. The exposition concludes merrily, and is often not repeated in performance, as strict adherence to sonata form would demand. Few performers, however, follow the tradition of repeating the ex-

Chromatic. Relating to tones foreign to a given key (scale) or chord; opposed to diatonic.

Cadenza (It.). An elaborate passage played or improvised by the solo instrument at the end of the first or last movements of a concerto.

Fortissimo (It.). Extremely loud.

Pianissimo (It.). Very soft.

Tutti (It.). The indication in a score that the entire orchestra or chorus is to enter.

Trill. The even and rapid alternation of two tones which are a major or minor second apart.

Da capo (It.). From the beginning.

position, for this practice slackens the listener's attention and interest.

The development presents some canonic interplay of themes. The return of the exposition, that is, the recapitulation, enters softly, with the principal theme again in the violins. It then blossoms forth into a brilliant orchestral display. The dreamy melody appears again in the violins, while the flute gently traces an ascending scale. An orchestral outburst follows, but soon yields to a woodwind trio, a flute and two oboes, exhibiting the main theme in rotation. The symphony concludes with a forceful restatement of the theme, in the splendor of full orchestral dress.

CONCERTOS

Concerto for Violoncello in C Major (c. 1765)

Concerto (It.). An extended multi-movement composition for a solo instrument, usually with orchestra accompaniment and using (modified) sonata form.

Violoncello (It.). A four-stringed bow instrument familiarly called the cello.

A veritable musicological cliff-hanger is the story of Haydn's two **concertos** for **violoncello** and orchestra. In the case of the C-Major Concerto, it is listed in all catalogues of Haydn's works accompanied by the forbidding mark "verschollen," irretrievably lost. That the work actually existed is attested by the musical quotation of the opening bars of the cello solo in Haydn's own catalogue, compiled by him toward the end of his life. In November 1961, the electrifying news came of the discovery of an eighteenth-century copy of the "verschollenes Konzert" in the National Museum of Prague. One can well imagine the thrill when the discoverer checked on the theme of the concerto with the Haydn catalogue, and found that the two excerpts were identical. This, of course, established the authenticity of the lost concerto beyond all doubt. Stylistic analysis suggested that the concerto was written about 1765. And so, after two centuries, the concerto received its first performance, on May 19, 1962, at the Prague Spring Festival. The soloist was Miloš Sadlo, with the Czech Radio Symphony Orchestra, conducted by Charles Mackerras.

The concerto is scored for two oboes, two horns, and strings. The wind instruments are engaged mainly in the introduction and the **ritornellos**, when the soloist participates only by duplicating the corresponding part in the ensemble. This type of reinforcement was necessary in eighteenth-century performances owing to the smallness of the performing groups. In the original score of the Haydn Concerto, the cello part is written in to help out the basses; in twentieth-century practice, with a plentiful supply of instruments, such duplication is unnecessary.

Ritornello (It.), ritornelle (Fr.). A repeat; in a concerto, the orchestral refrain.

From a formal standpoint, the concerto is entirely orthodox. The first movement, **Moderato**, in the principal key of C major, in 4/4 time, is typical of initial movements of most instrumental works of the time, with symmetrical structures determining the progress of the music. The soloist is given a melodious voice; technically brilliant passage work employs familiar Baroque devices. The middle movement, Adagio, is in **ternary** form in the key of F major, in 2/4 time; the third and last movement, Allegro di molto in C major and in 4/4 time, provides a fitting conclusion. There are some interesting modulatory digressions into neighboring keys, before the principal key is asserted with dynamic vigor.

Moderato (It.). At a moderate tempo or rate of speed.

Ternary. Composed of, or progressing by, threes.

Concerto for Violoncello in D Major (1783)

The problem of authenticity of Haydn's works has been a major concern of music scholars. In his old age Haydn compiled a list of his symphonies, but it proved grossly inaccurate; his memory played him false. But there have also been pleasant reaffirmations of authorship, a notable instance of which is the restoration of Haydn's D-Major Cello Concerto to the Haydn column after it had been credited for many decades to Anton Kraft, Haydn's first cellist in his orchestra at Esterháza, thanks to an assertion in a German musical encyclopedia

(1837). Kraft absorbed Haydn's melodic and contrapuntal techniques to perfection; since he wrote a cello concerto of his own, it is not surprising that the great D-Major Concerto was also ascribed to him. Fortunately, Haydn's original manuscript was eventually discovered in Vienna, and a new authentic edition, establishing Haydn's authorship beyond all doubt, was published in Vienna in 1962. The title page, in Haydn's own hand, bears the inscription "Concerto per il Violoncello, di me Giuseppe Haydn 1783." At the end of the manuscript, Haydn appended his customary valediction: "Laus Deo"— Praise be to God.

Kraft's name remains intimately associated with Haydn's concerto, because it was he who gave its first performance. It appears certain that Haydn wrote the concerto for the wedding of Prince Nikolaus Esterházy and Princess Maria Josepha Hermenegild Liechtenstein at the Liechtenstein Palace in Vienna on September 15, 1783. To judge by the almost stenographic rapidity of Haydn's handwriting in the concerto, the commission must have been given to Haydn with considerable urgency. After the discovery of the manuscript, the first performance of the concerto in its definitive form was given by Enrico Mainardi on May 19, 1957. Mainardi also composed the cadenzas for this performance.

The Violoncello Concerto is in three movements: Allegro moderato, Adagio, and Allegro. The writing is of extraordinary lucidity. The principal theme is stated without preliminaries. The violoncello is occupied without respite, either enunciating the subject or providing brilliant figurations, two to a beat, then four to a beat, six to a beat, and finally, eight to a beat. The result of this treatment is an energetic exposition of thematic material, in perfect balance with ornamental sonorities.

The theme of the Adagio is an exact reproduction, melodically and rhythmically, of a fragment of the original subject of the first movement. It progresses by measured accumulation of decorative **melismas**, concluding on a quiet cadence.

Melisma. A melodic ornament with more than one note to a syllable.

The Finale: Allegro, is set in the rhythmic style of a **gigue**. The subject is structurally related to the principal themes of both the first and the second movements. This cyclic affinity, rare in eighteenth-century music, provides an extraordinary feeling of musical unity. The concerto ends, as it began, in decisive tonal affirmation.

Gigue (Fr.), **giga** (It.). A jig.

Symphonie Concertante in B-flat Major (1792)

Multiple concertos for instruments with orchestra, so popular in the eighteenth century, lapsed into innocuous desuetude in the nineteenth. The twentieth century witnessed a revival of these concertos in modern dress. One of the most extraordinary multiple concertos is Haydn's Symphonie Concertante, a quadruple concerto for solo violin, oboe, cello, and bassoon, accompanied by a full symphony orchestra. Haydn wrote it when he was sixty, at the height of his creative strength, for the same organization for which he composed the "London" symphonies. Examination of the score has surprises in store for those who believe in the myth of "Papa Haydn," a benevolent and bewigged gentleman who wrote melodious music for easy listening. For in the Symphonie Concertante we find Haydn, the Musical Scientist, the man Beethoven went to for the study of counterpoint, the intellectual musician who found satisfaction in structural organization as well as in the art of melody.

The selection of two string instruments of high and low range, and two woodwind instruments, also of high and low pitch, as solo instruments in the Symphonie Concertante affords six possibilities for instrumental duets, and four combinations for trios, besides four-part **harmony** and solo passages for each instrument singly. These combinations are artfully exploited and provide constant variety of **timbre** and **range**.

The Symphonie Concertante is in three movements, in

Harmony. A musical combination of tones or chords; a composition's texture, as two-part or three-part harmony.

Timbre (Fr.). Tone quality.

Range. The scale of all the tones a voice or instrument can produce from the lowest to the highest.

the key of B-flat major. It opens with an Allegro in sonata form, 4/4 time. This first movement is of considerable length, and the exposition of principal subjects is detailed and complete. There is a flowery cadenza in the best rococo manner. The second movement is an Andante, in 6/8 time. The solo instruments are given ample opportunity to display both the singing and the technical quality of their genre. The figurations are brilliant and varied.

The last movement, Allegro con spirito, is in the form of a rondo. There is an interesting departure from the instrumental character of a concerto in recitatives for solo violin that follow the melodic and harmonic procedures associated with opera. These recitatives, in adagio, interrupt the spirited progress of the movement at frequent intervals. Other solo instruments contribute their **fiorituras** and little arias, as well as rapid figurations. There is an effective interplay between the solo instruments and the orchestra. Once more, a recitative of the violin intervenes, and the movement concludes in a brilliant finale.

Fioritura (It.). An ornamental turn, flourish, or phrase, introduced into a melody.

Concerto for Trumpet in E-flat Major (1796)

Haydn's catalogue is an inchoate body of titles and dates, monstrously overgrown and interspersed with exasperating question marks expressive of the editor's own state of confusion. Not a year passes without a discovery of an unknown Haydn manuscript, or—much worse—the demotion of a consecrated Haydn item to the list of works by a lesser composer, or to the realm of the Great Anon.

It is a relief to note that an overwhelming majority of Haydn's symphonies, concertos, choral works, and various instrumental pieces can be confidently embedded in the authentic division. Among these works is the Trumpet Concerto in E-flat Major, which Haydn wrote in 1796 for Anton Weidinger, the Viennese inventor of the *cornet à pistons* (cornet) capable of playing an entire chromatic scale.

The concerto is in three movements: Allegro, Andante, and Finale: Allegro. The first movement, in 4/4 time, in E-flat major, has a lengthy orchestral introduction presenting the principal subjects. The trumpet enters with fine bravado after this exordium. According to the traditions of sonata form, to the perfection of which Haydn contributed so importantly, the theme appears in various related keys. The contrasting section is remarkable because it contains a descending chromatic passage in the solo part to honor Weidinger's invention. There is a long cadenza for the trumpet before a businesslike ending.

The second movement, Andante, in 6/8 time, is in the key of A-flat major. It has the rhythmic lilt of a **serenade**, with a simple melody, which subsequently undergoes a series of amiable variations. The Finale: Allegro, in 2/4 time, returns to the principal key of E-flat major. The statement of the main theme is given to the orchestra, and is reintroduced by the trumpet. A dialogue ensues between the solo instrument and the orchestra. There is a trumpet cadenza, and the concerto comes, to the utmost satisfaction of the musical ear, to an explicit and brilliant close.

Serenade. An instrumental composition imitating in style an "evening song," sung by a lover before his lady's window.

VOCAL WORKS

The Seven Last Words of Christ *(1795–96)*

The story of the composition of *The Seven Last Words of Christ* was told by Haydn himself in one of the few explicit statements he ever made regarding his works: "About fifteen years ago," wrote Haydn in 1801 (so the time referred to must have been about 1786),

> . . . I was asked by a clergyman in Cadiz to write instrumental music to the Seven Words of Jesus on the Cross. It was then customary every year, during Lent, to perform an oratorio in the Cathedral at Cadiz, the effect of which

the following arrangements contributed to heighten. The walls, windows and columns of the Church were hung with black cloth, and only one large lamp, hanging in the center, lighted the solemn and religious gloom. At noon all the doors were closed, and the music began. After a prelude, suited to the occasion, the Bishop ascended the Pulpit and pronounced one of the seven words, which was succeeded by reflections upon it. As soon as these were ended, he descended from the Pulpit and knelt before the Altar. The pause was filled by music. The Bishop ascended and descended again a second, a third time, and so on; and each time the Orchestra filled up the intervals in the discourse.

My Composition must be judged on a consideration of these circumstances. The task of writing seven Adagios, each of which was to last about ten minutes, to preserve a connection between them, without wearying the hearers, was none of the lightest; and I soon found that I could not confine myself within the limits of the time prescribed. The music was originally without text, and was printed in that form. It was only at a later period that I was induced to add the text. The partiality with which this work has been received by scientific Musicians, leads me to hope that it will not be without effect on the public at large.

The "seven last words" refer strictly speaking not to separate words but to seven phrases. They are (1) "Father, forgive them; for they know not what they do." (2) "Verily I say unto thee, this day shalt thou be with Me in Paradise." (3) "Woman, behold thy son; Son, behold thy mother." (4) "Eli, Eli, lama sabacthani?" (5) "I thirst." (6) "It is finished." (7) "Father, into Thy hands I commend my spirit."

The original instrumental form of the oratorio consisted of an introduction, seven pieces in a free sonata form, and a finale. The most unusual part of the music was the final portion of the oratorio describing the earthquake after the death of Christ. The music is marked "presto e **con** tutta la **forza**," and contains characteristic chromatic progressions and **diminished-seventh chords**.

Haydn made an arrangement of *The Seven Last Words of Christ* for voices with instrumental accompaniment under most unusual circumstances. A German musician named Joseph Friebert made use of Haydn's score for a vocal composition. Haydn heard Friebert's version and became interested in the possibilities of expanding the work into a real oratorio. He selected a text and fitted it into the music. Haydn added the voice parts and several instruments to the original score. He also made other additions and emendations. The result was a remarkably homogeneous work that quickly took its place among the most popular religious oratorios of the concert repertoire.

Con forza (It.). With force, forcibly.

Diminished-seventh chord. A chord consisting of three conjunct minor thirds, outlining a diminished seventh between the top and bottom notes.

The Seasons *(1799–1801)*

Haydn's last work of large dimensions was *The Seasons*, an **oratorio** with a German text adapted from the eighteenth-century Classic poem by James Thomson (1700–1748). The project was suggested to Haydn by the Dutch-born nobleman and music patron, Gottfried, Baron van Swieten, who had also translated for Haydn the text of *The Creation*, after Milton's *Paradise Lost*. But whereas Haydn worked on *The Creation* with feverish enthusiasm (he said he had felt "one moment as cold as ice, the next as if on fire"), he hesitated to accept the new commission. Besides, he objected to van Swieten's treatment of the text, and nearly quarreled with him on that account. But once begun, *The Seasons* progressed quickly to completion. Its first performance took place at the Schwarzenberg Palace in Vienna, on April 24, 1801, a few weeks after Haydn's sixty-ninth birthday, and two years after the first per-

Oratorio (It.). An extended multi-movement composition for vocal solos and chorus accompanied by orchestra or organ.

formance in the same palace of *The Creation*. On May 29, 1801, Haydn conducted *The Seasons* at his benefit concert in Vienna. The new oratorio was a success, but Haydn said afterward: "*The Seasons* gave me the finishing blow."

The dramatis personae in *The Seasons* are Simon, a farmer, his daughter Jane, and a young peasant named Lucas. All four seasons are represented in James Thomson's original poem, as well as in Haydn's oratorio. When *The Seasons* became popular in English-speaking countries, the problem of retranslation from the German adaptation back into Thomson's native tongue presented formidable obstacles. There were several versions, each successive effort trying to salvage as many lines from the original as possible while leaving the melodic rhythm of Haydn's music intact.

Ἡ σοι γ'εκ γενεης τα δαμ' εσπείο Θαυμαία εργα ;
Ἡε τις αθάναίων, ηε Θνηίων ανθρωπων
Δωρον αγανον εδωκε, και εφρασε Θεσφιν αοιδην ;

HOMER'S Hymn on Mercury

WOLFGANG AMADEUS MOZART
(1756–91)
The Supreme

WOLFGANG AMADEUS MOZART (1756–91) was the supreme and prodigious Austrian composer whose works in every genre are unsurpassed in lyric beauty, rhythmic variety, and effortless melodic invention. The universal recognition of Mozart's genius during the two centuries since his death has never wavered among professional musicians, amateurs, and the general public, although those who preferred the larger-than-life qualities of Beethoven would fail to hear the proto-Romantic element amidst the Classic aesthetic in Mozart. In his music, smiling simplicity was combined with somber drama; lofty inspiration was contrasted with playful diversion; profound meditation alternated with capricious moodiness; religious concentration was permeated with human tenderness.

Mozart was the first great child prodigy. At a nursery age he knew public acclaim and the praise of kings and potentates. There was a sweetness and serenity in Mozart as a child unmatched by any other musical child in history. He was a miraculous player, and he was a composer of alluring charm even in his works written before he reached early adolescence.

Mozart's older sister, Maria Anna ("Nannerl"), took harpsichord lessons from their father, Leopold, and Mozart as a very young child eagerly absorbed the sounds of music. He soon began playing the harpsichord himself, and later studied the violin. Leopold was an excellent musician, but he also appreciated the theatrical validity of the performances that Wolfgang and Nannerl began giving in Salzburg. In 1762, he took them to Munich and Vienna to play for royalty and in 1763 to Frankfurt, where Wolfgang showed his skill in improvising on the keyboard. In November 1763 they arrived in Paris, where they played before Louis XV; it was in Paris that Wolfgang's first compositions were printed (four **sonatas** for harpsichord, with violin **ad libitum**). In April 1764 they proceeded to London; there Wolfgang played for King George III.

In London he was befriended by Bach's son Johann Christian Bach, who gave exhibitions improvising four-hands at the piano with the child Mozart. By that time, Mozart had tried his ability in composing serious works; he wrote two symphonies for a London performance, and the manuscript of another very early symphony, purportedly written by him in London, was discovered in 1980. Leopold wrote home with undisguised pride: "Our great and mighty Wolfgang seems to know everything at the age of seven that a man acquires at the age of forty." Knowing the power of publicity, he diminished Wolfgang's age, for at the time the child was fully nine years old. In July 1765, they journeyed to the Netherlands, then set out for Salzburg, visiting Dijon, Lyons, Geneva, Bern, Zurich, Donaueschingen, and Munich on the way.

Sonata (It.). An instrumental composition usually for a solo instrument or chamber ensemble, in three or four movements, connected by key, contrasted in theme, tempo, meter, and mood.

Ad libitum (Lat.). A direction signifying that the performer's preferred tempo or expression may be employed; that a vocal or instrumental part may be left out.

Arriving back in Salzburg in November 1766, Wolfgang applied himself to the serious study of **counterpoint** under the tutelage of his father. In September 1767, the family proceeded to Vienna, where Wolfgang began work on an opera, *La finta semplice*. His second theater work was a **singspiel**, *Bastien und Bastienne*, which was produced in Vienna at the home of Dr. Franz Mesmer, the protagonist of the famous method of therapy by means of "animal magnetism," later known as mesmerism. In December 1768 Mozart led a performance of his Missa solemnis in C Minor before the royal family and court at the consecration of the Waisenhauskirche.

Legends of Mozart's extraordinary musical ability grew; it was reported, for instance, that he wrote out the entire score of the Miserere by Allegri, which he had heard in the Sistine Chapel at the Vatican only twice. Young Mozart was subjected to numerous tests by famous Italian musicians; he was given a diploma as an elected member of the Accademia Filarmonica in Bologna after he had passed examinations in **harmony** and counterpoint. In 1770, the pope made him a knight of the Golden Spur. He was commissioned to compose an opera and conducted three performances from the harpsichord.

Two of his finest symphonies—No. 35 in D Major, the "Haffner," written for the Haffner family of Salzburg, and No. 36 in C Major, the "Linz"—date from 1782 and 1783, respectively. From this point forward, Mozart's productivity reached extraordinary dimensions.

In 1785, Mozart completed a set of six **string quartets**, which he dedicated to Haydn. Unquestionably the structure of these quartets owed much to Haydn's **contrapuntal** art, and Haydn himself paid tribute to his genius. Leopold Mozart reports Haydn's words about Mozart: "I tell you as an honest man before God that your son is the greatest composer I have ever known personally or by name. He has taste and, what is more, supreme science of composition." Despite the fact that

Counterpoint. Polyphonic composition; the combination of two or more simultaneous melodies.
Singspiel (Ger.). A type of eigtheenth century German opera; usually light, and characterized by spoken interludes.

Harmony. A musical combination of tones or chords; a composition's texture, as two-part or three-part harmony.

String quartet. A composition for first and second violin, viola, and cello.
Contrapuntal. Pertaining to composition with two or more simultaneous melodies.

Wolfgang Amadeus Mozart's Werke.

Kritisch durchgesehene Gesammtausgabe.

Serie 14.

QUARTETTE

für Streichinstrumente.

Serie 14.		Köchel's Verz. Nº	Seite.	Serie 14.		Köchel's Verz. Nº	Seite.
1.	Quartett G dur ¾.	80.	I.	13.	Quartett D moll C.	173.	96.
2.	Quartett D dur C.	155.	8.	14.	Quartett G dur C.	387.	106.
3.	Quartett G dur ⅜.	156.	15.	15.	Quartett D moll C.	421.	124.
4.	Quartett C dur C. Für	157.	21.	16.	Quartett Es dur C. Für	428.	137.
5.	Quartett F dur ¾. 2 Violinen,	158.	29.	17.	Quartett B dur ⅜. 2 Violinen,	458.	152.
6.	Quartett B dur C. Viola	159.	36.	18.	Quartett A dur ¾. Viola	464.	168.
7.	Quartett Es dur C. und	160.	45.	19.	Quartett C dur ¾. und	465.	186.
8.	Quartett F dur C. Violoncell.	168.	52.	20.	Quartett D dur C. Violoncell.	499.	206.
9.	Quartett A dur ¾.	169.	60.	21.	Quartett D dur C.	575.	226.
10.	Quartett C dur ¾.	170.	69.	22.	Quartett B dur ¾.	580.	242.
11.	Quartett Es dur C.	171.	77.	23.	Quartett F dur C.	590.	258.
12.	Quartett B dur ¾.	172.	86.				

Haydn was almost twice Mozart's age at the time, their friendship was on an equal footing. Haydn was generally accepted as the creator of the Classical quartet, a form that Mozart faithfully followed. But there was no condescension on Haydn's part when he expressed his opinion of Mozart's greatness, and there was no feeling of subservience on the part of Mozart. In short, the Haydn-Mozart relationship is a rare example of un-affected friendship between two men of greatness. It is interesting to add that both were members of the order of Freemasons. Mozart joined the Vienna Lodge in December 1784, and Haydn followed early in 1785.

A great number of Mozart's instrumental works were the products of commissions by wealthy patrons. This circumstance influenced even the form of Mozart's instrumental works. Thus, instrumental **divertissements**, **serenades**, and similar compositions often provided several extra **minuets** or other dances to fill in the time if the particular festivity for which such works were written lasted longer than expected, much as contemporary incidental music for movies provides extra sections, or is so arranged that the separate sections can be easily spliced.

Divertissement (Fr.). A light and easy piece of instrumental music.

Serenade. An instrumental composition imitating in style an "evening song," sung by a lover before his lady's window.

Minuetto (It.), **minuet**. An early French dance form.

Mozart's life and Mozart's music form an interlocking commentary. It is a strange reflection on eighteenth-century society that Mozart could not maintain the security that his early successes seemed to augur, and that in his later life he should have been dependent entirely on his commissions as composer, and when these failed to materialize in sufficient numbers, on borrowing without repayment and on undisguised begging. Composers have not been self-supporting at any time in any society based on profit, and have always been dependent on the benefactions of those in political or economic power—the kings in monarchical Europe, the wealthy art patrons in other parts of the world. But performers finding favor with the public were in a far better position than creative musicians. Why Mozart could not provide for himself and his family as a performer or a teacher is a puzzle not explained by the historians of musical society.

Still, melodramatic stories of Mozart's abject poverty are gross exaggerations. He apparently felt no scruples in asking prosperous friends for financial assistance. Periodically he wrote to Michael Puchberg, a banker and a brother Freemason, with requests for loans (which he never repaid); invariably Puchberg obliged, but usually granted smaller amounts than Mozart requested.

Mozart Timeline

1756	Born in Salzburg
1762	Performs with his sister Maria Anna ("Nannerl") for elector of Bavaria in Munich and Emperor Francis I in Vienna
1763	First compositions printed
1765	Tours the Netherlands, Salzburg, Dijon, Lyons, Geneva, Bern, Zurich, Donaueschingen, Munich
1768	Conducts performance of his Missa solemnis in C Minor before royal family and court
1769	Becomes Konzertmeister to Archbishop Sigismund von Schrattenbach in Salzburg
1770	Opera *Mitridate, re di Ponto* performed in Milan
1773	Composes first "mature" symphony, No. 25
1775	Supervises first performance of *Il Re Pastore* in Vienna
1778	Travels to Paris with his mother, who dies there
1780	Loses position in Salzburg; moves to Vienna
1782	Marries Constanze Weber; produces *Die Entführung aus dem Serail* at Burgtheater
1782-8	Composes symphonies No. 35, the "Haffner," and No. 36, the "Linz"
1785	Completes set of six string quartets dedicated to Haydn
1786	*Le Nozze di Figaro* (*The Marriage of Figaro*), produced in Vienna

(continued)

In literature, Mozart has been the subject of several novels and plays. Pushkin presented a tragic Mozart in a play, *Mozart and Salieri*, in which the Italian composer Antonio Salieri (1750–1825), the court Kapellmeister in Vienna, poisons Mozart to stop the flow of celestial harmony: "What if Mozart is allowed to live on and to reach new heights?" asks Salieri. "Will the art be maintained at that height? It will fall again as soon as Mozart disappears—he will not leave an heir. Like a cherub, he has brought down a few songs from paradise, which will only excite a wingless desire in us, the children of the dust, and he will then fly away. Fly then! and the sooner the better." Rimsky-Korsakov set Pushkin's tale of Salieri the poisoner to Mozartean music; his opera ends with Mozart playing his own Requiem. Salieri himself thought so seriously about the rumors he had had a hand in Mozart's death that in 1825 he sent a deathbed message to the pianist Ignaz Moscheles: "I did not poison Mozart." At least, Moscheles so reports. A fanciful dramatization of the Mozart-Salieri rivalry was made by Peter Shaffer into a successful play, *Amadeus*, and gained wider currency through a film version in 1984.

The notion of Mozart's murder also appealed to the Nazis: in the ingenious version propagated by some German writers of the Hitlerian persuasion, Mozart was a victim of a double conspiracy of Masons and Jews who were determined to suppress the flowering of racial Germanic greatness. In this version, the Masons were outraged by his revealing of their secret rites in *Die Zauberflöte* (*The Magic Flute*), and allied themselves with plutocratic Jews to prevent the further spread of his dangerous revelations.

Another myth related to Mozart's death that found its way into the majority of Mozart biographies and even into respectable reference works was that a blizzard raged during his funeral and that none of his friends could follow his body to the cemetery. This story is easily refuted by the records of the Vienna weather bureau for the day. It is also untrue that

Mozart was buried in a pauper's grave; his body was removed from its original individual location because the family neglected to pay the mandatory dues.

The parallel between Mozart and the Renaissance painter Raphael is often drawn. Both lived short lives. Raphael died on his thirty-seventh birthday; Mozart did not even reach his thirty-sixth. Raphael's art was marked by logical simplicity, and so was Mozart's. Raphael's subjects are serene and natural; Mozart, too, portrayed carefree moods in a carefree manner. This parallel was drawn for the first time by Franz Niemetschek in a biography of Mozart written a few years after his death and is sufficiently plausible to have engaged Mozarteans in successive centuries.

We are so familiar with the picture-book presentation of Mozart, a genius unconscious of his own powers, an eternal child with an angelic face in a frame of artificial curls, that it is naturally shocking to discover he could be mischievous in his art. He could be mischievous and sly also in his human relations. From the evidence of his letters, an entirely new Mozart emerges, cunning, shrewd, and not above borrowing money under false pretenses. Yet this Mozart is much more human than the tinseled creature of conventional biography.

Mozart used **dissonances** and forbidden **progressions** on purpose in a little parody that he called "A Musical Joke" ("Ein musikalischer Spass," subtitled "Die Dorfmusikanten," "The Village Musicians"), and which he wrote on the afternoon of June 14, 1787, for the amusement of friends. In this musical joke, Mozart deliberately used consecutive fifths and a **whole-tone scale** in the violin **cadenza** and, to top it off, finished the piece in five different keys. He could hardly foresee that the employment of several keys in simultaneous harmony would be taken seriously a hundred-odd years thence, and that it would even receive a scientific-sounding name—**polytonality**.

The variety of technical development in Mozart's works is all the more remarkable considering the limitations of in-

Mozart Timeline
(cont.)

1787 *Don Giovanni* first staged in Prague

1788 Composes last three symphonies, Nos. 39, 40, 41, "Jupiter"

1790 *Così fan tutte* (*Thus Do All Women*) is premiered in Vienna

1791 *Die Zauberflöte* first produced; dies in Vienna

Dissonance. A combination of two or more tones requiring resolution.

Progression. The advance from one tone to another.

Whole-tone scale. Scale consisting only of whole tones, lacking dominant and either major or minor triads; popularized by Debussy.

Cadenza (It.). An elaborate passage played or improvised by the solo instrument at the end of the first or last movements of a concerto.

Polytonality. Simultaneous use of two or more different tonalities found in modern music.

Recapitulation. A return of the initial section of a movement in sonata form.

Octave. A series of eight consecutive diatonic tones; the interval between the first and the eighth.

Modulation. Passage from one key into another.

strumental means in his time; the topmost note on his keyboard was F above the third ledger line, so that in the **recapitulation** in the first movement of his famous C-Major Piano Sonata, K. 545, the subject had to be dropped an **octave** lower to accommodate the **modulation**. The vocal technique displayed in his operas is amazing in its perfection; to be sure, the human voice has not changed since Mozart's time, but he knew how to exploit vocal resources to the utmost. This adaptability of his genius to all available means of sound production is the secret of the eternal validity of his music.

ORCHESTRAL MUSIC

Symphony No. 25 in G Minor, K. 183 (1773)

Mozart's Symphony No. 25 is dated October 5, 1773, that is, when Mozart was only seventeen years old. This is not too surprising, considering that he wrote his first symphony at the age of eight. Haydn's influence is easily detected in this Twenty-fifth Symphony, but there are also points of contact with Johann Christian Bach, the "London Bach," who showered attention on the child Mozart during the journey of Mozart's family to England. The presence of fine dynamic nuances in the work indicates Mozart's awareness of the innovations introduced by the Mannheim masters.

Con brio (It.). "With noise" and gusto; spiritedly.

The symphony is in four Classical movements. The first movement, Allegro **con brio**, in the principal key of G minor, in 4/4 time, opens with a strong rhythmic subject with repeated notes in syncopated rhythm. Its development follows the outline of sonata form, and there is a clearly defined reca-

Andante (It.). Going, moving; moderately slow tempo.

pitulation. The second movement, **Andante**, is in E-flat major, in 2/4 time. Here the interest lies in a balladlike sequential construction of the main theme for muted strings. The third movement, Minuetto, is in the traditional ternary form. The minuet proper is in G minor, the trio is in G major. The **Finale**: Allegro, in G minor, in 4/4 time, is a vivacious **rondo**. Once more, the construction by simple tonal sequences arrests attention.

Symphony No. 32 in G Major, K. 318 (1779)

Mozart wrote this work in Salzburg in 1779, when he was twenty-three. It is surmised that he intended it to be used as an overture to one of his operas planned for production there, which may explain the unsymphonic character of the work. It is in three movements, Allegro spiritoso; Andante; Tempo primo. There is no minuet. The finale constitutes a shortened recapitulation of the first movement, and it is played without a pause after the slow middle movement. The sequence of tempi—fast, slow, fast—is the formula of an overture rather than a symphony. There are dramatic incidents in the music— mounting **crescendos** over protracted **pedal points**, horn calls and **tremolos** in the strings—that suggest stage action.

Symphony No. 36 in C Major ("Linz"), K. 425 (1783)

On the way back from Salzburg to Vienna in late October of 1783, Mozart and his wife stopped over at the house of Count Thun in Linz. Mozart wrote on October 31, 1783: "On November 4, I am giving a concert at the town theater here, and since I do not have a single symphony with me I must work neck-and-head at a new one, which must be ready before then." It was indeed ready—the composition, the copying of the parts, and the rehearsals, all accomplished in four days. The work was performed on schedule and became known, rightly so, as the "Linz" Symphony.

The work is one of Mozart's most classically perfect compositions. It is in C major, and contains four movements. The first movement consists of an introductory **adagio** in 3/4

Finale (It.). The last movement in a sonata or symphony.

Rondo (It.). An instrumental piece in which the leading theme is repeated, alternating with the others.

Crescendo (It.). Swelling, increasing in loudness.

Pedal point. A tone sustained in one part to harmonies executed in the other parts.

Tremolo (It.). A quivering, fluttering, in singing; an unsteady tone.

Adagio (It.). Slow, leisurely; a slow movement.

SYMPHONY No. 36
in C Major, K.425 ("Linz")

Composed November 1783 in Linz.

time, leading to Allegro spiritoso, in 4/4, which evolves with poetic animation within the confines of Classical sonata form.

The slow movement, Poco adagio, in F major, in 6/8 time, is an air in the rhythm of **barcarole**. There follows a minuet, which moves along with typical Mozartean grace. The finale is a **Presto** in 2/4 time in rondo form, with the vivacious principal theme returning afresh after an intermittent series of melodious countersubjects.

Barcarole (Ger.). A vocal or instrumental piece imitating the song of the Venetian gondoliers.
Presto (It.). Fast, rapid; faster than "allegro."

Overture to Der Schauspieldirektor, *K. 486 (1786)*

While working on *The Marriage of Figaro*, Mozart took time off to write an engaging little theater sketch, *Der Schauspieldirektor (The Play Director)*, dated February 3, 1786. It was a commissioned work for a performance at the orangery of the royal palace in Schönbrunn, in Vienna, at a reception given by Joseph II for the visiting general-governor of the Netherlands. The slender story, from a contemporary play, dealt with a rivalry between two *prime donne*, in which the Impresario becomes embroiled, much against his will. They were named in the cast of characters Mlle Herz ("heart") and Mlle Silberklang ("sound of silver"). One of the parts was sung by Mozart's sister-in-law.

The score consists of an overture in C major (presto, 4/4 time), an **arietta**, a rondo, a vocal trio, and the finale. The text is in German. The most amusing number is the trio, in which the two *prime donne* sing in canon: "I am the prima donna, I am universally acclaimed, no other singer can approach me … adagio, allegro, **allegrissimo**, piano, pianissimo…"

The overture remains a popular item on concert programs. It is typically Italian in structure, and its vivacity is contagious. Several attempts have been made to titivate the simple story and the score for scenic purposes. A version of

Arietta (It.), **ariette** (Fr.). A short air or song; a short aria.

Allegrissimo (It.). Very rapidly.

1845 had Mozart himself put on the stage as a supernumerary character. The Italian title *L'Impresario* was adopted in the middle of the nineteenth century. In 1953 Eric Blom published a witty English version under the title *An Operatic Squabble, or The Impresario Perplext*, naming the warring singers respectively Mrs. Heartfelt and Miss Silvertone.

Overture to The Marriage of Figaro, *K. 492 (1786)*

Le Nozze di Figaro: *dramma giocoso in quadro atti; poesia di Lorenzo Da Ponte, aggiustata dalla commedia del Beaumarchais, "Le Mariage de Figaro"* was written by Mozart in Vienna in 1786. It was performed at the Imperial Royal National Court Theater in Vienna on May 1, 1786. Amazingly enough, the performance ran into all kinds of obstacles on account of the immorality of the comedy itself. Lorenzo Da Ponte reports in his memoirs that Mozart wrote the music as fast as the **libretto** was being prepared, and that the entire opera was completed in six weeks.

Libretto (It.). A "booklet"; the words of an opera, oratorio, etc.

The librettist, Lorenzo da Ponte, decided to approach the Emperor Joseph II himself for permission to have the opera performed. "But you know that I have already forbidden the German theatrical company to have this piece performed," the emperor told Da Ponte. The librettist acknowledged that it was so, but pleaded with the emperor, pointing out that he had cut out all objectionable scenes in making the Beaumarchais play into an opera libretto. He assured the emperor that nothing would be left that might shock the sensibility of the public. He courteously reminded the emperor of the high opinion in which Mozart's musical talent was held in the city.

The emperor relented and ordered the score to be sent to the copyists. Later, Mozart himself was summoned to the palace to play some numbers from the opera for the emperor in private. Joseph II was delighted by the music, and *The Mar-*

riage of Figaro started on its glorious road through the opera houses of the world.

The overture itself, in D major, is a presto. The basic movement remains unaltered throughout the overture, but marvelous contrasts and subtle variety of moods are created by rhythmic and melodic changes of musical phrases. The form is a projection of luminous symmetry. After the main themes have been stated, there is a **reprise**, culminating in a brilliant **coda**.

Reprise (Fr.). A repeat; reentrance of a part or theme after a rest or pause.
Coda (It.). A "tail"; hence, a passage ending a movement.

Symphony No. 38 in D Major ("Prague"), K. 504 (1787)

Mozart always loved Prague, and Prague loved him. He knew greater triumphs and heart-warming welcome in Prague than in his native Salzburg or in his adopted hometown of Vienna. Within the German and Austrian sphere of influence, Prague was a great cultural center in the eighteenth century. Confident of success, Mozart, accompanied by his wife and several friends, gladly undertook the tedious three-day journey from Vienna to Prague (150 miles, about twenty minutes by plane today) to conduct his freshly composed symphony, which came to be known as the "Prague" Symphony.

The *Prager Oberpostamtszeitung* (*Prague Post Office Newspaper*) reported on January 12, 1787:

> Last night our great and beloved composer Herr Mozard [a common spelling in Mozart's time] arrived here from Vienna. We do not doubt that in honor of this man, the well-loved work of his musical genius, *The Marriage of Figaro*, will be performed again and that the discerning inhabitants of Prague will surely assemble in large numbers, notwithstanding that they have already heard the piece frequently. We would dearly like to be able to admire Herr Mozard's playing for ourselves.

Mozart did not disappoint the expectations of Prague's music lovers, and he conducted a special performance of his opera. So delighted was he by the reception that within the same year, he gave Prague the honor of the first performance anywhere of his greatest opera, *Don Giovanni*, and came again to Prague to conduct it.

Mozart filed a necessary application "to hold a musical concert," which was duly granted by the office of the governor of Bohemia. On January 19, 1787, he conducted the "Prague" Symphony and, in response to applause, obliged with three **improvisations** on the piano. Mozart left Prague on February 8, arriving in Vienna, by stagecoach as before, in four days.

Improvisation. Offhand musical performance, extemporizing.

Mozart entitled the work simply Eine Sinfonie. A sad postscript: in the latest edition of Köchel's catalogue, there is an annotation: "Manuscript lost since the end of the war." Some Mozart lover in the Army of Occupation must have taken the "Prague" Symphony as a war souvenir from one of the deposits in various German towns where the manuscripts of the old Prussian State Library were distributed by faithful German librarians during the last days of the Third Reich.

The first movement begins with an adagio in D major, in 4/4 time, with dramatic upward runs in unison. The violin has a plaintive melody, echoed in the woodwinds. The mood darkens, with a shift to D minor. A syncopated figure, punctuated by the strokes of the kettledrum, alternates with light flourishes of the violins. The modulations are tense and follow a **chromatic** progression toward an extensive **cadence**. The principal Allegro opens with a syncopated figure on a repeated note in the first violins. The wind instruments enter, by way of contrast, and the strings return, while the oboe plays a short melody. The figure of the repeated note soon develops into a rhythmic pattern. The orchestra, now in full strength, plays a vigorous marching theme, leading to the **dominant** key. Again the figure of the repeated note appears, in different instruments and different keys, ending on a quiet cadence in the dominant.

Chromatic. Relating to tones foreign to a given key (scale) or chord; opposed to diatonic.

Cadence. Rhythm; also, the close or ending of a phrase, section, or movement.

Dominant. The fifth tone in the major or minor scales; a chord based on that tone.

The first violins carry a quiet melody. There is a sudden darkening into a minor key, with the bassoons echoing the violin theme. The major key returns, and the violins play a lively theme, leading toward the marching theme, this time in the dominant. This concludes the principal part of Allegro in sonata form. The development section that follows opens with a curious **canon** in the violins. The same canonic device is then taken up in the low register. The marching theme appears in different keys, in combination with the figure of the repeated note. There is a prolonged pedal point on the deep A, and the repeated note returns in the first violins: this is the recapitulation. However, in sonata form, recapitulation is literal repetition only in very orthodox writing. This is not early unsophisticated Mozart; and he is not content with unchanged forms. Accordingly, there are new modulations, and characteristic shifts from major to minor on the same keynote. This section ends on the quiet theme in the tonic, corresponding to the preceding quiet theme in the dominant.

From now on, the recapitulation follows its appointed course with little change. Again, there is a darkening into the minor key. The expressive violin theme reappears, and the animated marching section leads to a brilliant ending.

The second movement, Andante, follows after a brief pause. It is in 6/8 time, in the key of G major, with a rhythmic lilt suggesting a barcarole. The tenseness of the mood is indicated by frequent chromatic progressions. There is canonic imitation between the violins on the one hand and cellos plus the basses on the other. The modulatory scheme is bold, and there is a feeling of unrest. Finally, there is an intense drive toward the key of D, with the violins and the woodwinds playing preparatory figurations.

A new phrase of **pastoral** character is heard in the violins. The mood is sustained by the echoing of woodwind instruments. The violins play a concluding theme, and the **exposition** is ended. The development elaborates on the

Canon. Musical imitation in which two or more parts take up, in succession, the given subject note for note; the strictest form of musical imitation.

Pastoral. A scenic cantata representing pastoral life; an instrumental piece imitating in style and instrumentation rural and idyllic scenes.

Exposition. The opening of a sonata movement, in which the principal themes are presented for the first time.

ideas already presented. There are darker colors, frequent shifts from one key to another. The chromatic upward runs intensify the dramatic effect. The scoring is more full, and the contrasts are emphasized by dynamic changes.

A few remaining bars of the development lead to a recapitulation. But once more, recapitulation is here no literal repetition. The orchestration is supplemented, the coloring is sharper. However, the succession of keys follows the traditional formula. Both the principal and the second, pastoral theme are now played in the **tonic** key. The movement ends gently, in **pianissimo**.

The third and final movement, Presto, is appropriately optimistic. The tonality is clear D major, and there are no tortuous chromatics. The tempo, in 4/4, is light, the scoring diaphanous. Particularly fine are the color effects of woodwind interludes. The division of musical periods is symmetric: four, eight, or sixteen bars each. The melodic flow is free, the phrasing natural and simple. It is the Mozart of *Figaro*, intent on amusement, not the philosophical Mozart of the first two movements of this symphony.

The strings open the movement with the four-note principal theme. After a symmetric sixteen-bar period, the orchestra enters in full. By way of contrast, there follows a section in the woodwinds, imitating the principal theme in a modulatory period, from D Minor to F Major. The full orchestra is sounded again, and there is some darker, dramatic coloring here. Now the strings play the second theme, and the flute, accompanied by a bouncing bassoon, finishes it off. The interplay of these elements is repeated. The woodwinds play the principal theme in the dominant key of A major, and the strings enter in imitation.

Again, the full orchestra enters dramatically, in a minor key. The violins play the principal theme, varied in rhythm and intervals, and descending **arpeggios** bring the first section to a close. Full orchestra chords announce the second section,

Tonic. The keynote of a scale; the triad on the keynote (tonic chord).
Pianissimo (It.). Very soft.

Arpeggio (It.). Playing the tones of a chord in rapid, even succession.

and there is alternation with woodwind. The contrasts are sharp. A prolonged development, with keys shifting frequently in a wide modulation range, leads to the return of the second theme in the violins. Again, as in the first section, the woodwinds finish off the phrase. The tonality is now D major, the key of the entire symphony. The descending arpeggios bring the Presto (and the symphony) to a brilliant close.

Symphony No. 39 in E-flat Major, K. 543 (1788)

June 1788 was a very busy month in Mozart's life. On June 17, he moved with his wife and children to new lodgings in suburban Vienna, at Wäringergasse no. 135, at the sign of the Three Stars. He had left the previous quarters on the Landstrasse under unpleasant circumstances, for the landlord compelled him to pay the back rent before they moved out. Mozart liked the new rooms, which were comfortable and, what was particularly important, cheap. True, he had to pay the fiacre ten kreutzer to drive to town, but then he was more free to work, because visitors were less frequent at this distance from town. And he did accomplish in ten days in the new lodgings more than he had in two months in the old.

Mozart's Symphony in E-flat Major is the first of the stellar symphonic trilogy created in a state of quiet inspiration during the summer of 1788. The second and the third symphonies of the cycle are the intimate G Minor and the Olympian C Major.

The E-flat Major Symphony can be seen as a musical equivalent to the golden section in architecture. In it, each phrase relates to its associative period as that period relates to the entire movement, and as each movement relates to the entire work. There is an abiding symmetry in the noble macrostructure as in the minimotives of each of the four movements of the work. An opening adagio serves as an

SYMPHONY No. 39
in E-flat Major, K.543

Composed June 1788 in Vienna.

earnest declaration of purpose, introducing the main division of the first movement, Allegro. Its principal theme is built on the three notes of the tonic triad of E-flat major, exquisitely arranged in convoluted undulations.

A contrasting figure follows with a doubled quantitative rhythmic content. Then an energetic new motive makes its entry. These thematic elements engage in a lively interchange until the exposition is completed. There is no formal development; each variation, each modulatory digression, appears as a newly born idea, melodically and rhythmically associated with the basic subjects of the movement. The provocative suggestion of a famous modern composer that Mozart's symphonies could have been vastly improved by the elimination of the development section does not apply. The music here is irreducible in content and in impact.

The second movement, Andante, in 2/4 time, in the key of A-flat, is a **romanza** with varied contrasting clauses. Its syncopated rhythmic pattern lends itself to canonic imitation. The modulatory scheme is remarkably bold; by dint of artful **enharmonic** equations, the entire cycle of scales is circumambulated and the remotest keys are reached, before returning to the home base.

The Minuet: Allegretto, is far from a conventional courtly dance. The initial theme is arrayed in wide intervallic steps encompassing two octaves in a single measure. It is in this minuet that Prokofiev must have found the model for the brusque skipping melodies of his *Classical Symphony*. In the middle section of the minuet—the trio—the clarinet and the flute conduct a melodious dialogue.

The Finale: Allegro, is a rondo. The main motive, with its vigorous upbeat, sets the tone of Classical directness. The alternation of numerous ancillary motives provides variety without impeding the strong pulse of rhythmic motion. Canonic imitation between strings and woodwind instruments proceeds vivaciously. There are frequent excursions into distant

Romanza (It.). A short romantic song or a solo instrumental piece.

Enharmonic. Differing in notation but alike in sound.

Diminished-seventh chord. A chord consisting of three conjunct minor thirds, outlining a diminished seventh between the top and bottom notes.

tonalities, and they are effected without resort to the **diminished-seventh chord**, that passe-partout of enharmonic modulation. The ending is remarkable; the initial motive of the finale serves as the concluding measure of the symphony. Here the principle of cyclic construction finds its perfect application.

Symphony No. 40 in G Minor, K. 550 (1788)

Sacha Guitry, the French actor and playwright, who wrote a play about Mozart, said that Mozart flew across the skies of music like an archangel with wings of gold. In Pushkin's drama *Mozart and Salieri*, Salieri pours poison into Mozart's wine murmuring "So fly away to Paradise from whence you came." (This Mozartocidal tale is an unmitigated fantasy not supported by an atom of realistic evidence.)

The real Mozart, as revealed in his correspondence, had little of an angel in him. He was an honest artisan trying hard to earn enough money to support himself and his growing family. He was even, horribile dictu, given to profanity. His scatological canons have been issued on records, now that there is no censorship of German four-letter words. Nor is Mozart's music uniformly serene. There is enough drama in its somber harmonies and its throbbing rhythms to conjure up a vision of Mozart the Tragedian.

Mozart's Symphony in G Minor, his fortieth, was written in the summer of 1788, after the one in E-flat major, and preceding the great C-Major Symphony, the "Jupiter." The creation of three symphonies, each one sublime in its art, within a single year was an unparalleled achievement even for Mozart. The four movements of each of these three symphonies are in the Classical mold: a fast first movement, Allegro molto, followed by an Andante, a Minuet, and a rapid Finale: Allegro assai.

The symphony opens with Allegro molto, in G minor. Its palpitating principal subject sets the tone for the entire movement. The form is that of a sonata allegro, which is worked out

SYMPHONY No. 40
in G Minor, K.550
Completed July 25, 1788 in Vienna.

with superlative clarity and dramatic contrasts. The second movement, Andante, in the key of B-flat major, is characteristic of Mozart's "Italian" style, songful and decorative in its ingratiating melodic variations. The third movement, Minuett, in the principal key of G minor, is uncommonly brief. The middle part, trio, is based on the fanfare figures of hunting horns. The movement is set in a Classical three-part form, without elaborations or variations.

The Finale: Allegro assai, is full of kinetic energy. In the development section, there are bold enharmonic modulations to remote keys. The diminished-seventh chord (which the Italians called *accorde di stupefazione*, "chord of stupefaction") plays a crucial role in the modulatory scheme. In one intriguing episode, three mutually exclusive "chords of stupefaction" form a series of twelve different notes, used consecutively in various instruments of the orchestra. Some modern commentators cite this section as a prophetic anticipation of dodecaphonic usages. Mozart, it appears, was a composer for all seasons. And in his music there are to be found roots of future idioms and future techniques.

CONCERTOS

Concerto for Violin No. 5 in A Major, K. 219 (1775)

In 1775, at the age of nineteen, Mozart wrote five violin concertos, probably intended as exercises to satisfy the paternal urgings of Leopold Mozart, himself an eminent violinist and teacher, and possibly with a view toward a performance by a Salzburg virtuoso. The manuscript of the Fifth Violin Concerto is now in the Library of Congress in Washington; it was formerly owned by the famous violinist Joseph Joachim (1831–1907), and before that by the publisher Johann Anton André, who acquired it from Mozart's widow.

The Fifth Concerto is a fine distillation of Mozart's stylistic qualities, a paradigm of his instrumental art in composition. There is the characteristic vivacity of a musical optimist in the rapid portions of the music; elegiac inspiration in songful passages; and a graceful gait of a court dance in the finale.

The first movement, in A major, is set in the energetic meter of 4/4. It comprises three sections: an "openhearted" allegro aperto, in which the subject based on the notes of the tonic triad is introduced jointly by the soloist and orchestra; a brief adagio, with an expressive theme in the solo part accompanied by the shimmering murmurations of innumerable semi-demi-quavers; and another "open" (aperto) allegro, not as a literal recapitulation, but as a greatly expanded presentation of germane thematic materials in a new melodic and rhythmic mold.

The second movement, Adagio, in E major, in slow 2/4 time, is remarkable for its varied melodic figurations, in which Mozartean **syncopation** seems to reinforce the main beat by metrical anticipation. A series of tonal sequences leads to an unaffected ending.

Syncopation. Shifting of accents from strong beat to weak beat or between beats.

The third and last movement, in A major, is a minuet, an unusual selection for a finale. The violin solo introduces the gentle dancing theme, with an upbeat and a note échappée, falling down on the unprepared suspension on the leading tone. The place of a traditional trio is taken by an allegro set in a totally different metric scheme, in 2/4 time, in the minor tonic. Melodic patterns are most curious in this middle section; there is a fascinating ascending chromatic phrase within a **tetrachord**, reciprocated by a symmetric descending chromatic phrase, in a manner suggesting a peasant stomping dance of Central Europe.

Tetrachord. The interval of a perfect fourth; the four scale-tones contained in a perfect fourth.

In fact, some musicologists have published learned essays on Mozart's utilization in this and other violin concertos of such peasant dance tunes. However that might be, the effect produced by this display of elastic resilience in chromatic progression is extraordinary. The Tempo di minuetto re-returns, and the concerto concludes with reverberating gusto.

Concerto for Three Pianos in F Major, K. 242 (1776)

Mozart composed his Concerto for Three Pianos in Salzburg a few days after his twentieth birthday, as a commission for Countess Antonia Lodron and her two daughters. Mozart's father, always mindful of the prime necessity of pleasing aristocratic patrons, wrote out a flowery dedication in Italian: "Dedicated to the incomparable merit of Her Excellency the Signora Contessa Lodron and her two daughters, Countesses Aloisa and Giuseppa, by their most devoted servant Wolfgang Mozart." But apparently the three ladies never performed the concerto. The first hearing was given in Augsburg on October 22, 1777. Mozart played the second piano part, with a local organist at the first piano, and a piano manufacturer at the third.

Like so many of Mozart's concertos, this concerto consists of three movements, Allegro, Adagio, and **Rondeau**, the latter marked Tempi di minuetto. The first and last movements are in F major, and the slow movement is in B-flat major. The concerto has 565 bars, of which Allegro numbers 280 bars, Adagio 73 bars, and Rondeau 212 bars. Although the slow movement has the smallest number of bars, the reduced tempo equalizes it with the fast movements in duration.

Rondeau. A medieval French song with instrumental accompaniment, consisting of an aria and a choral refrain.

Concerto for Flute and Harp in C Major, K. 299 (1778)

A major part of Mozart's meager revenue came from commissions to write music for amateur musicians of the nobility, dukedom, or royalty. The Concerto for Flute and Harp was composed in April 1778 for the duc de Guines and his daughter. The duke played the flute and the daughter, the harp. Mozart wrote in a letter that the duke was a very good flutist and that the little duchess played the harp "magnifique."

Being a superior workman capable of satisfying any kind of customer, Mozart adopted in his concerto a French salon manner. He was also careful not to write passages that might overtax the technique of the duke and the duchess, and he wrote the concerto in the key of C major unencumbered by sharps or flats in the key signature. But despite all of Mozart's eagerness to please, the duke was uncivil enough to have delayed the payment for the commission for fully four months after the delivery of the manuscript, a fact of which Mozart, always pressed for money, complained to his father.

The concerto is in three movements, Allegro, **Andantino**, and Rondeau (the latter spelled in French in the manuscript). Mozart had written cadenzas for both the flute and the harp in the concerto, but they were lost. The concerto numbers 775 bars of music in all, Allegro taking 265 bars, Andantino 118 bars, and Rondeau 392 bars.

Andantino (It.). A little slower than andante, but often used as if meaning a little faster.

Sinfonia Concertante for Violin and Viola in E-flat Major, K. 364/320d (1779)

So brief was Mozart's life that Mozartologists are compelled to classify his successive styles and manners of composition in periods of a very few years each. Mozart's productivity was prodigious. Neither the heartaches of his amorous youth nor disheartening failures to obtain satisfactory employment interfered with the steady flow of music from his magical pen. It may be said that composition for Mozart was a bodily function, as natural as respiration and the oxygenation of venous blood.

Mozart's gifts were universal. He was superb in all genres of musical composition: opera, symphony, chamber music, solo works for various instruments, and concertos. He mastered the art of keyboard playing to perfection; but he was also an expert violinist; at one time he applied himself to the viola, and played in a string quartet with Haydn. His double concerto for violin, viola, and orchestra, known as Sinfonia Concertante, bears testimony to his ability to write for these instruments with a virtuosity based on personal practice.

The work, written in 1779, is the culmination of a series of double concertos that Mozart wrote between the ages of twenty-one and twenty three, and is regarded as one of his greatest achievements in this particularly difficult form. He wrote it upon his return to his native Salzburg from a visit to Paris. On his way he stopped over in Mannheim, a locality of great importance in music history, for it was there that the "Mannheim sound," characterized by a wealth of dynamic instrumental effects, originated; among these the total orchestral crescendo and **diminuendo** were of particular expressive power. Mozart was very much taken with the Mannheim innovations and adopted them in his subsequent works.

Diminuendo (It.). Diminishing in loudness.

In Salzburg, Mozart held a position with the archbishop's court and drew a modest salary. His letters indicate that he had little love for his employment there; he wrote to his father that "the Archbishop cannot pay me enough for this Salzburg slavery."

The Sinfonia Concertante in E-flat Major is more in the nature of a **concerto grosso** than a symphony. The two solo instruments perform the function of the concertino, contrasted with the **tutti** of the orchestra. It is in three movements: Allegro maestoso, Andante, and Presto. The work opens with a declaration of tonality in assertive chords of the tonic E-flat major. A procession of triadic tones in the solo violin supports this declaration. The immediacy and the freshness of the thematic material have forced the critics to exhaust their supply of superlatives. The tonus of the music is muscular, determined by the prevalence of major keys. It is in this movement that the "Mannheim crescendo" makes its debut with great effect. Another remarkable feature is the proliferation of persistent pedal points on the dominant, with chromatic passing notes forming the connective tissue for modulatory digressions. After a double cadenza for the soloists, the movement comes to a close.

Concerto grosso (It.). An instrumental composition employing a small group of solo instruments against a larger group.

Tutti (It.). The indication in a score that the entire orchestra or chorus is to enter.

The second movement, Andante, is in C minor. It is in the nature of a ballad, with expressive melodic suspensions imparting a poignant sentiment to the melody. The tonality is gradually turned toward E-flat major through a series of daring cross-relations. There are truly Beethovenian anticipations in the somberness of sonorities reposing on deep pedal points.

The Finale: Presto is a festival of rhythm, a dance of many connected refrains. Both soloists and orchestra are active in melodious and harmonious cooperation. As in the preceding movements, the pedal point on the dominant occupies a strategic position in the progress of the music. The ending reasserts the declaration of tonality in the basic E-flat major.

Concerto for Piano No. 24 in C Minor, K. 491 (1786)

Mozart completed this concerto in Vienna on March 24, 1786. It represents his "dramatic" period, notable for the somber quality of his harmonies and a considerable increase of enharmonic modulations in comparison with his earlier works. There are fascinating points of similarity between the material of this concerto and some arias and orchestral **ritornellos** of *The Marriage of Figaro*, which occupied Mozart's creative imagination at about the same time as the concerto. In fact, the opera bears the next K. number, 492. The resemblance between the two formally unrelated works is revealed sometimes in the intervallic turn of the melodic phrase, sometimes in characteristic tonal sequences, sometimes in harmonic progressions, and quite often in rhythmic figures. One can almost hear an echo of an aria from *The Marriage of Figaro* in the concerto, and the Italian words almost fit some of the concerto's themes.

Ritornello (It.), **ritornelle** (Fr.). A repeat; in a concerto, the orchestral refrain.

There are three movements in the concerto. The first, Allegro, in C minor, in 3/4 time, opens with a long orchestral introduction. Owing to the basic minor key and the prevalence of chromatic modulations, the coloration of the music appears to be in the dark part of the tonal spectrum. The piano enters without accompaniment, and soon plunges into a series of energetic passages of a fine rococo character. In the recapitulation, the principal theme of the movement appears in the relative major key; the second theme is, as required by tradition, in the tonic key of C minor. The movement ends quietly.

The second movement, **Larghetto**, is set in E-flat major, in **alla breve** time. The piano solo again appears without accompaniment; the mutual responses between the soloist and the orchestra set the mood of the music, in **antiphonal** dialogue. The thematic materials are developed in fluent variations, and the movement concludes without ostentation.

The third and last movement, Allegretto, in C minor, alla breve, is a rondo with variations. The themes are stated with utmost clarity, with variations developing by rhythmic diminution so that the number of notes within a given beat increases steadily and produces a state of tension, which is further enhanced by the use of chromatic modulations. Then, with characteristic Mozartean ease, the intensity of the musical texture is suddenly relaxed. The concerto comes to a close without undue prolixity or Baroque garrulity.

Larghetto (It.). The diminutive of largo, demanding a somewhat more rapid tempo.

Alla breve (It.). In modern music, two beats per measure with the half note carrying the beat; also called cut time.

Antiphonal. Responsive, alternating.

Concerto for Piano No. 25 in C Major, K. 503 (1786)

Mozart was very punctilious in noting down the exact date of completion of most of his works, but he never numbered his symphonies and concertos, which makes the task of cataloguers difficult and leads to discrepancies and duplications. Considering also the influx of spurious scores ascribed to Mozart and later exposed as not authentic, the numeration of his works becomes even more complicated.

Mozart completed his Piano Concerto in C Major in Vienna on December 4, 1786, and played its first performance at the Vienna Academy on March 7, 1787. A Ph.D. thesis ought to be written on the significance of C major in Mozart's music, but the writer should be careful to take into consideration the important fact that the standard of **pitch** was much lower in the eighteenth century than it is now. Mozart's C-Major Concerto as played by himself in 1787 would sound somewhere between B and B-flat major to most American musicians accustomed to the high pitch of American orchestras. Conversely, it would register in Mozart's ear higher than D-flat major were he to hear it as performed in America. The symbolism of C major, the key that Robert Browning described as the essence of life, its immaculate whiteness, its chaste freedom of all chromatic impurities, is largely a matter of **notation**: no sharps, no flats in the key signature, only white keys on the piano keyboard.

> **Pitch.** The position of a tone in the musical scale.

> **Notation.** The art of representing musical tones, and their modifications, by means of written characters.

The concerto is one of Mozart's most ingratiating scores, pre-Raphaelite in its natural simplicity. It is in three movements. The first movement, Allegro maestoso, in gentle 4/4 time, introduces the principal theme, which is derived from the component tones of the C-major triad. A development follows, with thematic phrases embellished by graceful **arabesques**. Occasionally the tonality darkens; the **mediant** and the **submediant** are flatted, and the key assumes the somber coloring of C minor. There are numerous piano vignettes, replete with pearly scales and flowing arpeggios.

> **Arabesque.** A type of fanciful pianoforte piece; ornamental passages accompanying or varying a theme.
> **Mediant.** The third degree of the scale.
> **Submediant.** The third scale tone below the tonic; the sixth degree.

The second movement, Andante, in F major, in 3/4 time, is a songful eclogue. It evolves as a theme with variations. The flute, the oboe, and the clarinet are given prominence, contributing to the pastoral character of the music. The third movement, Allegretto, in C major, in 2/4 time, is a vivacious rondo. Once launched, it progresses with unabated celerity toward a brilliant ending.

At the time of the composition of the concerto, Mozart's financial situation was far from being in C major. It was rather in F double-sharp minor, what with sharp reminders from his Vienna landlord regarding the payment of past due rent. In his distress, Mozart turned for help to a friendly banker, one

Michael Puchberg, who was a fellow member of Mozart's in the Vienna branch of the Free Masonic Order, which gave Mozart an opportunity to address him as a fraternal soul. Once, receiving no reply from Puchberg to one of his begging letters, Mozart enclosed a pair of pawnbroker's tickets as collateral. Mozart never asked for outright gifts, but always termed his requests as applications for a loan. As far as can be established, Puchberg never got back a kreutzer.

But in exchange for his florins Puchberg received a measure of immortality in the name index of Mozart's biographies. In fact, had he bequeathed Mozart's begging letters to his descendants, they would have made a fortune selling them to autograph dealers for several thousand times the sum originally asked by Mozart. The finances of Mozart's family did not improve much after his death. Mozart's widow could not even place many of his manuscripts with publishers. She printed the C-Major Concerto in 1798 at her own expense.

Concerto for Piano No. 27 in B-flat Major, K. 595 (1791)

The manuscript of this piano concerto, the last that Mozart wrote, is dated January 5, 1791. Mozart played it in Vienna at a concert of the clarinetist Josef Bähr on March 4, 1791. He died at the end of that year.

The concerto is in three movements, in the key of B-flat major. The first movement, Allegro, in 4/4 time, is thematically evolved from a simple triadic formation in the gentlest Mozartean manner. Musical phrases are formed in symmetric tonal sequences, and the periods are usually **binary**.

Binary. Dual; two-part.

The second movement, Larghetto, in 4/4 time, is in E-flat major. Here, too, utmost serenity prevails. No diminished-seventh harmonies, so conspicuous in Mozart's dramatic works, darken the diatonic lucidity of the thematic design, and the melodic and harmonic progress is charmingly predictable.

The third and last movement, Allegro, in the key of B-flat

major, in 6/8 time, is a vivacious rondo, which has an air of bucolic festivity. It forms a perfect counterpart to the more spa-
cious first movement, rounding off the formal equilibrium of
the cyclic structure.

The original manuscript of the concerto was preserved in
Berlin for a century and a half after Mozart's death. The 1964
edition of the Köchel catalogue of Mozart's works carries the
melancholy note, "Missing since the end of the war."

Concerto for Clarinet in A Major, K. 622 (1791)

Mozart's production was of a universal quality. He was equally
resourceful in opera, symphony, **chamber music**, and solo
works. He composed concertos for piano, for violin, for flute,
for clarinet, for bassoon, for horn. His concerto for clarinet
and orchestra is his last written for any instrument; he composed it in the year of his death, 1791.

Chamber music. Vocal or instrumental music suitable for performance in a room or small hall.

In Mozart's time, the clarinet was a relative newcomer in
orchestral usage, and Mozart himself did not include clarinets
in the scene until his later symphonies. It is therefore all the
more remarkable that he was able to use the entire range of
the clarinet, particularly its deep register, with such beauty
and perfection. The concerto became a model for subsequent
works for solo clarinet and orchestra, and firmly established
the clarinet as a fine solo instrument in operatic overtures, in
symphonies, and in chamber music.

CHAMBER MUSIC

String Quartet No. 15 in D Minor, K. 421 (1783)

Before Mozart's time string quartets were a novelty. The more
common forms of instrumental writing in four parts were the
so-called *sinfonie a quattro*, in which each instrumental part

Opening of Mozart's String Quartet No. 15 in D Minor, K. 421

could be played by any number of similar instruments. It was Haydn who established the now familiar composition for two violins, viola, and cello. Goethe poetically described his impressions of quartet playing in a remark to the composer Carl Friedrich Zelter on February 9, 1829: "We hear four intelligent people converse with one another; we seem to profit from their discourse, and, at the same time, become acquainted with the characteristics of each instrument." The composer Carl Maria von Weber (1786–1826) described the string quartet as a "musical consommé" in which the expression of every musical idea is reduced to its most essential property, a musical idea in four-part harmony.

As for the succession of movements, the string quartet in the form that it assumed in the hands of Haydn and Mozart is similar to the symphony. This similarity was brought about by the inclusion of the minuet (or **scherzo**, in Beethoven), and by the use of sonata form in the opening movement.

Scherzo (It.). A joke, jest; an instrumental piece of a light, piquant, humorous character.

Mozart composed his first quartet at the age of fourteen. At that time he was entirely under the influence of Italian masters. The subsequent development of Mozart's style is closely connected with the guiding direction of Haydn's quartets. Hermann Abert, in his illuminating article on Mozart in *Cobbett's Cyclopedic Survey of Chamber Music*, suggests that Mozart was entirely independent of extraneous considerations only in his chamber music. He wrote his operas for the public; his concertos were expressions of his vital energy; his symphonies, a manifestation of masculine energy; but his chamber music, and particularly this most intimate and least spectacular form of chamber music—the string quartet—was the revelation of his inner soul. Harmonically speaking, Mozart's string quartets contain the boldest progressions he ever applied. Abert also finds in the quartets a premonition of the tragic Mozart—the brooding, contemplative, fatalistic Mozart.

Mozart acknowledged his great indebtedness to Haydn in

the dedication to him of six quartets written between the years 1782 and 1786, when Mozart was in his late twenties. Haydn himself greatly praised these quartets, and Mozart's father credibly reports that Haydn spoke to him of these quartets as being without rivals.

The D-Minor Quartet is the second of the six quartets dedicated to Haydn, and the only one in a minor key. Its companions breathe energy in various forms: the first quartet, in G, is masculine; the third, in E-flat, romantic; the fourth, in B-flat, aggressively energetic, with the hunting-song theme; the fifth, in A, glowingly gay; and the sixth, in C, vigorous and buoyant.

The Quartet in G Minor was written in Vienna in June 1783, when Mozart was twenty-seven years old. The first movement is an Allegro in 4/4, and in recognizable sonata form. The first subject is stated at once by the first violin, and repeated an octave higher. The harmonic progressions follow the Classical alternation of the tonic and the dominant, but soon the Mozartean plaintive harmonies of the augmented sixth appear, with their inevitable resolutions into the octave. Simultaneously with the chromaticization of the harmonic texture, the rhythmic pattern is quickened in the second section of the exposition. There are bold modulations in the development, transitions to remote keys, at one juncture connecting E-flat minor and A minor by a sudden chromatic move. It is of such enharmonic changes that Robert Browning wrote:

> And music: what? that burst of pillar'd cloud by day
> And pillar'd fire by night, was product, must we say
> Of modulating just by enharmonic change,
> The augmented sixth resolved.

The variety of keys in this section of Mozart's D-Minor Quartet, and the persistent enharmonicism, are revelations of a Mozart who was not all sweetness and light. The recapitulation of the Allegro is, however, entirely on the Classical model.

The second movement, Andante, is in 6/8 time. The harmonic succession of keys is here characterized by an alternation of major and minor. The third movement is a Minuet, following the example set by Haydn. The trio is written in the folksong style, and the last movement, Allegro ma non troppo, is a set of variations in the key of the quartet, D minor.

String Quartet No. 17 in B-flat Major ("Hunt"), K. 458 (1784)

Mozart's "Hunt" Quartet is the third of the six dedicated to Haydn. It was written in one day, on November 9, 1784, in Vienna. Mozart sold all six quartets to the publishers for 100 ducats, and they were published almost immediately.

Sending his six quartets to Haydn, Mozart wrote, in Italian, in an affected, half-humorous manner:

> A father who had once decided to send out his sons into the great world deemed it his duty to entrust them to the protection and guidance of a man of great fame who, moreover, was also his best friend. In like manner I send my six sons to you, most celebrated and very dear friend. They are indeed the fruit of a long and painstaking endeavor; but the hope, corroborated by many friends, that this toil will be in some degree rewarded, flatters me and encourages me in the belief that some day these children may prove a source of consolation to me.
>
> During your last stay in this capital you, my very dear friend, personally expressed to me your approval of these compositions. Your kind opinion encourages me to present them to you, and lets me hope that you will find them not entirely unworthy of your favor. I pray you, then, receive them kindly, and be a father, guide, and

friend to them. From now on I surrender my rights over them to you. I beseech you not to be severe to faults that may have eluded a father's partial eye, and to preserve your generous friendship toward one who so highly treasures it.

The sobriquet "Hunt" is justified by the opening theme of the first movement, which is based on a well-known figure of the so-called horn fifths, based on the natural tones of a hunting horn; they are used whenever it is intended to picture a hunting episode, a journey, or leave-taking. Schubert uses it in his song "Die Post," from Schwanengesang (Swan Song), Beethoven in his "Les Adieux" Piano Sonata, Mendelssohn in his "Hunting Song" from the Songs Without Words. And it is interesting to observe that these hunting-horn intervals are mostly used in the key of B-flat major, the key in which natural bugles, trumpets, and postilion horns were actually constructed. It is not unnatural, then, that Mozart's "Hunt" Quartet is written, too, in the key of the hunting horn.

The "Hunt" quartet follows the Haydn model. There are four movements. The first and the last movements are fast, and the two middle movements are, respectively, a Minuet and an Adagio. There are no unusual harmonic procedures, no dissonant tonal encounters that baffled early Mozarteans, and moved some of them to the thought of correcting these rough spots in order to achieve smoothness in harmony. It is a serene Mozart, free from the strife and preoccupations of his later life.

String Quartet No. 19 in C Major ("Dissonant"), K. 465 (1785)

Mozart's Quartet in C Major, the last of the six quartets he wrote for Haydn, was composed in Vienna in one day, January 14, 1785. Mozart's earliest biographer, one Franz Niemetschek, a teacher at the Prague Gymnasium, wrote: "Mozart could not

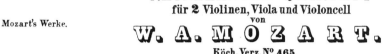

NEUNZEHNTES QUARTETT
für 2 Violinen, Viola und Violoncell
von
Mozart's Werke. **W. A. MOZART.** Serie 14. No. 19.

Köch. Verz. No. 465.

Componirt am 14. Januar 1785 in Wien.

Stich und Druck von Breitkopf & Härtel in Leipzig. W.A.M.465. Ausgegeben 1882.

Opening of Mozart's String Quartet No. 19 In C Major, K. 465

honor Haydn more with any other work than with these quartets, which are a treasure of the finest thought, a model, and a lesson in composition."

The C-Major Quartet is a celebrated one in the annals of Mozartology. In the opening adagio, Mozart uses combinations of chromatics that create what is known in harmony textbooks as "cross relations." Natural and altered tones brush each other in closest proximity, and there is a strange feeling of the absence of key. C major is expressed only by the initial tonic in the cello, while the viola and the two violins hover perilously on the fringe. All kinds of subtle explanations have been advanced to account for these chromatic vagaries, but Haydn, to whom the quartet was dedicated, merely remarked: "If Mozart wrote it, he must have had a good reason to do so."

After the quartet's famous ambiguous introduction, the key of C major asserts itself in an Allegro in common time (4/4). The following slow movement, in triple time, Andante cantabile, is regarded as one of the finest examples of Mozart's lyricism. Then follows a minuet in C major. The last movement is a brilliant Allegro in duple time.

"Eine kleine Nachtmusik" (Serenade in G Major), K. 525 (1787)

The year 1787 was crucial in Mozart's life. His father Leopold, who was also his teacher and partly a provider, had died. Also, one of Mozart's infant sons died, following the natural average of infant mortality in those days. In 1787, Mozart wrote his greatest opera, *Don Giovanni*. He made a successful visit to Prague, where he conducted his new Symphony in D ("Prague," K. 504). It was one of the few lucrative engagements that Mozart ever had in his life. Upon his return to Vienna, he was appointed chamber musician by the emperor.

And yet he remarked to the Bohemian composer Adalbert Gyrowetz that he envied him his concert engagements in

Italy and elsewhere, for Mozart himself could make his living only by teaching and by writing occasional pieces to be played at social functions. Even the appointment as chamber musician did not secure a necessary minimum for Mozart and his growing and ailing family. The emperor was strangely frugal despite the success that Mozart had in Prague. When some time later the king of Prussia offered Mozart a better salary and a more enviable position, Mozart refused out of loyalty to the emperor and to Vienna, but the gesture was little appreciated.

Great as was Mozart's fame even in his day, it seems from contemporary reports that he was not the most successful composer in Vienna as far as public reception and appreciation is concerned. A Vienna correspondent, writing in the *Magazine für Musik* in 1788, gives the palm of priority to Leopold Koželuh (1752–1818): "Koželuh's works hold their ground and are always acceptable, while Mozart's are not by any means as popular." Incidentally, Koželuh succeeded Mozart, after his death, as chamber musician, and at a higher salary. And where is Koželuh now? One finds him only in very complete music dictionaries.

Mozart composed the so-called "Eine kleine Nachtmusik" in Vienna on August 10, 1787, as a piece of the order we now would call *Gebrauchsmusik*, "utilitarian" music, to be played by students or amateurs. "Eine kleine Nachtmusik" is classified as a serenade, which in Mozart's usage was not much different from a little symphony. In fact, the piece is entirely symphonic. It is built in four movements. The initial Allegro in G major, and in common time (4/4), is couched in the orthodox sonata form. The development is exceedingly brief, and there is nothing experimental in the use of different keys. The second, slow, movement, Romanze, is in C major, in duple time. It is in **ternary form**. The phrases are sharply subdivided into four-bar **phrases**, or their multiples. The middle section of the Romanze is in C minor, with characteristic simple figures imitated by one instrument after another. Then the C-major

Ternary form. Rondo form; ABA form, such as the minuet and trio.

Phrase. Half of an eight-measure period.

theme returns, and the movement is concluded with the feeling of a perfect ending.

The following movement is a Minuet in G major, with a trio in the dominant. The minuet is repeated, according to usual ternary form. The last movement is an allegro, which is called Rondo by Mozart himself, although the structure is close to sonata form. The initial vivacious theme dominates the movement, appearing in the tonic, then in the dominant, and in the middle section also in other keys. The movement is further consolidated by an extended coda.

LUDWIG VAN BEETHOVEN
(1770–1827)
The Fervent Genius

THE GREATEST MUSICAL NAMES have a harmonious sound all their own, as though they were intentionally shaped to impress themselves on the minds of humanity. The family name of Beethoven possesses such a ringing sound; yet it is derived from nothing more lofty than the Dutch word for a beet field. Beethoven's grandfather was a Dutchman who settled in Bonn, where Beethoven was born. Beethoven's family was a democratic one; yet Beethoven was proud of his nobiliary particle "van," which had an air even more aristocratic than the German "von."

Many musical biographies begin with the words: "His father opposed music as a profession and desired his son to be a lawyer." Beethoven's early biography needs no such negative introduction. His father was himself a musician in the employ of the prince-elector of Cologne, and he thought highly of his social position. When he discovered that Beethoven had instinctive musical ability, he taught him to play the violin and piano and to read music. Often Beethoven would stray away from the notes before him and play some inventions of his own. His father would then discipline him and admonish him to attend to the printed music.

Soon father Beethoven decided that it was time to present his young son to the world. He arranged a joint concert for him with another of his pupils, a **contralto** singer, and announced in the local press that his "little son would give complete enjoyment to all ladies and gentlemen" with his playing on the piano. Beethoven progressed rapidly; when he was thirteen years old, he wrote three piano **sonatas**. His father, always mindful of practical matters, arranged for publication of these youthful works with a flowery dedication to the prince-elector, in which the young composer (aided no doubt by his father) expressed himself with becoming modesty and deference to princely powers:

> May I venture, most illustrious Prince, to place at the foot of your throne the first fruits of my youthful inspiration? And may I venture to hope that you will bestow on them the benevolent paternal mark of your encouraging approval? Accept them as a pure offering of childlike homage, and look graciously on them, and on their young author.

Beethoven was not quite fourteen when he was appointed assistant court organist, while his father held the position of first organist. Young Beethoven was given a salary, which was a token of recognition of his professional standing. Three years later he had enough funds to undertake a journey to Vienna. There he was introduced to Mozart, and played for him, not from written music as he was told to do when he was

Contralto (It.). The deeper of the two main divisions of women's or boys' voices, the soprano being the higher; also called alto.

Sonata (It.). An instrumental composition usually for a solo instrument or chamber ensemble, in three or four movements, connected by key, contrasted in theme, tempo, meter, and mood.

a child, but from his own unfettered imagination. To improvise freely was a mark of true musicianship in the age of Mozart and Beethoven. Mozart listened to the passionate and artful **roulades** from another room with some friends. "This young man will soon make much clamor in the world! Watch him in the future!"

His first works are Mozartean in melody and in gentleness of harmonies. Gradually the untamed passion of Beethoven's musical spirit would break through the eighteenth-century grace. And yet he was still a student; he felt that he needed more musical and general education. He settled in Vienna, where he took lessons from Haydn, at eight groschen each, a sum that corresponded to about twenty-five cents. He wrote exercises in **counterpoint**, which Haydn patiently corrected. Beethoven's artistic independence grew. "I wish to learn the rules well, the better to break them," he confessed to a friend.

Beethoven's refusal to bow before men of power found expression in another story: one summer, when Beethoven met Goethe in the spa town of Teplitz, Archduke Rudolph passed by in a carriage. Goethe stopped, took off his hat, and bowed deeply; Beethoven pulled his hat down, buttoned up his overcoat, and folded his arms. Then he explained to Goethe that they, as men of intellect and imagination, should not defer to men whose only greatness resides in their uniforms and titles. Perhaps this story, too, is an elaboration of what might well have happened. But even an imaginary episode has its place in a great man's biography if it is in character. It is undoubtedly true that to Beethoven, aristocracy of the mind was at least as important as nobility of title. When his brother came to visit him and, not finding him at home, left a note signed "Carl van Beethoven, landowner," Beethoven returned the visit and, his brother being absent, left a similar note, signed "Ludwig van Beethoven, brain owner."

Beethoven was a giant, and he was a child. He was constantly oppressed by the consciousness of his insufficient ed-

Roulade (Fr.). A grace consisting of a move from one principal melody tone to another; a vocal or instrumental flourish.

Counterpoint. Polyphonic composition; the combination of two or more simultaneous melodies.

ucation. He had some Latin in school, and he learned to write ungrammatical French and passable Italian, but arithmetic was his nemesis, and he could never manage to compute his domestic expenses. Having already reached fame, he surreptitiously acquired a book entitled *The Easiest Method of Teaching Arithmetic to Children in a Pleasant Way*. His nephew, of whom he was very fond and whose guardian he eventually became, explained to him that multiplication was a simplified form of addition, but this Beethoven could never manage to master. And when he attempted complicated rhythmic divisions in one of his later sonatas, the note values did not add up correctly, a fact that a contemporary critic scornfully pointed out.

Then came the severest trial in any musician's life. Beethoven had known for a long time that his hearing was failing; at the peak of his creative activity, he became almost totally deaf and was forced to resort to a "conversation book" for communication with friends. A greater misfortune can hardly be imagined, and yet, by an extraordinary self-assertion of genius, Beethoven wrote sublime music, which he himself could not hear. The mighty Fifth Symphony, the joyful and poetic Pastoral Symphony, the transcendental "Choral" Symphony (the Ninth), were all written during the period of external deafness. But it was also the time of inner illumination, and it enabled Beethoven to form musical images of striking power and beauty.

Considering the fact that Beethoven had many friends and worshipful followers who realized the opportunity that fate had offered them in being with Beethoven, irritatingly little is known about Beethoven's intimate life, his method of work, or even the dates of his compositions. His conversation books are singularly lacking in important details. Beethoven wrote relatively few letters, and most of them were business communications, or letters relating to his incessant personal quarrels. There is, of course, one celebrated exception in

Beethoven's correspondence: his letter addressed to an unknown woman, whom he called the "Immortal Beloved." Who the Immortal Beloved was still remains unsolved by the Beethoven scavengers (the expression was used by the American music historian Oscar Sonneck in his painstaking but futile 1927 essay "The Riddle of the Immortal Beloved").

The advent of Beethoven in music history marked the transition from pure classicism to a more concentrated, more expressive type of music, which we know as romanticism. Nothing illustrates Beethoven's romantic musical nature better than the progressive change of style and idiom from his early works to his last instrumental compositions, which presage the development of modern music. Mozart and Haydn wrote symphonies in quantity, and the style of these symphonies remained within a general concept without transcending the established tradition. Each Beethoven symphony, however, each successive piano sonata or **string quartet**, is a step forward in the direction of a new musical language. Excelsior! For Beethoven could not conform, not even to his own greatness, nor to his own reputation in the world of music. He was the passionate genius who broke the bounds of conventionally pleasurable art to reach the realm of musical expression yet to come.

String quartet. A composition for first and second violin, viola, and cello.

SYMPHONIES

Symphony No. 3 in E-flat Major (Eroica), *Op. 55 (1804)*

On August 26, 1804, Beethoven wrote to his publishers, Breitkopf & Härtel, in a letter accompanying the shipping of several new works, among them the Third Symphony: "The symphony is really entitled Bonaparte, and, in addition to the usual instruments, there are three **obbligato** horns. I believe

Obbligato (It.). A concerted (and therefore essential) instrumental part.

Beethoven Timeline

1770	Born in Bonn
1783	First published work, Nine Variations for Piano on a March of Dressler
1784-92	Deputy court organist in Bonn
1792-94	Studies with Haydn in Vienna
1795	First concert in Vienna
1796-99	Tours Prague, Dresden, Leipzig, Berlin
1801-5	Composes several piano sonatas, including the Sonata in D minor ("Tempest"), Sonata in C ("Waldstein"), Sonata in F ("Appassionata"), Sonata in C-sharp minor ("Moonlight")
1802	Plagued by increasing deafness, writes the "Heiligenstadt Testament"
1803-8	Completes the Fourth, Fifth, and Sixth Symphonies
1805	Attends first performance of his *Fidelio* at the Theater an der Wien
1805-6	Composes the three string quartets ("Razumovsky")
1809	Composes Fifth Piano Concerto ("Emperor"), String Quartet in E flat ("Harp"), Seventh and Eighth Symphonies, three piano sonatas
1811	Composes "Archduke" Trio
1811	Writes letter to the mysterious "Immortal Beloved"
1818	Begins using "conversation books" as primary means of communication

(continued)

it will interest the musical public." Breitkopf & Härtel, however, declined the symphony, and it was subsequently published by the Verlag für Kunst und Industrie, with the new title "Sinfonia Eroica composta per festeggiare il sovvenire di un grand' Uomo," that is, "Heroic Symphony, composed to celebrate the memory of a great man." On the title page of the manuscript used for publication there were two words after the title, which were carefully erased. But the second word is legible: it is "Bonaparte." The first word, in all probability, is "Napoleon."

Between the completion of the symphony and its publication occurred the most celebrated episode in music history: the dramatic elimination of the title *Bonaparte* from the symphony. The story is related in substantially identical features by two intimates of Beethoven: Ferdinand Ries and Anton Felix Schindler. "The original idea of the symphony is said to have been suggested by General Bernadotte, who was then French Ambassador at Vienna," writes Schindler,

… and had a high esteem for Beethoven, so I was informed by several of his friends. Count Moritz Lichnowsky, who was frequently with Beethoven in Bernadotte's company, and who is my authority for many circumstances belonging to this period, gave me the same account. In his political sentiments Beethoven was a republican; the spirit of independence natural to a genuine artist gave him a decided bias…. He lived in the firm belief that Napoleon entertained no other design than to republicanize France…. Hence, his respect and enthusiasm for Napoleon. A fair copy of the musical work for the First Consul of the French Republic, with the dedication to him, was on the point of being dispatched through the French Embassy to Paris, when news arrived in Vienna that Napoleon Bonaparte has caused himself to be proclaimed Emperor of the French. The first thing Beethoven did on receiving this intelligence was to tear off the title-leaf of this symphony and to fling the work itself to the floor, from which he would not allow it to be lifted, with a torrent of execrations against the new French Emperor, against the new tyrant. It was a long time before Beethoven recovered from the shock and permitted this work to be given to the world with the title of Sinfonia Eroica.... I shall only add that it was not till the tragic end of the great Emperor at St. Helena, that Beethoven was reconciled with him, and sarcastically remarked that, seventeen years before, he had composed appropriate music to this catastrophe, in which it was exactly predicted musically, alluding to the Funeral March of the symphony.

Beethoven Timeline (cont.)

1820	Wins custody of nephew, Karl
1824	Ninth Symphony premiered in Vienna; Missa Solemnis premiered in St. Petersburg
1784-92	Composes late string quartets
1827	Dies in Vienna

It must be noted that Schindler himself was a mere boy at the time and in his story relies entirely on Ries and Lichnowsky. There is no evidence that Ries recorded the story before he published his short memoir of Beethoven, that is, before 1837. Napoleon was proclaimed emperor in May 1804, and the news must have reached Vienna within a fortnight after the event. It is quite possible that between 1804 and 1837, Ries might have unconsciously embellished the incident. The evidence of the manuscript score with the dedication to Napoleon laboriously erased, and Beethoven's calm mention, in his August 1804 letter to the publisher three months after Napoleon assumed the title of emperor that the symphony was entitled *Bonaparte*—all this points to a different interpretation. Ries asserts in his memoir that the copy he saw on Beethoven's table bore Napoleon's name in the Italian form, "Buonaparte," at the extreme top of the title page, and, at the extreme bottom the signature, also in the Italian form, "Luigi van Beethoven." Yet it is very unlikely that Beethoven would have used the Italian form, which at the time was not in favor with the adherents of Napoleon, and this alone lessens the reliability of Ries's testimony.

Half note. A note one-half the value of a whole note.

Overture. A musical introduction to an opera, oratorio, etc.

Aria (It.). An air, song, tune, melody.

Concerto (It.). An extended multi-movement composition for a solo instrument, usually with orchestra accompaniment and using (modified) sonata form.

The Third Symphony was finally dedicated to Beethoven's patron, Prince Franz Joseph Lobkowitz, and was performed numerous times at his palace. Ries records an occasion when Beethoven conducted and became so confused in the second half of the first movement, where the **half notes** are tied over the bar line, going against the beat, that the orchestra had to stop and start over again. The first public performance took place in Vienna on April 7, 1805, under Beethoven's direction. The symphony was announced simply as "a new grand symphony," and the key was given, curiously enough, as D-sharp instead of E-flat. The audience and critics thought that the symphony was too long, and that Beethoven was not sufficiently courteous to the public in acknowledging the applause. This complaint caused Beethoven to write on the violin part of the symphony: "As this symphony somewhat exceeds the usual length, it should be played nearer the beginning rather than the end of a concert, after an **overture**, an **aria**, or a **concerto** lest it lose some of its effect on an audience fatigued by preceding pieces." In the same letter from Beethoven in Vienna to his publishers, Breitkopf & Härtel in Leipzig, in which Beethoven referred to the composition of the *Bonaparte* Symphony, he also wrote:

I hear that the symphony which I sent you last year and which you returned to me has been roundly abused in the *Musikalische Zeitung*. I have not read the article, but if you think that you do me harm by this, you are mistaken. On the contrary you bring your newspaper into discredit by such things—all the more since I have not made any secret of the fact that you sent back this symphony.

The article referred to was a review published in the May 21, 1806, issue of the *Allgemeine Musikalische Zeitung,* which was the house organ of Breitkopf & Härtel. "It is to be hoped," the article stated, "that this symphony makes no claim to be included among Classical works. It begins with a March à la Russe, after which follows an **Allegro** which is the very essence of wantonness, where trumpets and drums reign supreme, and where all other instruments are thrown into dust by this domination."

The *Eroica* is in four movements. The first, Allegro con brio, is the heroic movement par excellence. Interestingly enough, it is in triple measure, not in the martial accents of 4/4 time. The famous opening theme is derived with utmost simplicity from the triadic configurations of the E-flat chord. The form is that of sonata; the traditional sections include a full-fledged **recapitulation** and an extended **coda**.

The most significant movement of the *Eroica* is the Marcia funebre: Adagio assai. The story is told that when Napoleon died in exile on St. Helena, Beethoven exclaimed, "I predicted this catastrophic end when I wrote the funeral march in the Eroica!" Formally, the Funeral March is a set of **variations**; the miracle of its composition is that it never loses its mournful beat through all the harmonic **modulations** and rhythmic modifications of the music. The Marcia funèbre is followed by a lighthearted **Scherzo**. The **Finale**: Allegro molto is the most complex movement of the entire work. It contains elements of variations with numerous episodic interpolations suggesting the form of a **rondo**; in addition there are fugal developments of great intricacy. The coda, **presto**, provides a fittingly heroic ending.

Symphony No. 5 in C Minor, Op. 67 (1807–8)

"So knocks Fate on my door!" This famous exclamation, supposedly made by Beethoven to describe the opening theme of the Fifth Symphony, belongs to a rapidly expanding anthology of spurious winged phrases. Beethoven himself denied that he had ever used the simile. Upon investigation, it appears that the rhythmic pattern of the theme, consisting of three short notes followed by a long one, occurs in a number of Beethoven's

Allegro (It.). Lively, brisk, rapid.

Recapitulation. A return of the initial section of a movement in sonata form.

Coda (It.). A "tail"; hence, a passage ending a movement.

Variations. Transformations of a theme by means of harmonic, rhythmic, and melodic changes and embellishments.

Modulation. Passage from one key into another.

Scherzo (It.). A joke, jest; an instrumental piece of a light, piquant, humorous character.

Finale (It.). The last movement in a sonata or symphony.

Rondo (It.). An instrumental piece in which the leading theme is repeated, alternating with the others.

Presto (It.). Fast, rapid; faster than allegro.

works dating from the period of the composition of the Fifth Symphony: the "Appassionata" Sonata for Piano in F Minor, Op. 57; the Fourth Piano Concerto in G Major, Op. 58; and the String Quartet in E-flat, Op. 74. Most remarkably, the tonalities of these works are related to C minor, the key of the Fifth Symphony. It is obvious, therefore, that it was present in Beethoven's mind as a purely musical invention for a long time, free of any psychological or phraseological associations. Another theory of the origin of the motive is that Beethoven used the notes of a birdcall, specifically of a goldfinch. Beethoven did use birdcalls in the *Pastoral* Symphony, which was written at the same period as the Fifth, and so the hypothesis is not entirely improbable.

The most natural supposition is that the four notes are of a purely musical, nonprogrammatic origin. The catalogue of all Beethoven's themes, published by the Beethoven House in Bonn in 1932, lists nineteen examples of the rhythmical figure of the Fifth Symphony, under the heading of "triple repetition in the **upbeat**, followed by a skip." It must be assumed, therefore, that this rhythm was part of Beethoven's natural vocabulary. However, there is no instance of the use of this rhythm in Beethoven's works with the downward skip of a major third, in a minor key, from the **dominant** to the **mediant**, except in the Fifth Symphony.

Beethoven was thirty-eight years old when the Fifth Symphony was presented to the public, but sketches of the symphony refer to a considerably earlier period. The original four notes are present in the earliest jottings in Beethoven's notebooks, but other thematic material is amazingly different from the final shape.

The Fifth Symphony occupies the midway point in Beethoven's creative life. In it the link with the eighteenth century is not entirely severed. The traditional form of a Classical symphony is observed, yet there are constantly erupting flames of the Beethoven of the last, his greatest, period, the

Upbeat. The raising of the hand in beating time; an unaccented part of a measure.

Dominant. The fifth tone in the major or minor scales; a chord based on that tone.
Mediant. The third degree of the scale.

Beethoven who used the medium of music to express the drama of turbulent emotion, the essence of human struggle, rather than the formulas and usages of the Classical art, however exquisite. There are coloristic effects, such as the kettledrum episode in the protracted deceptive cadence of the Scherzo, before the clarifying explosion of the C-major fanfare of the finale, when, for the first time, the trombones enter the scene. There is the accumulation of power through the persistent repetition of notes and figures, pursued even where the laws of contrast might dictate a different course, as, for instance, in the use of the same four-note motive in the second subject, with a change of **interval** and **key**.

Interval. The difference in pitch between two tones.
Key. The series of tones forming any given major or minor scale.

Long after Beethoven's death, young Mendelssohn visited the aged Goethe, and played the first movement of Beethoven's Fifth Symphony for him. "This is very great," Goethe remarked, "and quite mad. One fears that the house would come down on us if all instruments were to play it together." Schumann wrote after hearing a performance of the symphony: "So often heard, it still exercises its power over all ages, just as those great phenomena of nature, which, no matter how often they recur, fill us with awe and wonder. This symphony will go on centuries hence, as long as the world and world's music endure."

And Berlioz, the great Romantic and great individualist, saw in the Fifth Symphony the revelation of Beethoven's soul: "He develops in it his own intimate thought. His secret sorrows, his concentrated rage, his reveries charged with a dejection, oh, so sad, his visions at night, his bursts of enthusiasm—these furnished him the subject; and the forms of melody, harmony, rhythm, and orchestration are as essentially individual and new as they are powerful and noble." He saw in its first movement, Allegro con brio, a conglomeration of "disordered sentiments which oppress a great soul." He compared the **syncopated** alteration of chords in the wind instruments and strings to hiccups, and their dynamic con-

Syncopation. Shifting of accents from strong beat to weak beat or between beats.

trasts to a sudden change from the breathing of a dying man to a desperate outburst of human violence. The coda of the first movement represented to him "two burning unisons forming twin torrents of lava."

The first performance of the Fifth Symphony took place in Vienna on December 22, 1808. The program must have been an exceptionally long one, for it included, in addition to the Fifth Symphony, Beethoven's Sixth Symphony, the *Pastoral* (but the numbers were exchanged, so that the Fifth, the C-Minor Symphony, was billed as No. 6, and the *Pastoral* as No. 5), and the Fourth Piano Concerto, with Beethoven as soloist.

The first movement is in Classical sonata form. The instrumentation of the "fate" motive is surprising: it is scored for two clarinets and strings in unison. The entire melodic material of the exposition is evolved from this basic phrase. The second subject is lyrical in nature, but the "fate" figure lurks in its contrapuntal background. The development follows the Classical model with the inevitability of a syllogism. The recapitulation arrives in a blaze of symphonic glory. The coda is succinct and energetic.

The theme of the second movement, Andante con moto, in A-flat major in 3/8 time, is one of the most beautiful slow melodies created by Beethoven. When a scientific melometer is perfected, we may be able to define in concrete terms the secret of esthetic gratification derived from such melodies. The form of the movement is that of a set of variations, combined with the characteristics of a rondo.

The third movement, Allegro vivace, in C minor, is a brilliant essay in scherzo form. The extraordinary rapid figuration in the trio, when the cellos and double basses make a virile entry in the bland key of C major, reminded Berlioz of "the gambols of a frolicsome elephant." The rhythm of the "fate" motive is heard again. There follows a mysterious kettledrum solo in steady triple rhythm, holding the listener in mounting suspense, which is resolved by the climactic fanfare inaugurating the finale, Allegro, in C major, in festive duple time.

It is in the Finale: Allegro that the trombones make their tremendous appearance for the first time in a Beethoven symphony. A comparison with the ominous trombones that announce the terrifying presence of the statue of the Commendatore in Mozart's *Don Giovanni* suggests itself. The scherzo is recollected with its thematic four-note motive. Then the Allegro returns, leading to a precipitous coda, presto. The ending constitutes the most emphatic reiteration of tonic triads in symphonic literature. Here the music creates the sense of psychological subjection, a melosomatic catharsis.

Symphony No. 7 in A Major, Op. 92 (1811–12)

Wagner called Beethoven's Seventh Symphony the apotheosis of the dance, with reference to the last movement, in which, so Wagner thought, nature itself danced with Beethoven. Other romantic commentators solemnly examined the score and found in it the expression of exultation at the deliverance of Europe from French domination; the famous second movement, in which the melody grows out of the rhythmic pendulum on a single note, inspired visions of the catacombs to some. Beethoven left no hint as to pictorial or literary associations with the music, and so deprived his admirers of authorized speculation.

Beethoven began the composition of his Seventh Symphony in 1811, and dedicated it upon completion to the "High-born Count Morits von Fries." The first performance of the Seventh Symphony took place in Vienna on December 8, 1813. There was a previous private hearing at the Archduke Rudolph of Austria's palace in Vienna on April 20, 1813.

The public performance of the Seventh Symphony was given on the same program with a curious work that

Beethoven wrote to celebrate the victory of the duke of Wellington over the French, written especially for a mechanical instrument, called the panharmonicon, an invention of Johannes Nepomuk Maelzel. Both Maelzel and Beethoven hoped for great financial rewards, which failed to materialize, despite the musical flattery to Great Britain, with quotations from "God Save the King" and "For He's a Jolly Good Fellow." The Seventh Symphony, without such artificial fanfares, survives as a great work, while *Wellington's Victory* is relegated to a museum of musical curiosities.

Maelzel was also the inventor of the **metronome**, and his name is immortalized in the markings "M. M." (Maelzel's Metronome) preceding the figure indicating the number of beats per minute. Beethoven was very much taken by Maelzel's invention, and in his letter to him expressed his determination never to use the old-fashioned Italian designations of **tempo**. He even set metronome marks for all of his symphonies. But his enthusiasm was short-lived. In one of his works he indicated a metronome figure, but added a word of caution, that "feeling also has its tempo and cannot be entirely expressed in figures."

The first movement of the Seventh Symphony opens with poco sostenuto, in 4/4 time, serving as an introduction to the main part, **Vivace**, in 6/8. The music is full of kinetic energy accentuated by dotted rhythms. The progress is interrupted on several occasions by extraordinary silences of two bars each, silences that give Beethoven an opportunity for instantaneous modulations into remote keys.

The second movement is marked **Allegretto**, but it registers in the listener's perception as being slow, as a result of an aural illusion produced by the measured progress of **quarter notes** and **eighth notes** and a sustained growth of the theme from a single note. The form is ternary, with a section in A major embanked between the principal divisions in A minor. An interesting **fugato** develops toward the recapitulation.

Metronome. A double pendulum moved by clockwork and provided with a slider on a graduated scale marking beats per minute.

Tempo (It.). Rate of speed, movement; time, measure.

Vivace (It.). Lively, animated, brisk.

Allegretto (It.). Quite lively; moderately fast.

Quarter note. Half a semitone; equal to one beat in any time signature with a denominator of 4.

Eighth note. Equal to one-half of the duration of a quarter note.

Fugato (It.). A passage or movement consisting of fugal imitations not worked out as a regular fugue.

The third movement, Presto, is a scherzo, with the trio section containing characteristic horn calls of the type used by Beethoven in all his symphonies.

The Seventh Symphony ends with the impetuous dance movement, Allegro con brio. The two contrasting melodic and rhythmic themes, the dance theme and an explosive figure in dotted rhythms, constitute the elements of sonata form. The main rhythm of the dance returns with tremendous vigor. The symphony ends, indeed, as an apotheosis of nature dancing.

Symphony No. 8 in F Major, Op. 93 (1812)

Beethoven wrote his Eighth Symphony in 1812 in his brother Johann's house in Linz. He revised and completed it while traveling by stagecoach to various health resorts, because his doctor recommended hydrotherapy to relieve the ailments from which he suffered all his life. A feud between the two brothers started in that year, when Beethoven objected to his brother's marrying a woman whom he violently disliked. In his letters, Beethoven often referred to his hated sister-in-law as the Queen of the Night, with the allusion to the sinister character in Mozart's last opera, *The Magic Flute*.

The Eighth Symphony was first performed in Vienna on February 27, 1814. The Seventh Symphony was also played on the same program. It was already familiar and well liked, and was received with considerable enthusiasm. An account of the concert in the prestigious musical journal *Allgemeine Musikalische Zeitung* noted that the new symphony had aroused much interest and expectations, which were not quite gratified. The writer explained this adverse reaction on the part of the audience by the length of the program featuring two symphonic works.

The Eighth Symphony is in four movements, a traditional division of Beethoven's symphonies. The first movement, Allegro vivace e con brio, justifies its designation: it is gay, vivacious, and noisy. The noise is euphonious, of course, with shining brass and dancing violins. This is the music of Beethoven in his rustic mood. A typical postilion's horn, always a favorite with Beethoven and so easily imitated by natural French horns, is a leading motive here. Beethoven must have heard this call very often while changing his stagecoach.

The principal theme of the second movement, Allegretto **scherzando**, a sort of circular canon, is supposed to have been inspired by Maelzel's metronome. Beethoven was enthusiastic about Maelzel's invention, and liked him personally. An apocryphal story goes that Beethoven improvised a text for this canon: "Ta, ta, ta, Lieber Maelzel," containing the word "metronome" in another line. But there is an anachronism involved, because Maelzel's rhythm machine was originally called a musical chronometer, and only much later was patented under the name "metronome."

Scherzando (It.). In a playful, sportive, toying manner; lightly, jestingly.

The third movement, Tempo di menuetto, does not present any innovations. But it departs from the traditional melodic and rhythmic figurations of the old court dance and suggests rather a scene of merrymaking in the country. The last movement, Allegro vivace, is set in a festive mood. Some commentators believe that there is a Gypsy mood in the finale, inspired by itinerant Gypsy bands that Beethoven might have heard at country fairs.

Beethoven himself described the Eighth Symphony as "a little symphony." Posterity disagreed. Berlioz had this to say about the work: "It is one of those inspirations for which there is no antecedent. Such music falls directly from heaven into the composer's brain."

Symphony No. 9 in D Minor ("Choral"), Op. 125 (1822–24)

First performed in Vienna on May 7, 1824, the program described the Ninth Symphony, Beethoven's last, as a "Grand

Symphony with a finale in which solo voices and chorus enter, on the text of Schiller's Ode to Joy." The choral ending is notoriously difficult to sing, because its **tessitura** lies very high. Attempts were made to obviate the difficulty by transposing the chorus a tone lower, but there is no record of an actual performance using such a device. There are indications that the choral ending was an idea that came to Beethoven when the preliminary sketches of the symphony were already written. The sentiments expressed by Schiller must have been dear to Beethoven, for the "Ode to Joy" preaches the universalization of humanity in joy and happiness.

Tessitura (It.). The range covered by the main body of the tones of a given part, not including infrequent high or low tones.

Wagner, in his book on Beethoven, interprets the Ninth Symphony as the culmination of all instrumental music and a natural transition to a Wagnerian music drama. But music critics in Europe and in America found much fault with it. An American publication had this to say in 1853:

> If the best critics have failed to find the meaning of Beethoven's Ninth Symphony, we may well be pardoned if we confess our inability to find any. The last movement appeared to be an incomprehensible union of strange harmonies. Beethoven was deaf when he wrote it. It was the genius of a great man upon the ocean of harmony, without the compass which had so often guided him to his haven of success; the blind painter touching the canvas at random.

The violinist Ludwig Spohr (1784–1859), a great musician and a close contemporary of Beethoven, wrote in his autobiography:

> The fourth movement of the Ninth Symphony seems to me so ugly, in such bad taste, and the conception of Schiller's Ode so cheap that I cannot understand how such a genius as Beethoven could write it down. I find in

it another proof of something I had always suspected, that Beethoven was deficient in aesthetic imagery and lacked the sense of beauty.

Beethoven had intended to dedicate the Ninth Symphony to Czar Alexander I of Russia, the conqueror of Napoleon, but changed his mind and inscribed the score to the king of Prussia, Friedrich Wilhelm III. The king sent to Beethoven a diamond ring as a token of gratitude. But when the ring reached Vienna, it turned out to be a less precious stone, and Beethoven sold it to a local jeweler for three hundred florins. What happened to the original diamond ring? Possibly the Prussian functionaries to whom the affair was delegated substituted a cheaper stone. It is also possible that the Viennese customs officers made this profitable switch.

When the Ninth Symphony was first performed by the Philharmonic Society of London, it was advertised as a "New Grand Characteristic Sinfonia, in manuscript, with vocal finale, composed expressly for this society." Obviously, Beethoven must have promised the first performance to both Vienna and London; he was always confused in his practical arrangements. In 1827, when the news reached London of Beethoven's grave illness, the Philharmonic Society sent him one hundred pounds. The money was used to pay a portion of the funeral expenses.

The opening measures of the first movement, Allegro ma non troppo, in D minor, with a time signature 2/4, are arresting. The theme consists of falling fourths and fifths, before committing itself to a complete triadic progression in D minor. A development follows by the process of accumulation, typical of Beethoven's music. Eight distinct motives can be found in the first movement, but they are so closely interwoven that an impression of continuous motion is firmly maintained.

The second movement, Molto vivace: Presto, is still in D minor, in 3/4 time. It corresponds to a scherzo, and is marked by a forceful rhythmic pulse with energetic syncopation. The third movement, Adagio molto e cantabile, is in B-flat major, in 4/4 time. There are two discernible themes, each giving rise to a series of variations. Beethoven reversed the order of the middle movements in the traditional symphony, in which the slow movement follows the opening section, and a **minuet** or a scherzo is the third movement.

Minuetto (It.), **minuet**. An early French dance form.

The finale is like an **oratorio** in its magnitude. It contains numerous sections, instrumental and vocal, opening with a chord of tremendous majesty, containing as it does every note of the D-minor harmonic scale. Of course, it resolves immediately into a D-minor chord, but the combination dismayed many musical purists. After recitatives in the cellos and double basses, the baritone enters with an exhortation to humanity to raise their voices in song. The tenor has a solo in an episode marked vivace alla marcia. The chorus becomes active, first in allegro assai and then an andante maestoso. An adagio follows, yielding soon to an allegro energico. There are many adumbrations to the famous tune of the "Ode to Joy," materializing in its entirety in the final **prestissimo**. There are several false endings which may mislead the audience into premature applause. The coda is a veritable festival of D-major chords.

Oratorio (It.). An extended multi-movement composition for vocal solos and chorus accompanied by orchestra or organ.

Prestissimo (It.). Very rapidly.

OVERTURES

Overture to The Creatures of Prometheus, *Op. 43 (1801)*

It is difficult to imagine Beethoven in the role of a ballet composer, but he did write danceable music. Of his ballet *Die Geschöpfe des Prometheus*, only the overture survives in frequent performances. The libretto is based on one of the several myths concerning the legendary bringer of fire. Prometheus molds two beautiful human figures out of clay and water. He steals the fire from the sun to animate them, and sends his creations to Apollo. The latter in turn sends them to the muse Melpomene, who teaches them the art of dramatic emotion. The muse of comedy, Thalia, shows them how to laugh, and the muse of choreography, Terpsichore, instructs them in dancing. To complete their education, Bacchus initiates them into wine drinking. But Prometheus realizes that all men are mortal and is saddened by the thought of the inevitable death that awaits his creations.

Beethoven wrote the ballet in 1801 on commission from the famous Italian dancer Salvatore Vigano (1769–1821). The score contains an overture, an introduction, and sixteen ballet numbers. The original opus number was 24; when Beethoven revised the score, it was assigned a later opus number, 43. Vigano produced the ballet in Vienna on March 28, 1801; it was described in the program as a "heroic-allegorical ballet in two acts." Interestingly enough, much of the material that eventually went into the finale of the *Eroica* Symphony was originally written for *The Creatures of Prometheus*.

The overture is in C major. It opens with an adagio. The main part of the overture is the Allegro molto con brio, a movement charged with kinetic energy. There is a contrasting lyrical subject. The development of the materials is businesslike and unfailingly effective. A series of **tonic** chords marks the ending.

Tonic. The keynote of a scale; the triad on the keynote (tonic chord).

Leonore *Overture No. 3, Op. 72a, no. 3 (1806)*

Beethoven wrote only one opera, but he supplied it with four overtures. The title of the opera is *Fidelio*, but only the fourth overture bears that name. The remaining three overtures are known respectively as Leonore Overtures Nos. 1, 2, and 3. The riddle of the double name is easily solved when we recall that in the opera, Fidelio is the male pseudonym of Leonore, the faithful wife (as the derivation of the word Fidelio implies, *fides* being Latin for "faith") of an unjustly imprisoned man; *Leonore* was also the original title of the opera. Leonore, dressed as a youth, secures the position of an assistant to the warden and succeeds in saving her imprisoned husband's life by interposing her own body between him and a murderous governor of the fortress. The rescue comes to both husband and wife when a trumpet is heard from afar (in the overture this trumpet call is usually sounded off-stage for better effect), and the Minister of State arrives to reestablish justice, and Leonore's happiness. There is a minor complication when the warden's daughter falls seriously in love with the transvestite Leonore.

Beethoven was not the first composer to write an opera to this highly romantic and highly incredible story. An opera, *Léonore, ou l'Amour conjugal*, was produced in Paris on February 19, 1798, music by Pierre Gaveaux, libretto by Jean Nicolas Bouilly. Then Ferdinand Paër wrote an Italian opera, *Leonora, ossia L'Amor conjugale*, which was produced in Dresden on October 3, 1804. Beethoven used a German text by Josef Sonnleithner, and the opera was produced in Vienna on November 20, 1805, under the name of Leonore's male avatar, Fidelio. That was a few days after the occupation of Vienna by Napoleon's armies, and the audience consisted mainly of French officers and diplomatic agents. The opera ran for three performances, and its incomplete success was attributed not only to the French occupation, but also to the fact that it was longish. Beethoven was persuaded, after a long night session with persons concerned about the production, to cut the opera from three to two acts. This curtailed version was produced in Vienna on March 26, 1806, and ran for five days. It was revived at the Vienna Opera on May 23, 1814, in a considerably revised version, and with a new overture, which Beethoven composed specially for the revival. This was the Overture No. 4, the only one that is known as the *Fidelio* Overture. It was in

E major, in contradistinction to the three *Leonore* Overtures, which are in the key of C major. Beethoven conducted, as on previous occasions, but in 1814 he was considerably deafer, and the synchronization of his gestures and the orchestra's playing was much more difficult. As a safety measure, the regular conductor, Michael Umlauff (1781–1842), was stationed behind Beethoven's back, and it was to him that the orchestra looked for guidance in emergency.

The overture opens with a **scale** majestically descending in unison. A lyrical phrase is heard. The flute plays ascending **arpeggio** figures, imitated by the violins. They gradually gather force, and lead to a climax, with powerful chords alternating in the strings and wind instruments. The mood changes suddenly, in the typical Beethoven manner; a tender phrase is sounded in the **woodwinds**, and is repeated with more insistence. The adagio ends in the air of anticipation of the principal movement, Allegro.

The principal theme in C major is presented in the violins. It is full of action, incessantly striving forward. Its rhythmical aspect (dot-dash-dot, in 4/4) enhances its melodic dynamism. From a cautious **pianissimo** it grows to brilliant **fortissimo** in the high register of the strings. Then the woodwinds take over the theme. The key shifts, and heavy accents underscore the syncopated rhythm. A horn call ushers in a lighter mood. The violins, and then the flute, sound a lyrical phrase, but soon a tension appears, and the dot-dash-dot rhythms are telescoped in canonic imitation. The dynamics are in black and white, sudden outbursts of power contrasted with brief periods of calm.

The Allegro is in a mood of transition. The basses mount **chromatically**, still preserving the familiar rhythms of the principal theme. There are running scale passages, presaging a significant entry, and the long trumpet call is heard, which in the opera signals the advent of the Minister of State, and the liberation of the prisoner. The trumpet call is repeated after a

Scale. The series of tones which form (a) any major or minor key (*diatonic* scale) or (b) the *chromatic* scale of successive semitonic steps. Also, the compass of a voice or instrument.

Arpeggio (It.). Playing the tones of a chord in rapid, even succession.

Woodwind. Wind instruments that use reeds, and the flute.

Pianissimo (It.). Very soft.
Fortissimo (It.). Extremely loud.

Chromatic. Relating to tones foreign to a given key (scale) or chord; opposed to diatonic.

lyrical phrase in slow, even notes. After the second trumpet call there is an increase in tempo, the even notes appear in double, then quadruple, time, in preparation of a new entry. The flute introduces the principal theme in G major, instead of the customary C. The solo of the flute is of considerable length. Then the strings in pianissimo start a chromatic trek upward, which eventuates in the reentry of the principal theme in full orchestral splendor.

The allegro is the recapitulation, the repetition of the principal section, the exposition. As the regulations of the sonata form prescribe, the recapitulation is in the original key throughout. But there is also some additional material. The flute plays in short insistent phrases, which are echoed, with more emphasis, by the strings, oboe, and bassoon. The violins play a figure of three ascending notes which seem to spell "excelsior." Then the violins, violas, and cellos with basses, one group after another, break forth in rapid scale passages, leading to a triumphant coda.

The three *Leonore* Overtures and the *Fidelio* Overture were performed on one program by Mendelssohn in Leipzig on January 9, 1840. Schumann delved deeply into the relationship between the overtures: "Here the composer can be plainly watched in his own workshop. What he altered, what he discarded, what ideas he followed, what instrumentation he used, all is revealed to us. How unwilling he is to give up the trumpet call backstage! To observe and to compare is a most fascinating and instructive task for any student of the art."

Coriolanus *Overture, Op. 62 (1807)*

Beethoven wrote the overture to *Coriolanus* in 1807. It was not inspired by Shakespeare's play of that name, but by the tragedy of a minor poet, Heinrich Josef von Collin. Coriolanus, the valiant Roman soldier of the fifth century B.C., turned against Rome and remained deaf to the entreaties of his fam-

Overture to *Coriolanus,* Op. 62

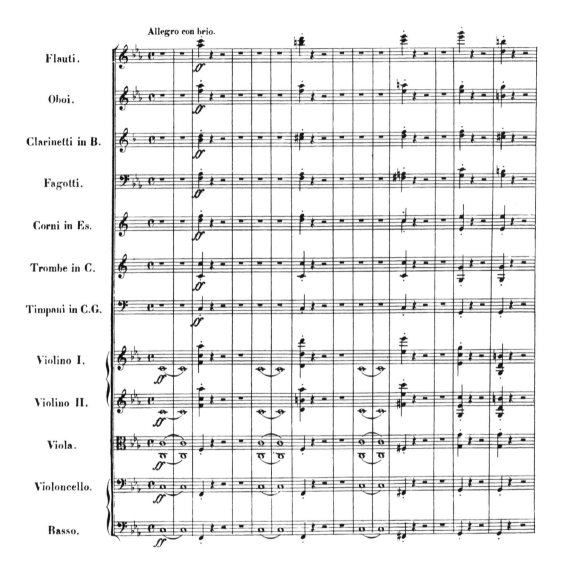

ily to lift the siege. In Collin's play, Coriolanus commits suicide. Some writers speculate that Beethoven felt a spiritual kinship with the Roman hero in his intransigence, pride, self-assertion, and self-righteousness. Like Coriolanus, Beethoven believed that his genius was not appreciated. He wrote to Collin, urging him to collaborate on a grand opera: "Take my music for your poetry, and you can be sure that you will gain thereby." The opera project did not materialize, but the overture is acknowledged as one of Beethoven's finest works.

The overture, in the key of C minor, is in one continuous movement, Allegro con brio. It is set in martial time of 4/4. The opening is announced by unisons on C in the strings, dramatically enhanced by powerful and resonant chords in the full orchestra. The first theme seems to portray the turmoil of the soldier's heart. The second theme is in the relative key of E-flat major. There is femininity in the lyrical passion of this melody, and it may well represent the implorations of Coriolanus' wife. The time-honored form of sonata, much modified, is in evidence here, for there is a development section and a full-fledged recapitulation, in which the first subject returns in the key of F minor and the feminine theme appears in C major. There is an elaborate coda, and the mighty chords of the opening are heard again. The closing bars are in C minor, suggesting a lament at the death of the hero.

Egmont *Overture, Op. 84 (1810)*

Beethoven's musical mind was that of a giant, and his creative imagination encompassed the loftiest and noblest visions in sound. He was a symphonic philosopher. The music of the theater was not his chosen domain; his opera *Fidelio* was a symphonic drama. But being Beethoven he injected some of his profoundest thoughts into incidental music for the theater. Such was the score he wrote for Goethe's drama *Egmont*. Its subject was close to Beethoven's heart, for it concerned the struggle for freedom. Count Lamoral d'Egmont was a Dutch patriot who led the people of the Netherlands against the oppressive Spanish rule. He was tried for treason by the infamous Council of Blood and was executed in 1567. But his martyrdom spurred his countrymen to continued action against tyranny, resulting in the eventual liberation of the Netherlands.

Goethe's drama with Beethoven's music was first per-

Overture to *Egmont,* Op. 84

Interlude. An intermezzo; an instrumental strain or passage connecting the lines or stanzas of a hymn, etc.

formed in Vienna on May 24, 1810. The score comprised an introduction, four **interludes**, two songs, and a concluding "Triumph Symphony." From these materials Beethoven fashioned an overture, which became a standard piece of symphonic concert repertory. The opening measures, in F minor, in 3/2 time, set the tone for dramatic action. The ponderous chords, separated by pregnant silences, reflect Egmont's brooding spirit on the eve of his decision to lead his people against the oppressor. This serves as a preamble to the main section of the overture, Allegro, in 3/4 time. The first subject is rhythmically agitated, portraying the mass action on the political scene. The second theme is a courtly **sarabande**, which may be interpreted as the symbol of the Spanish duke of Alva, for a sarabande is reputedly a dance of Spanish origin. Some literal-minded analysts attempt to follow the fortunes of Egmont through the thematic development of the music, so that the falling **octaves** in the violins at the interval of a perfect fourth at the end of the principal section of the overture are taken as illustrating the beheading of Egmont. The concluding part of the overture, allegro con brio, in F major, in 4/4 time, depicts the triumph of the people, with jubilant fanfares carrying the oriflamme of victory in the brass, reinforced by the penetrating sound of the piccolo like a full-throated voice of the people in the streets.

Sarabande (Fr., Ger.). A dance of Spanish or Oriental origin; the slowest movement in the suite.

Octave. A series of eight consecutive diatonic tones; the interval between the first and the eighth.

Overture to King Stephen, *Op. 117 (1812)*

Beethoven wrote occasional pieces for the theater, among them a score of incidental music for the opening of a grand theater in Pest, the capital of Hungary. The opening took place on February 9, 1812, with a drama by the famous German playwright August von Kotzebue, dealing with St. Stephen, king of Hungary, who fought the pagan noblemen in the early eleventh century. Beethoven's overture to *King Stephen* was performed after the drama, as a postlude; his overture to *The Ruins of Athens* (also by Kotzebue) served as a prelude to the drama.

In a letter to his older brother, who was often an intermediary between him and his publishers, Beethoven specifically mentioned the honorarium for the overture and other incidental music for the occasion. There were twelve numbers in all; Beethoven wanted 20 ducats each for four of them; 10

ducats apiece for seven others, and only 5 ducats for the shortest number. Adding them up, Beethoven arrived at the *summa summarum* (Beethoven used the Latin words), 155 ducats.

The overture opens with a preamble in C minor, in a deliberate slow tempo. Martial fanfares are heard in the horns introducing the main section, Presto, in E-flat major. The brass instruments are very busy, maintaining a rapid march tempo. While the work is not of major importance in Beethoven's catalogue, there are some interesting features in the score. Particularly intriguing are the passages in the violins anticipating the main theme of the choral finale of Beethoven's Ninth Symphony, almost note for note. After a return to the initial section in C minor, there is a decisive recapitulation in E-flat major, continuing in rapid tempo to the end, with drums and brass playing fortissimo supported by the entire orchestra.

Overture to The Consecration of the House, *Op. 124 (1822)*

Beethoven wrote the overture to the play *Die Weihe des Hauses* for the opening of the Josefstadt Theater in Vienna, and it was performed on that occasion on October 3, 1822. Beethoven conducted the orchestra himself. He could still hear a little with his left ear, and he directed the performance from the piano bench, turning his good ear toward the stage. But he could not command the players unassisted. Fortunately, his disciple and biographer Anton Schindler was at his side, leading the violin section and helping to maintain the proper tempo. Socially, the opening of the Josephstadt Theater was a great success. Four hundred reserved seats and fourteen boxes were sold in advance, and the crème de la crème of Vienna society was in attendance.

The overture is set in a festive mood; its hymnal strains are positively Handelian in their lofty utterance. There are some melodic and rhythmic figures reminiscent of the *Pas-*

toral Symphony, and there are other earmarks of Beethoven's familiar style. The ending is a joyous celebration in the immaculately white key of C major.

CONCERTOS

Piano Concerto No. 2 in B-flat Major, Op. 19 (1785; revised 1794–95, 1798)

In 1852, a Latvian-born Russian writer of German descent named Wilhelm von Lenz published in St. Petersburg a book in the French language entitled *Beethoven et ses trois styles*. In it he arbitrarily divided the creative catalogue of Beethoven's works into three periods: from Opera 1 to 21, entirely Classical in style; from Opera 22 to 95, truly Beethovenian in spirit and noble in expression; and the last, from Opus 96 on, marked by an attempt to scale unattainable heights. This artificial but convenient division's obvious defect relates to the fact that Beethoven distributed his opus numbers not chronologically but according to the publishers' convenience. As a result, wide divergences exist between the opus numbers and the time of composition in Beethoven's list of works. For instance the two "easy" piano sonatas, which are among Beethoven's earliest works, bear the incongruous opus number 49.

Beethoven's Second Piano Concerto in B-flat Major, is assigned the opus number 19, and thus belongs to the first "Classical" period. In fact, it was written before the First Concerto in C Major, which bears an earlier opus number, 15. Beethoven completed his Second Piano Concerto when he was twenty-three; it was one of the earliest works he wrote in Vienna after his arrival there from his native city of Bonn. The title of the first edition, published in Vienna in 1795, reads in the original French: "Concert pour le pianoforte avec deux violons, viole, violoncelle et basse, une flute, 2 hautbois, 2 cors et 2 bassons, oeuvre XIX." There are no clarinets in the score.

Piano Concerto No. 2 in B-flat Major, Op. 19

This abstinence is indeed very Classical, pre-Mozartean, in fact. The original orchestration has reduced strings, according to eighteenth-century usage.

The B-flat Major Concerto has no number in the original

edition. Its classification as the Second Piano Concerto was adopted in later editions. To reverse the numbering in order to reestablish proper chronology is now impractical. (Incidentally, the numbering of Chopin's two piano concertos is also reversed; his Second was written before the First.)

The concerto is set in three movements, in the cyclic succession of tempi: fast, slow, fast. The first movement, Allegro con brio, opens with a lengthy introduction for orchestra, bringing out the dotted rhythm characteristic of the principal theme of the first movement. The piano enters with a brief episode and then plunges into the energetic **exposition** of the subject. The contrasting lyrical theme appears in the dominant, according to the time-honored sonata form. In the development, the modulatory scheme carries the music to more remote keys. The recapitulation contains a number of episodes in which great rhythmic variety is achieved by the use of two, three, four, and six notes to a beat. Beethoven wrote a special **cadenza** for this movement, in which the dotted rhythm is greatly emphasized.

The second movement, Adagio, is an air with variations. The tonality, E-flat major, remains firm throughout; the thematic material is distributed **antiphonally** between the solo piano and the orchestra. The ending is in pianissimo.

The third and last movement, Allegro molto, is a rondo. It starts brilliantly in piano solo, and is set in jig time with strong off-accents. The orchestra picks it up, while the piano provides a background in bravura passages. The alternative themes of the rondo, lacking the sharp accents of the opening, are more serene. The conclusion is terse and vigorous.

Piano Concerto No. 3 in C Minor, Op. 37 (1800)

Beethoven wrote his Third Piano Concerto during the last year of the eighteenth century. He completed the score on December 15, 1800, on the eve of his thirtieth birthday. The

Exposition. The opening of a sonata movement, in which the principal themes are presented for the first time.

Cadenza (It.). An elaborate passage played or improvised by the solo instrument at the end of the first or last movements of a concerto.
Antiphonal. Responsive, alternating.

piano writing of the concerto represents a transition between the facile virtuosity of the era of Mozart and Haydn and the dramatic, massive style of the mature Beethoven. The nature of melody and harmony is also indicative of this transition. Time and again, in the midst of a hedonistic development, there is a glimpse of the somber image of Beethoven of his future tragic years. The first performance of the concerto took place in Vienna on April 5, 1803. Beethoven himself played the piano part.

The concerto is in three movements, with a slow movement placed between two fast sections. There is a lengthy orchestral introduction, which summarizes, like an overture to an opera, the entire content of the first movement, Allegro con brio. Both principal subjects, the dramatic first theme in C minor and the romantic contrasting subject in E-flat major, are explicitly stated. After the introduction is completed, the piano enters without accompaniment. As the exposition progresses, the piano and orchestra share the thematic substance. The movement ends brilliantly in unison.

Largo (It.). A slow and stately movement.

The second movement, **Largo**, in E major, in 3/8 time, is unmistakably marked with Beethoven's stylistic expression. The piano solo introduces a songful theme supported by resonant deep harmonies. The melody is decorated with harmonious arpeggios and melodious **trills**. As the piano falls silent, the orchestra, with strings muted, echoes the subject. This dialogue forms the substance of the music. Gradually, the piano intensifies the rhythmic variety of its filigree ornamentation. So fine does the fabric become that Beethoven is impelled to use passages of quintuple-stemmed 128th-notes, so that the full complement of these microrhythmic notes numbers 48 units in a single minuscule bar of 3/8.

Trill. The even and rapid alternation of two tones which are a major or minor second apart.

The finale is a rondo; the tempo is Allegro; the time signature is 2/4. Here Beethoven is completely unbuttoned, speeding in a rustic mood with hardly a pause to prepare for the next step. After an extraordinary cadenza, traversing the entire range of the piano from bass to treble, the concerto ends in a display of sonorous fireworks.

Romance in G for Violin and Orchestra, Op. 40 (1802)

In 1802 Beethoven's brother, who took care of his affairs, wrote to his publisher: "We have also two Adagios for violin with accompaniment for several instruments, which will cost 135 florins." One of these adagios was a piece published subsequently under the title "Romance, Op. 40." There was no dedication, an unusual omission among Beethoven's works. This Romance preceded by three years the composition of Beethoven's Violin Concerto. There is, however, very little in the music of the Romance that presages the concerto. Rather, the composition of the Romance should be set down as an addition to the supply of short solo pieces for the then growing class of virtuoso performers on the violin.

The score of the Romance opens with a passage for violin unaccompanied, with double stops that suggest a kinship with the opening of the "Kreutzer" Sonata (Op. 47), composed at about the same time. The violin passage is repeated by the orchestra. In this, too, there is analogy with a similar procedure in the "Kreutzer" Sonata, where the piano and the violin are antiphonally treated. Further development includes ornamentations and variations of the theme. The melodic interest is sustained throughout; the treatment is concise and clear, and the ending is simple, without superfluous climaxes.

In Beethoven's biography, the year 1802, when the Romance was composed, was one of the darkest. It was the year of the Heiligenstadt Testament, in which he expressed his despair that he was growing deaf, a document that revealed Beethoven as being close to suicide. It would be futile to try to find a counterpart to this gloomy testament in music composed at the same time. Certainly, there is nothing of the Heiligenstadt philosophy in the innocent Romance for Violin and Orchestra. But it is psychologically interesting that this Romance was written immediately before or immediately after these lines penned by Beethoven on October 6, 1802: "You men who think or say that I am malevolent, stubborn, or misanthropic, how greatly do you wrong me. O how harshly was I defeated by the doubly tragic experience of my bad hearing, and yet I could not say to people, speak louder, shout, for I am deaf. Ah, how could I possibly admit an infirmity in the one sense which should have been more acute in me than in others, a sense which I once possessed in highest perfection, a perfection such as surely few in my profession enjoy or have enjoyed!"

Concerto in C Major for Violin, Cello, and Piano, Op. 56 (1804)

Beethoven wrote his triple concerto for violin, cello, piano, and orchestra in 1804, the year of the *Eroica*, but its melodic and harmonic style bears the hallmark of an earlier period. There is a Baroque dalliance in symmetric rhythmic sequences and in the luscious display of expansive arpeggios in the piano part. The antiphony of the violin and the cello is clearly outlined. But the orchestra participates in the proceedings to a much greater degree than in the traditional Baroque ensembles, and has a distinctly symphonic character.

The concerto is in three movements. The opening Allegro, in C major, is in sonata form. The violin and the cello assume a virtuoso character as soon as the main themes are introduced, while the piano occupies a subsidiary position. The development section and the recapitulation are elaborated according to tradition, but Beethoven's hand is revealed in bold modulations led by chromatic expansions in enharmonic progressions. A roulade of decorative melodic figurations leads to the coda on the **pedal point**. The ending is assertive.

Pedal point. A tone sustained in one part to harmonies executed in the other parts.

The second movement, Largo, in A-flat major, is a typical Beethoven romance, with a long protracted melody serving as the point of departure for instrumental variations in filigree texture. The dynamic design is a model of Classical perfection, providing a natural alternation of moods. After a stationary and foreboding passage there is a transition without pause to the last movement, Rondo alla polacca. The propulsive rhythm of the **polonaise** is struck immediately, imparting a festive air to the music. The sonorities are enhanced by a cascade of scales in the solo instruments, gradually subsiding into a series of echoes, followed by coquettish trills and ponderous unisons. Once more there is a discursive interlude; meaningful **diminished-seventh chords** create a temporary suspense, and a brilliant coda is launched in vigorous 2/4 time. The last hurrah is sounded, bringing the triple concerto to a most satisfying close.

Polonaise (Fr.). A dance of Polish origin, in 3/4 time and moderate tempo.

Diminished-seventh chord. A chord consisting of three conjunct minor thirds, outlining a diminished seventh between the top and bottom notes.

Piano Concerto No. 4 in G Major, Op. 58 (1805–6)

Beethoven began his Piano Concerto No. 4 in the year 1805, but apparently the composition proceeded slowly. He was in the habit of writing several works concurrently and intermittently, without a definite chronology, in which respect he was very unlike Mozart, Haydn, or Schubert, who turned out symphonies in a matter of days, rarely weeks. Thus, while at work on the concerto, Beethoven was engaged in the composition of the Fourth and Fifth Symphonies; and it is probable that the similarity between the rhythmical figure of the first phrase of the concerto and the famous "knocks" of the Fifth is not just a coincidence. In 1805 Beethoven was thirty-five years old. His deafness was already a serious affliction, he was dramatically conscious of it, and he had already confided his fears to friends. In his everyday affairs he was highly irritable, and suspicious of everyone. Yet these years marked the peak of his powers.

Beethoven disliked playing his own compositions in public. When the Fourth Concerto was completed, he asked his pupil and friend Ferdinand Ries to play it. There were only five days left for Ries to learn it before the performance, and Ries begged Beethoven to let him play the C-Minor Concerto instead. But the great man could tolerate no opposition to his desires. He left Ries in a rage, and turned to another young pianist, who agreed forthwith. At the last moment, however, the audacious pianist demurred, and substituted in the program the selfsame C-Minor Concerto that Ries wanted to play. Beethoven, though raging, had to submit. The first performance of the Fourth Concerto took place much later—at one of Prince Lobkowitz's palace concerts, in March 1807—and Beethoven played the piano part. The orchestral parts were published in 1808. The concerto was dedicated to the Archduke Rudolph.

The concerto opens in an unusual manner, with the piano solo. The theme has a rhythmic pattern similar to the opening of the Fifth Symphony, without its dramatic significance. The strings imitate the rhythm, with immediate modulation. Gradually the entire orchestra is brought into play, while the principal theme undergoes various modifications, until only two notes of it remain, alternating in vigorous rhythmic figures. After the climax there is a moment of calm, and a curious modal transition brings in a new theme in a minor key, given first to the violins. Then the oboe is heard, and the flute, seconded by the bassoon. The sonority grows, the rhythm is more incisive, the accents are sharper, and the rumbling basses prepare another climax, punctuated by the full chords in the orchestra. As an aftermath, the woodwinds play the concluding figure, based on the pattern of the principal theme. Four energetic chords round off the orchestral interlude, and the piano finally enters with a rhythmic figure, again formed of four notes. There is brilliant passage work, the orchestra sounds four powerful chords in the key of the concerto, G major, and the piano resumes its solo. Now it is give-and-take between the

Piano Concerto No. 4 in G Major, Op. 58

soloist and the orchestra, with the principal subject embellished and varied. The piano part covers the entire range of the
instrument and in one place the distance between the right
and left hands exceeds five octaves. This is a typical device of

Beethoven, met with also in the "Appassionata," composed at about the same time as the concerto.

Then the strings announce a lively theme. The bassoon and later the clarinet take it up, while the piano plays rhythmical figurations, trills, arpeggios, and freely rhythmed ornaments. The theme in a minor key, heard at the beginning of the movement, reappears, and merges with the four-note motto of the principal theme. The oboe and the bassoon hold the foreground, while the piano continues its passage work, spiced with vigorous cross-accents. After a four-octave chromatic run, the piano has a short interlude in the treble. There is a crescendo. The orchestra enters in full strength, and there is the concluding figure in the woodwinds. This section corresponds to the similar section in the middle of the first part. It is here in the key of D major, while at its first appearance the key was G major, the tonic. As before, the piano solo enters with the four-note motto, and there is a great deal of elaboration on this figure. A climax is reached with a chromatic run, followed by trills in the piano part. A quiet theme is sounded, punctuated by the four-note figure in the lower strings.

The woodwinds and the horns now have the four-note figure, with the piano still contributing the accompanying flourishes. The mood is quiet, but there are cross-accents. A quick and vehement crescendo brings about a climax. The orchestra is cut off, after a series of powerful chords, and the piano solo announces the principal theme, as in the beginning of the concerto. This is the recapitulation, but the theme is played an octave higher, and with considerable enhancement, rhythmic and melodic. Such highly modified recapitulations are characteristic of the middle and late period of Beethoven's art of form. The secondary theme appears in G minor and, through a series of modulations, is headed for a climax in G major. There are powerful chords in the full orchestra and a piano cadenza.

Beethoven composed two cadenzas for the first movement. As every cadenza should, each includes flourishes, arpeggios, and trills. All these ornaments bear a definite thematic relationship to the principal theme, and the four-note motto is clearly recognizable. After the cadenza, the piano continues playing, with the orchestra accentuating the thematic material. After some extended scale passages, the four-note motto is reiterated in the full orchestra, and the movement comes to an end.

In the second movement, Beethoven marked expressly in the score that the piano part should be played throughout with the soft pedal down. This fact alone imparts a characteristic color to the movement. To be sure, the orchestra is given a wide range of dynamics, from triple piano to **forte**. Even the piano part, in its final short cadenza, bears an indication, "*à 3 corde*," which means, in effect, soft pedal off. Beethoven was notoriously inconsistent in such small matters, and would rarely observe his own specifications. The interesting feature of this movement is also the fact that the piano and orchestra do not play together, but alternate antiphonally. The orchestra is given a sharply rhythmed phrase, while the piano responds with a lyrical period. The key of the movement is E minor, the time, slow 2/4.

The Rondo at the beginning of the third movement is in quick 2/4 time. Thus, all three movements are in duple metrical division, which may be not without a special significance, as implying energy and vigor. The key is G major, but the incisive three-note motto opens in C major. There is an interchange of phrases between the strings and the piano, at an increasingly rapid pace. The full orchestra now plays the principal theme, and there is a new four-bar phrase, with the rumbling basses giving it vigor. The piano echoes the new phrase, and the interplay is repeated in another key. The contest between the orchestra and the piano is now narrowed to a one-bar figure. In this connection it is well to recall that the word "concerto" comes from the Latin word signifying a competition. This meaning of the word was very clear in the minds of the early composers of instrumental concertos; much later, Stravinsky deliberately revived the original meaning in his Concerto for Two Pianos.

Forte (It.). Loud, strong.

The piano solo has a brilliant cross-accented passage in sixteenth notes, which subsequently slows down to triplets in eighths. Follows a quiet theme in the piano part, which is taken up by the clarinet and strings in pianissimo. Beethoven's rondo form was extremely flexible, and such interludes as this were quite in the manner. The piano solo now runs wide-ranged arpeggios, with incisive cross-accents in the woodwind. The motto of the Rondo is heard, the movement slackens, and the piano has a short cadenza: a C-major scale downward, and a chromatic scale upward. The Rondo is now resumed pianissimo in the strings, and follows the scheme of the beginning. There is an extensive modulation, and short rhythmic phrases are bandied from the orchestra to the piano. But the three-note Rondo theme persists.

The piano plays rapid figurations, corresponding to similar figurations in the first section of the Rondo. The movement slows down to triplets in eighth notes. The key is D, while the previous appearance of the triplet figure was in A. The quiet theme is heard, and once more the strings and the clarinet echo it in the orchestra. There are arpeggios, with syncopated chords in the woodwinds. The motto of the Rondo is heard again, and soon is proclaimed by the entire orchestra. The cadenza covers less range this time and, after a brief lull, with a clarinet solo against the background of plucked strings and percussive piano passages in broken octaves, the orchestra resumes with great vigor. The piano imitates the second phrase of the orchestra, and there is an alternation of lyrical phrases between the piano and the woodwind instruments. The strings repeat the quiet theme. Then the full orchestra sounds the phrase, modified and invigorated by cross-accents. Four short chords in fortissimo prepare the cadenza.

The cadenza was written by Beethoven himself. It is relatively short, containing references to the quiet theme, and there are some arpeggios. The piano continues with long trills. The Rondo theme returns, without the three-note motto, in the woodwinds, while the piano plays arpeggios in the treble. The movement becomes more animated, and once more there is a long trill in the piano. The concluding section is marked presto. Starting in pianissimo, the dynamic range is quickly covered up to fortissimo, and the Rondo theme is given in full by the orchestra. The piano then plays arpeggios in the treble, and once more there is a crescendo, reaching the final climax, the three-note motto being sounded with crashing effect.

Violin Concerto in D Major, Op. 61 (1806)

Beethoven wrote five piano concertos, but only one violin concerto. The latter was written for a popular Vienna violinist named Franz Clement. Beethoven inscribed the manuscript, in a mixture of Italian and French, "Concerto per clemenza pour Clement." Why did Beethoven have to beg Clement for clemency? There must have been a reason behind the pun. Perhaps he felt conscience-stricken, for he did not deliver the manuscript until the last moment for its first performance in Vienna, on December 22, 1806, and poor Clement had to play it practically at sight. The program was arranged in a most peculiar manner. Clement played the first movement of the concerto and, before going on with the work, presented a violin fantasy of his own, holding the violin upside-down. He completed the concerto in the second part of the program. Such interpolations of solo pieces of the "virtuoso" type between the movements of a concerto or a symphony were not uncommon at the time. Anyway, there is no evidence that Clement's fantastic stunt shocked anyone in the audience, or for that matter Beethoven himself.

The first movement, Allegro ma non troppo, in D major, in 4/4 time, begins in a startling way, with four strokes on the kettledrum on the tonic D. A story is told that these drumbeats were inspired by a neighbor knocking at Beethoven's door late at night, but there is as little verisimilitude in it as in the legend that the initial four notes of Beethoven's Fifth Symphony represent Fate knocking at the door. (It may have been the same door, for Beethoven was working on the Violin Concerto and the Fifth Symphony at about the same time and in the same lodgings.) The orchestral introduction is unusually long; it forms a summary of the thematic content of the entire movement. The first theme is introduced by the woodwinds. The beautifully proportioned second theme is sung out by the violins.

A remarkable phenomenon occurs in the transition: four D-sharps, set at the same measured pace as the opening four drumbeats, and left in suspended animation without a resolution into their natural outlet on E. With malice aforethought, or so it seems, Beethoven leads them to a dominant-seventh chord of D major, in which the crucial E is misplaced; the four D-sharps are then repeated and intentionally misdirected to the dominant-ninth chord, again minus the hoped-for E.

The mystery deepens, and the plot thickens, when we discover that in the preliminary sketches of the Violin Concerto the impertinent D-sharps are enharmonically notated as E-flats—many arcs removed, on the quintal cycle of scales, from the basic tonality of this concerto. Then there is this neat circumstance that E-flat, as well as its enharmonic equivalent D-sharp, stands in the **tritone** relationship to the dominant of the principal key of the concerto, the tritone being the "diabolical" interval which the musical theologians of the Middle Ages called "diabolus in musica." There is enough material in this note grubbing for a musicophilosophical essay full of cavernous profundities. Fortunately, relief from analytical tension is provided on heuristic grounds: enharmonic substitution was common in Beethoven's notational modus operandi. To cite an amazing example, the *Eroica* was described in the announcement of its first performance as a symphony in D-sharp rather than E-flat major. Were it in fact set in that improbable key, the signature would have required nine sharps, two of them double! The Case of the Four D-sharps is solved at a later

Tritone. The interval of three whole tones.

occurrence of the suspension in question, when they are pointedly led to their legitimate exit on E.

When the solo violin is at last introduced after the lengthy orchestral prolegomenon, its entrance is oblique, masked by allusive arpeggios and decorative scale passages. It is only after a great deal of virtuosic perambulation that the soloist gains prominence in melodious presentations. The orchestra accommodates itself to the harmonious soloist, and the movement concludes without prolixity or supererogation.

The second movement, **Larghetto**, is set in G major, in 4/4 time. As in the first movement, the thematic initiative is given to the orchestra, which states the principal subject in muted strings. Once again the soloist assumes the role of the exterior decorator, furnishing some exquisite purfling. But when in due time the solo part rises to its rightful dominance, it resounds with magnificent eloquence. A cadenza perlustrates the pertinent thematic materials, leading to a decisive plunge into the third and last movement, Rondo, in D major. Here Beethoven finds himself in his natural environment, under the open harmonious skies, happily pursuing a pastoral echolalia in the folkish rhythm of 6/8.

The music is full of fanfares, suggesting the sound of a postilion horn announcing the departure of a stagecoach, or of a distant hunting scene. A poignant balladlike tune in a minor key brings about a change of mood. But soon the rollicking rhythms of the country dance reassert themselves. An upward run of two and a half octaves along the chord notes of the D-major triad in the solo part gives the signal for an applause-provoking ending.

Larghetto (It.). The diminutive of largo, demanding a somewhat more rapid tempo.

Piano Concerto No. 5 in E-flat Major ("Emperor"), Op. 73 (1809)

Beethoven wrote his fifth, and last, piano concerto in Vienna in 1809. The city was under the siege of Napoleon's armies in

August of that year, but surrendered quickly after the French howitzers opened fire. Beethoven spent most of the time during the bombardment in the cellar of his brother's house with pillows pressed against his ears to protect him from the noise of the artillery.

The E-flat Major Concerto has somehow acquired the nickname "Emperor" Concerto, perhaps in connection with the fact that it was composed during Napoleon's drive on Vienna. An imperial link may also have been suggested by the "military" tonality of E-flat major, the key of the *Eroica* Symphony, which was inspired by Napoleon. Incidentally, the concerto's nickname, "Emperor," is unknown in Germany and Austria.

The first performance of the concerto took place in Leipzig on November 28, 1811; it had its first Vienna hearing on February 12, 1812, when Carl Czerny, famous for his piano exercises, who was a pupil of Beethoven's and the teacher of Liszt, was the soloist. The Vienna concert was a social affair, and its ostensible purpose was a benefit for the Charitable Society of Noble Ladies. Popular entertainment was provided on the same program by three living tableaux representing paintings by Raphael, Poussin, and Troyes. For this type of audience the music of the concerto was too difficult, and it was indifferently received.

The concerto is in three movements. The orchestra strikes a powerful tonic chord in the first movement, Allegro, and it triggers a sonorous display of arpeggios in the piano part. Another orchestral chord, in the **subdominant**, is struck, and the piano responds with a series of harmonic figurations. The dominant follows, and once more the piano fills in the harmonic outline. The introduction is completed with the resolution into the tonic. The orchestra then presents the principal "imperial" subject in its most authoritative utterance, set in martial 4/4 time, in the main key of E-flat major. A lyric melody in G major in the piano part serves as the second subject. Bravura passages follow, with a piano and orchestra fully

Subdominant. The tone below the dominant in a diatonic scale; the fourth degree.

Piano Concerto No. 5 in E-flat Major, Op. 73 ("Emperor")

engaged. Chromatic sequences provide colorful elaboration of the principal subjects, but the key of E-flat major dominates the harmonic scheme in its porphyrogene majesty.

The second movement, Adagio un poco mosso, in 4/4 time, is in the key of B major; it is set in the form of instru-

Chorale. A hymn tune of the German Protestant Church, or one similar in style.

Submediant. The third scale tone below the tonic; the sixth degree.

mental variations on a **chorale**-like melody. A remarkable modulation is effected at the end of the movement through the enharmonic identification of the tonic of B major with the flatted **submediant** of E-flat major. The spirit of improvisation reigns in the transitional chords, softly played by the pianist, in anticipation of the main subject of the finale, Rondo. There is a sudden dash forward, unleashing an explosive series of tonic chords and harmonic embellishments, allegro ma non tanto. The tonal scheme of the finale is crystal clear. Cascades of chords and arpeggios, cataracts of scales, rivulets of pearly figurations fill the air with music. The piano reaches the high E flat in the treble, a key that had not been available to Beethoven on the instruments he used to compose his early works. The "Emperor" Concerto ends with a coruscating scattering of brilliant sonorities.

CHAMBER MUSIC

String Quartet No. 1 in F Major, Op. 18, No. 1 (1799–1800)

Beethoven was a late beginner in composition. He wrote his first string quartets at the age of twenty-nine. At the same age, Mozart had already gone through more than half his voluminous catalogue of works. Also, Beethoven worked laboriously. While Mozart could turn out a string quartet in one afternoon, it took Beethoven months to bring his early quartets into shape, after many revisions.

The Quartet in F Major, Op. 18, No. 1, is the first of Beethoven's published quartets, although not the first in the order of composition. Opus 18 includes six quartets in all, dedicated to Beethoven's friend and financial benefactor, Prince Franz Joseph Lobkowitz, who was an amateur musician and patron of the arts. Many of Beethoven's instrumental compositions were performed for the first time at Lobkowitz's home. Such private performances arranged by a rich music lover were very frequent in the Vienna of Beethoven's time, whereas public performances in public halls were rather exceptional.

Beethoven's notebook reveals five attempts at the composition of the very first theme of this quartet. Curiously enough, they were all in 4/4 time, while the final product crystallized itself in 3/4. Beethoven completed the composition of the quartet on June 25, 1799, but a year later, in June 1800, he wrote to Karl Friedrich Amenda, his friend to whom he had given the manuscript: "Don't play my quartet—I have modified it very much. I am only now learning how to write quartets, as you will observe when you receive the music." And Beethoven was already in his thirtieth year at the time!

In his student days Beethoven practiced strict counterpoint diligently, using for a textbook the famous Latin treatise on counterpoint, *Gradus ad Parnassum (Steps to Parnassus)*, by the celebrated composer and theorist Johann Joseph Fux (1660–1741). Beethoven's own music book with 245 exercises, some of them corrected by Haydn, who was Beethoven's teacher for a time, is extant, and testifies to the fact that he applied himself thoroughly to the science. But strict counterpoint never appealed to Beethoven, although he felt great admiration for master contrapuntists of his day. In actual composition Beethoven made use of counterpoint as he saw fit, without being much concerned about the strictness of the interval and the pedantry of the science. He humanized counterpoint. In quartet writing, he individualized separate instruments by lending melodic interest to their parts and, in common with all contrapuntal practice, he made ample use of the device of imitation. But it was mostly imitation of pattern rather than strict transposition of intervals.

The Quartet Op. 18, No. 1, is in the orthodox four movements. The first movement, Allegro con brio, in F major, in 3/4 time, is based on one single motive, which is used 102 times in 313 bars, an amazing proportion for a movement that is not a set of variations. This rhythmic theme appears in every instrument, in various melodic forms. There is a contrasting second theme and a development—a fact which makes it possible to approximate this movement to sonata form.

The second movement, Adagio affettuoso ed appassionato in D minor, in 9/8, is also in sonata form, but with considerable modifications. Thus the return to the first time in the original key is embellished with figuration, which serves to enliven the closing part of the movement. We catch a glimpse of the future nineteenth-century Beethoven in characteristic explosions of dynamic force and lightning flashes of rapid notes. We find here also an instance of the use of extremely rare 128th notes. Amenda tells us that this movement was inspired by the scene in the tomb in Romeo and Juliet; this statement is plausible in view of the fact that a sketch of this movement, dated 1799, bears the programmatic designation "*Les derniers soupirs*," "the last sighs," as the end.

The third movement, a Scherzo, is used by Beethoven in place of the Classical minuet. As in the minuet there is a trio, so named because in the original Classical form three instruments used to play the middle section. The Scherzo is in the key of the quartet, F major, and the trio is in the dominant, C major, in conformity with common usage. The principal part of the Scherzo is repeated, completing the **ternary form**. Donald Francis Tovey is the authority for the statement that Beethoven always used the word "scherzo" in its etymological sense, the German *Scherz*, or "jest," thus suggesting a humorous composition.

Ternary form. Rondo form; ABA form, such as the minuet and trio.

The last movement is a lively Rondo, in duple time, in F major. The principal theme returns three times, and there are episodes with new material between the appearances of the principal theme. The coda is extensive, and leads to a brilliant close.

String Quartet No. 8 in E Minor, Op. 59 ("Razumovsky" Quartets), No. 2 (1805–6)

The tenuous thread existing between the Immortal Beloved and the three Op. 59 Quartets (called the "Razumovsky" Quartets) hangs on the question of chronology. Beethoven was extremely careless in his dates. The letter to the Immortal Beloved was dated Monday, July 6, but without the year. Among the years in which July 6 fell on a Monday, the most probable is 1807, that is, if Beethoven was not mistaken in setting down the day of the week. Now on April 20, 1807, Beethoven signed an advantageous contract with the London-based Italian composer and publisher Muzio Clementi, by the terms of which he sold Clementi the British rights on his Quartets Op. 59, the Fourth Symphony, the Overture to *Coriolanus*, the Fourth Piano Concerto, and the Violin Concerto for the sum of two hundred pounds sterling. But the quartets were in the hands of Count Franz von Brunsvik, and Beethoven, eager to deliver all the items to Clementi in due time, wrote in May 1807 an urgent note to Brunsvik requesting him to return the quartets to him at once. This letter contains the phrase "Kiss your sister Therese." This kiss, taken in conjunction with the letter to the Immortal Beloved written two months later, makes Therese an important candidate.

Psychologically it is unlikely that Beethoven should have included this kiss in a letter of prosaic contents, if it had any emotional significance, but confronted with the riddle of the Immortal Beloved, Beethoven scavengers are willing to grasp at a straw. No Beethoven scholar has considered the most likely solution of the riddle: that Beethoven played with his own fantasy, as he very often did; that he invented a nonexistent voyage which he described in that letter, and that he did not destroy the letter precisely because it had no object in the real world.

The three Quartets, Op. 59, are usually known under the name "Razumovsky" Quartets. Count Andreas Razumovksy was the Russian ambassador to the Austrian court in Vienna. He was also an amateur violinist, who played the second violin in a quartet he organized for his pleasure. That the quartets were written at Razumovsky's request, or were without such a request destined for Razumovsky, is shown by the fact that Beethoven introduced Russian themes in the music. The dedication to Razumovksy appears in the third printing of the quartets, in these characteristic words in French:

> Trois Quatuors très humblement dédiés a son Excellence Monsieur le Comte de Razumovksy, Conseiller, privé actuel de Sa Majesté l'Empéreur de toutes les Russies, Senateur, Chevalier des ordres de St. André, de St. Alexandre-Newsky, et Grand-Croix de celui de St. Vladimir de la 1re Classe, etc., etc., par Louis van Beethoven.

There is no trace of any money transaction between Beethoven and Razumovksy, but it may be assumed that this dedication, and the joint dedication of the *Pastoral* Symphony to Count Razumovksy and Prince Lobkowitz, were made in consideration of a sum of money. This was a perfectly legitimate and sanctioned procedure, no more objectionable in Beethoven's time than in our own.

The Russian melodies that Beethoven used in the Quartets Op. 59 were taken from a collection of Russian songs compiled by one Ivan Pratch and first published in Russia in 1790. Beethoven must have had a copy of this compilation, for he adhered to the type of the melody faithfully. In the Quartet Op. 59, No. 2, he makes use of the same Russian tune that was later used by Modest Mussorgsky (1839–1881) in the coronation scene of *Boris Godunov*. Pratch has this tune in 3/8 time and in A major. Beethoven uses it in the trio section of the third movement, alternately in E major and A major, setting the time signature as 3/4. The theme is treated fugally, with a **stretto** toward the end. The accompanying figure of the tune is in triplets, and the entire presentation is extremely logical and symmetric. Thus, the subject appears in each of the instruments, and is kept in its original melodic form. The Russian words of the theme—which Beethoven could not have understood, for there were no translations given in Pratch's collection—are in conflict with Beethoven's light conception. The song is in fact a hymn to the glory of the czar, and was used on solemn occasions in Russia: "Glory be to you, our Lord in Heaven! Glory be to our Czar on this earth. His beautiful robes will not be worn out! His faithful servants will not grow old! His valiant steeds will not tire out! We sing this song to our Lord! We render him his glory."

Stretto (It.). A division of a fugue in which subject and answer follow in such close succession as to overlap.

A brief notice in the *Allgemeine Musikalische Zeitung*, published after the performance of the quartets in Vienna, referred to them as "of great length and difficulty." The view was expressed that they "will be found perhaps too obscure for general acceptance, though finely constructed and deeply conceived." The quartets were performed in St. Petersburg at a private house early in 1812, a few months before Napoleon unleashed his armies on Russia. In 1857, the Russian writer Alexander von Oulibichef, in his book on Beethoven directed against Wilhelm von Lenz, the initiator of the theory of three styles of Beethoven, assailed the quartets of Beethoven's later period in vehement language:

Few people liked the quartets at the time of their first appearance in St. Petersburg. Today the Op. 59 are called the "great" Beethoven quartets; soon the Opp. 127, 130, 131, 132, and 135 will be called the very great. These titles will undoubtedly be exact since the score of the longest in Op. 18 is thirty pages in length, the longest in Op. 59 is thirty-eight, and the longest of the last, sixty-two. Certainly no one can quarrel with this arithmetic.

String Quartet No. 13 in B-flat Major, Op. 130 (1825–26)

Beethoven's string quartets marked by opus numbers 127, 130, 131, 132, and 135 are usually bracketed under the group of "last" quartets or "late" quartets. They belong to Beethoven's last three years, and in them the greatness of inspiration is reflected in the greater length of the music itself, as though Beethoven needed a larger canvas and more manuscript paper to develop the dramatic expression of his last period.

The tragedy of Beethoven's last years of life, his "quartet years," was not only the Grecian tragedy in which the most precious line of communication, from the ear to the brain, was destroyed. His was also the lesser tragedy, the annoying lack of funds, which was magnified by Beethoven's inability to manage his daily life, and his susceptibility to minor distress. His hopes were set on England, the proverbial land of shopkeepers, which proved unsuspectingly and amazingly the land of generous and far-sighted customers for culture and genius.

In a letter dated September 20, 1824, Charles Neate wrote to Beethoven on behalf of the Philharmonic Society of London, offering him three hundred guineas to come to London to conduct the performance of the Ninth Symphony, which had been written for the Society. Beethoven asked for one hundred guineas more, to buy a coach in which to travel in greater comfort. For this extra money, he offered Neate a string quartet. Neate was receptive to this suggestion: "If you bring the quartet, it is as good as one hundred pounds more," he wrote, "and you can be quite sure, I see no obstacle to it that you should earn a sufficient sum of money to take back with you, enabling you to pass your whole life pleasantly and free from care."

This quartet was the B-flat Major Quartet, Op. 130. Beethoven was agitated by the thought of possible prosperity: "If God would only give me health, I shall be able to accept all commissions I receive from every country in Europe and even from North America." Beethoven's sketchbooks show that he went on from one quartet to another almost without an interval. It was a state of feverish activity; the extraordinary rhapsodic quality, the un-Classical fluidity of modulation, the innovating spirit of instrumental writing of the last quartets are explained by the fact that Beethoven ran a musical temperature when he was writing them. He was eager to market them, of course; but the pressure of work freed Beethoven from restrictions that he might have imposed on himself were he writing for familiar patrons who, as he knew, preferred a Mozartean Beethoven to the truly Beethovenian one. But his old patrons were gone. New patrons were from England, from Russia. They were not parading as benefactors, but approached Beethoven in full appreciation of his greatness.

The Quartet Op. 130 is the thirteenth in the order of Beethoven quartets. It was sketched in the spring and summer of 1825, and the scoring was completed by November of the same year. As so often in Beethoven's creative habits, he was working on all movements at once. The fourth movement of the B-flat Major Quartet, the Danza tedesca, was originally sketched in A major and apparently was to be made part of the A-minor Quartet, but later was transposed into G major, and entitled "Allemande," the French word for the Italian *tedesca*, a German dance; but the Allemande has also a special function and character as the opening dance in the Classical suite. The *Grand Fugue*, Op. 133, was originally intended as the finale of the B-flat Major Quartet, but its length (745 bars) and its polyphonic grandeur were regarded as deterrents to success by the publisher, who persuaded Beethoven to compose another finale. Beethoven followed the publisher's advice. The new finale was probably the last thing Beethoven wrote. He sent it to the publishers on November 26, 1826, four months before he died. The B-flat Major Quartet was performed with the original *Grand Fugue* for the first time on March 21, 1826.

The B-flat Major Quartet is in six movements, and the order of these movements is unusual. The first and the last movements are Allegros, the second movement is a Presto; the third movement is an Andante scherzoso; the fourth movement, an Allegro assai. The only truly slow movement is the fifth, Adagio molto espressivo. The characteristic markings of Beethoven's last period are observable in this quartet even to the eye: the shifting key signatures, the expressive silences, the dramatic instrumental solos. The first movement is in sonata form, with its two themes anticipated in the slow introduction in a truly Beethovenian manner. The Presto is a scherzo in the tonic minor, with a trio in the tonic major. The third movement, in the remote key of D-flat major, has been called by Schumann an "intermezzo." Harmonically, melodically, rhythmically, it is extraordinary, anticipating as it does the future development of Romantic music. There is drama in the uncertainty of key, in the shimmering use of tremolo, in the abrupt ending.

The fourth movement is the Danza tedesca of the sketchbook. There is no organic connection between this German dance and the rest of the quartet. It is an insertion, an interpolation.

The fifth movement is a Cavatina (short aria or song). Beethoven's friends reported that it was written in tears and agony. An indirect confirmation of this may be seen in Beethoven's expression mark *Beklemmt* ("agonized"), with which he marked an episodic passage.

The finale is in the original key of B-flat major. Like the Danza tedesca, this finale might well bear a lower opus number. It is a rustic dance in 2/4 time, with a contrasting lyrical theme in A-flat major. The climactic coda is in Beethoven's first style, imaginative and brilliant, with episodic ideas constantly brought into play. This finale, written in Beethoven's last months of life, demonstrates that the division of Beethoven's music into three styles, originated by Lenz and accepted by all Beethoven scholars, is at best a convenient chronology. In his third period, Beethoven had not relinquished the youthfulness, vigor, and simplicity of the first.

String Quartet No. 14 in C-sharp Minor, Op. 131 (1825–26)

Immortality was available at the price of fifty ducats in Vienna before 1827. Beethoven, who lived and died there, in a state of constant financial insecurity, was willing to dedicate an overture or a string quartet to anyone rich and beneficent enough to pay. And a Beethoven dedication was a ticket to immortality. Who would now retain the name of a Russian ambassador to Vienna during Napoleonic times, were it not for the fact that Beethoven wrote the "Razumovsky" Quartets? An even more obscure Russian, one of the innumerable tribe of princes, Nikolas Galitzin, also bought a ticket for immortality. His case is particularly interesting because he did not even pay in full for the privilege. Beethoven dedicated three quartets to him, at fifty ducats each, but never collected the entire money, for Galitzin went to war in Persia, and failed to keep his promise to send Beethoven the rest of the money through his bank in St. Petersburg. The inability to get this money preyed on Beethoven's mind during the months of his illness. After Beethoven's death, Galitzin tried to prove that the money had been paid, but finally closed the controversy by sending the required sum to Beethoven's heir, his unworthy nephew, Carl.

Beethoven was not as poor as he made himself out to be. After his death, several Austrian securities were found in the drawer of his desk. He could have lived better than he did, and that he did live in poverty during his last years cannot be doubted. Carl Maria von Weber's son, who visited him, described "a bare and poorly furnished room in terrible disorder: money, clothes, all scattered on the floor; a pile of linen on the bed, dust thick on the piano, cups and cracked plates strewn over the table."

Beethoven was constantly writing letters to friends bemoaning his condition. He wrote to the Italian composer Cherubini in 1823: "My situation is so critical that I can no longer keep my eyes fixed on the stars; I have to concentrate upon the barest necessities of life." He received no reply to this letter. While appealing for help, Beethoven would not yield in any of the disputes that he was getting into, and spent money on litigations with his brother's wife for the custody of his nephew, Carl; with the heirs of Prince Lichnowsky; even with the inventor of the metronome, Johannes Maelzel.

During the last ten years of his life, Beethoven wrote his greatest works, the Ninth Symphony and the "last quartets." Yet his life, his health, and his mental state were in the worst condition imaginable. His deafness was almost complete. His domestic life was made intolerable by his nephew, custody of whom he won after a court fight. We catch glimpses of the nephew's character from Beethoven's letters and notes. "Last Sunday, you again borrowed money from the housekeeper, that cheap old harlot," he writes to his nephew in desperation. But when his nephew shot himself in an unsuccessful suicide attempt, Beethoven forgot everything and begged him to come back to his "loving father Beethoven." He always signed his notes to his nephew as a loving father, not a mere uncle.

The String Quartet in C-sharp Minor, Op. 131, one of the "last quartets" embodying Beethoven's "third style" of creative development, had an indirect bearing on his nephew. Beethoven asked his publishers, in a letter written two weeks before his death, to inscribe the score to Baron von Stutterheim, the colonel of the regiment in which Beethoven's nephew was enlisted. The quartet had been completed and sent to the publishers in October 1826, a few months earlier.

In several of his letters, Beethoven refers to having finished this quartet, but his statement often was the expression of a determination, not the actual fact.

Musically speaking, the Quartet in C-sharp Minor represents the highest development of Beethoven's new style. It contains elements of innovation, extraordinary for his time. The selection of the key itself was unusual, if not unprecedented. The quartet has seven movements, linked so that there is no distinct separation between the component parts, but a liquid transition from one mood to another. There is an element of experimentation in the use of such effects as the **violoncello** playing on the bridge in the high treble register, or pizzicato in isolated notes, creating the impression of an intrusive drumbeat. The form is extremely free, and yet in the Presto Beethoven reverts to his manner, and employs a simple harmony and rhythm of a country dance.

Violoncello (It.). A four-stringed bow instrument familiarly called the cello.

That the quartet was conceived, on the whole, as an expression of Beethoven's brighter side is borne out by Beethoven's own inscription on the manuscript: "zusammengestohlen aus verschiedenem diesem und jenem": "fashioned [literally, "stolen together"] from various this and that." Beethoven was in the habit of writing several movements, or several different pieces, at once, and the seeming eclecticism (or synthesis, if a more dignified word is desired) may be explained exactly by Beethoven's "zusammengestohlen."

The opening movement is Adagio ma non troppo e molto expressivo, in common time (4/4), in C-sharp minor. It is a fugue with episodic development, ending on the tonic major. Wagner described this movement as "revealing the most melancholy sentiment ever expressed in music." The following movement is Allegro molto vivace, in D major, in 6/8 time. The third movement is Allegro moderato, in B minor, in common time (4/4). A short adagio serves as an introduction to andante ma non troppo e molto cantabile, which is a theme with variations, which Wagner characterized as "the incarnation of perfect innocence, revealed in countless aspects." The fifth movement is Presto, starting in E major, in common time, "a vision embodied in material form," to quote Wagner once more. This movement is similar in character to the Scherzo from the Ninth Symphony, composed during the same period. There is surprising boisterousness in this movement that belies the picture of Beethoven as an unchangeably gloomy hypochondriac.

The concluding part is an adagio in the key of the quartet, C-sharp minor, in triple time, leading to the final Allegro in cut time (2/2), which suggested to Wagner the picture of "the indomitable fiddler, whirling us on to the abyss."

String Quartet No. 16 in F Major, Op. 135 (1826)

The String Quartet Op. 135 is the last complete work written by Beethoven. It bears the date in Beethoven's hand: October 30, 1826. Beethoven died on March 26, 1827. The quartet was performed posthumously in Vienna, on March 23, 1828. This quartet has caused more flow of commentators' ink than all the rest put together, mainly because of Beethoven's curious inscription at the head of the last movement, over the musical quotation of the two principal themes: "Muss es sein? Es muss sein!" ("Must it be? It must be!"). The musical quotation bears a special title, also written in Beethoven's own hand: "Der schwer gefasste Entschluss" ("the very difficult resolution").

Schindler offers a prosaic explanation of this mysterious quotation. Beethoven's housekeeper had asked him for money. "Must it be?" Beethoven inquired. "It must be," the housekeeper answered with emphasis. An alternate explanation, also offered by Schindler, is that Beethoven had asked his publishers for money and, anticipating a query, answered it in a musical theme. A more probable version is offered by Maurice Schlesinger, the son of Beethoven's publisher, namely that Beethoven did not care to write this quartet, which is, in its extension and inner significance, on an inferior scale to the quartets opp. 127, 130, 131, and 132, but, needing money, and having promised the work to the publisher, was conscience-bound to write it. The difficulty in accepting Schlesinger's version lies in the fact that he stated it thirty-two years after the event, and quoted from memory a letter that Beethoven was supposed to have written to the publishers in explanation of the "must it be" quotation, a letter that was lost during a fire at the publisher's premises, and of which no copy was kept. A simpler explanation suggests itself in the absence of plausible report, namely that Beethoven, thinking about the possibilities of the themes already selected by him, fitted the question and answer to them, and set them down in the spirit of a ponderous joke of the kind to which he was addicted.

The first movement is an Allegretto. This is the only quartet that opens with an Allegretto; the rest begin with an Allegro in sonata form, sometimes prefaced with a slow introduction. This departure from rule indicates the lighter nature of the quartet as a whole. The mood is established at once by a whimsical melodic squib in the viola. This melodic fragment has a questioning character underlined by its harmonization. Half a dozen more motives appear in free succession. There is hardly any development, and the form as well as the mood here point toward late Romantic music; this Allegretto might well be regarded as a direct predecessor of Richard Strauss's *Till Eulenspiegel*, which is also in the key of F major.

The following movement is a Vivace, and corresponds to a scherzo. It is in fast 3/4 time. The movement opens in canon so that the two violins and the viola enter on different beats, while the cello plays an independent melody staccato. The middle part contains a succession of forty-seven bars with an unchanging figure in the second violin, viola, and cello, while the first violin disports itself over this insistent background.

Beethoven's early critics saw in this display of Beethovenian humor a sign of mental decline, and the consequences of deafness. Yet, this repetition of figures is obviously part of a design, and is quite in keeping with the spirit of the whole scherzo.

The slow movement is a different Beethoven. Joseph de Marliave, in his book *Les Quatuors de Beethoven*, which is a model of conscientious presentation of facts and careful analysis, here gives way to the besetting temptation of all writers on music, and explains the movement as a premonition of approaching death. Even if unconscious knowledge of the end has come to be accepted, there is no more evidence in this particular movement than in any other slow movement in Beethoven's music that he felt that it would be his last **Lento**. If anything, a case can be made against all powers of premonition in Beethoven's life. When he wrote his last will and testament, he did not die. And his last quartet has three movements full of life and gaiety, as against one contemplative movement. The very last music he wrote, a new finale to the Quartet Op. 130, overflows with youthful energy. The slow movement of the present quartet had better be analyzed without excursions into the mysteries of foreknowledge.

Lento assai, cantante e tranquillo is in the remote key of D-flat major, with the middle part in a minor key on the same tonic, enharmonically changed to C-sharp. This short middle part is dramatic, even mysterious; there are gaps or silences typical of Beethoven's third style of writing. When the movement is resumed in the major key, the pastoral mood reigns, with flashes of distant lightning in the first violin. Beethoven's sketchbook bears these words in relation to this Lento: "gentle song of peace."

The finale is based on the motives "Must it be?" and "It must be," the first with an upward and questioning inflection, the second, in the affirmative interval of a fourth, in downward movement, resting on F, the tonic of the quartet. There are rapid changes of mood, alternating between doubt and affir-

Lento (It.). Slow; calls for a tempo between andante and largo.

mation. The casual and light nature of the movement is emphasized by Beethoven's note at the end of the development: "The second part to be repeated if desired." Elsewhere, in his sonatas and quartets, Beethoven is much more categorical about his repeats.

Beethoven's last quartet opens the era of Romantic music. Beethoven's near contemporaries condemned the quartet for its looseness in construction, and judged it a work of the decline. Others acclaimed it as a prophetic vision of the Romantic future. Perhaps it is neither. The quartet is typical Beethoven, and there are elements of his great style, as exemplified in the Lento, and also the lesser art of brilliant humor. Although Beethoven noted "the last quartet" at the end of the manuscript, he could not foresee it was to be his last work. This quartet was Beethoven's **intermezzo**, which death converted into a finale.

Intermezzo (It.). A light musical entertainment alternating with the acts of the early Italian tragedies; incidental music; a short movement connecting the main divisions of a symphony.

PIANO WORKS

Piano Sonata No. 14 in C-sharp Minor ("Moonlight"), Op. 27, No. 2 (1801)

The writer of the Beethoven entry in the ninth edition of the *Encyclopedia Britannica*, published when there were still people alive who had known Beethoven, describes Beethoven's relationship with women in the following manner:

> Although by no means insensible to female beauty, and indeed frequently enraptured, in his grand chaste way with the charms of some lady, Beethoven never married, and was, in consequence, deprived of that feeling of home and comfort which only the unceasing care of refined womanhood can bestow. . . . He was a favorite with the ladies of the court, and many of the reigning beauties of Vienna

adored him and would bear any rudeness from him. These young ladies went to his lodgings or received him at their palaces as it suited him. He would storm at their least inattention during their lessons, and would tear up the music and throw it about. He may have used the snuffers as a toothpick in Madame Ertmann's drawing-room, but when she lost her child, he was admitted to console her. He was constantly in love, and though his taste was very promiscuous, Beethoven made no secret of his attachments. . . . One thing is certain, that his attachments were all honorable, and that he had no taste for immorality.

Afterwards, Beethoven's famous letter addressed to the Immortal Beloved was published. The greatest confusion was precipitated by it among Beethoven biographers. The letter was never sent, and possibly was never intended to be sent, but who was the presumptive addressee? One of the strongest candidates was Beethoven's pupil, Giulietta Guicciardi, later the Countess Gallenberg. To her Beethoven dedicated his most poetic and most personal work, the "Moonlight" Sonata. The nickname originated with the Berlin music critic and publisher Johann Rellstab (1759–1813) who, in his criticism of the work, said it reminded him of the moonlight on Lake Lucerne.

Beethoven wrote the Sonata quasi una fantasia in C-sharp Minor, Op. 27, No. 2, as the "Moonlight" Sonata is properly titled, in 1801, in the full vigor of his manhood, at the age of thirty-one. Was this sonata a musical declaration of love? The theory was destroyed by the Countess Gallenberg herself, who told Alexander Thayer (1817–1897), Beethoven's greatest biographer: "Beethoven gave me the Rondo in G, but wishing to dedicate something to the Princess Lichnowsky, he took the Rondo away and gave me this Sonata in C-sharp minor instead." The dedication was thus a makeshift gift, and nothing more.

The first movement, Adagio **sostenuto**, was principally responsible for Rellstab's impression of the moonlight. The

Sostenuto (It.). Sustained, prolonged; may also imply a tenuto, or a uniform rate of decreased speed.

tranquil mood of this Adagio sostenuto is established by the slow, wavy motion of harmonic progressions in the right hand against the deep organlike octaves in the left. The melody, sounded above these harmonies, is built on only two essential notes, followed by a cadence. Depending on where the cadence leads, the key shifts with the conclusion of every phrase. Soon the melody ceases, and the underlying harmonies spread over several octaves in an ever-heightening emotional sweep. Then the calm mood returns. But while in the beginning the melodic direction was downward, toward lower keys, here the melody strives higher and higher, before coming to rest on the tonic. The characteristic pulse of the melody is then heard in the bass, under the wavy harmonies of the right hand. The close is in a perfect mood of tranquillity.

The second movement, Allegretto, in D-flat major, is written in a light manner. It is a scherzo, regularly constructed, with a trio for a middle part. What makes it typically Beethovenian is the use of cross-accents, which inject new vigor into the rhythmic scheme. Dynamic contrasts in this movement are essential to the music.

The third and last movement, Presto agitato, is in true sonata form. There are two contrasting sections, the stormy first and the lyrical second. The scheme for modulation also follows the broad lines of the Classical sonata form, with such modifications as Beethoven applies in all but his very early sonatas and symphonies. Thus, there is not one first theme, but several subjects that can be bracketed together to form a first section.

The second subject is more easily isolated and recognized. But it appears over the bass of rapid passages which characterize the whole mood of the movement. It is heard variously, in the left hand and in the form of syncopated octaves in the right hand. In Beethoven's later sonatas, the development section is the scene of much contrapuntal activity, canonic imitation, and fugal interlocking. In this sonata there is no formal complexity—new themes are added freely as the inspiration prompts. The sonata's title, Sonata quasi una fantasia—"Sonata in the style of a fantasia"—suggests the procedure. The mood of a fantasia is magnificently displayed in the final section of the last movement. Technically, it takes the place of a coda, but as Beethoven conceives this final section, it is a long meditation on the themes of the sonata. It abounds in cadenzas, trills, arpeggios, meaningful pauses, dramatic transitions.

It is often said that Beethoven is the most personal composer among the great, and that one can read his soul in his music. The stormy pages of the conclusion of the "Moonlight" Sonata seem to justify this common notion. It is easy to connect this music with the picture of Beethoven as presented by Romantic painters, deep in meditation, with flashes of explosive power anticipated in the knitted brow. Even if Beethoven's features had never been seen, painted, or described, his physical appearance could have been plausibly reconstructed from his music.

Piano Sonata No. 28 in A Major, Op. 101 (1816)

In 1816 and 1817, in the wake of the Napoleonic Wars, there was in Europe a general resurgence of the national spirit. One trait of this resurgence was the emphasis laid on the purity of national languages. Beethoven, who always followed, in his impetuous way, the changes of political sentiments, decided that in music, too, the vernacular should be used in preference to the internationally accepted Italian terms. He had experimented in this direction, and even coined some substitute words, such as *Luftsang* for **aria**, *Kreisfluchtstück* for canon, and *Grundsang* for bass. In January 1817, Beethoven, in a formal letter, announced his decision to change the Italian term *pianoforte* to *Hammerklavier*. It was not a translation, but a mere designation of the type of sound production, by hammers, actuated from a keyboard. The first composition desig-

Aria (It.). An air, song, tune, melody.

nated for the Hammerklavier was the Piano Sonata No. 28, Op. 101. Apparently, Beethoven felt there were compelling reasons for the change, for he expressed willingness to pay for a new title page of the sonata, which had been engraved with the use of the word "pianoforte." The indications of tempo and mood were given in both languages, and the German was usually more explicit and more expressive. Beethoven used the term "Hammerklavier" for three sonatas, and after that apparently lost interest in verbal quibbles, letting his publisher use the commonly established phraseology.

Dorothea von Ertmann, to whom the sonata is dedicated, was a Beethoven pupil, and one of the best interpreters of his music. There is a tendency among biographers to seek romantic implications in every dedication Beethoven made to a woman. In the case of Dorothea von Ertmann, there were definitely no such developments. She was married to an Austrian Army officer. When Mendelssohn visited the Ertmann family in 1831, this officer, now a general, gave some interesting sidelights on Beethoven's habits, such as, for instance, the use of candle snuffers for a toothpick during a music lesson with Dorothea. Less authenticated is the story that when the Ertmanns lost a child, Beethoven invited Dorothea to his house and played for an hour, talking to her in tones instead of words.

To place the Sonata Op. 101 in Beethoven's creative catalogue, it should be sufficient to note that it was written during the long interval of years between the Eighth and Ninth Symphonies. The exact dates of composition are unknown, but may be tentatively given as 1815, 1816, and/or 1817. Beethoven was not in the habit of dating his manuscripts, and was careless in dating his letters, particularly in the early months of every year, when he would inadvertently set down the year just passed, a habit which worked havoc with the Beethoven chronology, and confused his biographers.

The indications in German for the first movement read, "somewhat lightly, and with innermost feeling." The time signature is 6/8. Although the key of the sonata is A major, the tonic triad does not make its appearance until the last section of the first movement. The opening phrase begins in E major, considered as the dominant of A, but the cadences are deceptive, leading into minor keys, and away from the designated key of the sonata. From the musical, and even psychological, point of view, such studied ambiguity is interesting, particularly since it is not found in any of Beethoven's other sonatas. The rhythmical scheme of the movement is a slow **barcarole**-like motion, which is reduced in transitional passages to a series of syncopated chords, without the main beat. The initial phrase furnishes most of the thematic elements used in the first movement. The coda is unusually extensive.

The indication in German for the second movement is "lightly, marchlike." The movement is energetic, suggesting a drumbeat rhythm. The key is F major. The middle section, in the subdominant, is written in the form of a two-part **canon**, which imparts a quality of sparseness. In canonic imitation, the right hand leads, the left following a half bar behind; then the left hand leads, and the right follows a whole bar behind; and after a brief noncanonic interpolation, the left hand leads the right by half a bar, using the subject of the first period of the canon, where the right hand led the left by the same length. These formal devices are characteristic of the Beethoven of the last sonatas. After the middle section, the march is repeated without modification.

The indications, in German, for the third movement are "slow, and full of yearning." The adagio serves as an introduction to Allegro. The initial phrase is repeated in various forms, accumulating strength with every repetition. There is a slow cadenza. Then, the opening phrase of the first movement is quoted, as if to point out the unity of the whole sonata. Three long, chromatically rising trills lead to the Allegro, in A major, in 2/4 time, which is launched vigorously. The indications, in German, read: "fast, but not excessively so, and with determination." A figure of a falling third, from the upbeat to the downbeat, is the motto of Allegro, which is used later in the

Barcarole (Ger.). A vocal or instrumental piece imitating the song of the Venetian gondoliers.

Canon. Musical imitation in which two or more parts take up, in succession, the given subject note for note; the strictest form of musical imitation.

fugue. The structure is canonic, the right and left hand moving in free imitation. There is an emotional melodic section, warningly marked "non lirico," "not lyrically." After another canonic episode, the second theme of a spirited character is played in the dominant, which is in agreement with Classical usage. A cadence confirms the dominant key.

In the fourth movement, a short interlude is played; instead of a development, as in Classical forms, there is a fugue, based on the figure of the falling third, the motto of the principal subject of Allegro. But Beethoven's fugues were no mere exercises in polyphony. Beethoven himself is quoted (and the remarks sound authentic) in these words: "To make a fugue requires no particular skill. But the imagination ought to assert itself, and a new poetic element should be injected into the traditional form." In the fugue of this sonata, the subject and the answers do not follow the absolute rule of the tonic and dominant. Instead, they appear on various degrees of the scale, as used in the middle section of the Bachian fugue. The freedom of the form contributes to the cumulative dynamic force; the voices telescope; there is a stretto, a narrow progression of thematic fragments. The dominant is reached in the bass, preparatory to the return of the initial section of the Allegro. As usual in Beethoven's later sonatas, the recapitulation has many additional details. The succession of keys is, however, according to the Classical formula. The "nonlyric" theme of the first section, then heard in the tonic, now recedes into subdominant, and the spirited second theme is played in the tonic, bringing the sonata to an easy conclusion. The coda is built on a swelling trill in the deep bass, and the ending is in fortissimo.

Piano Sonata No. 29 in B-flat Major ("Hammerklavier"), Op. 106 (1817–18)

The full title of Beethoven's Sonata op. 106 is Grosse Sonate für das Hammerklavier. Its principal key is B-flat major. The name Hammerklavier is nothing more than the German word for "hammer keyboard," which Beethoven adopted as a concession to the rising tide of German nationalism of the post-Napoleonic times. The "Hammerklavier" Sonata is the longest of all Beethoven's sonatas. Its tonal range exceeds six octaves, and extends from D in the low bass register to F in the highest treble, over an octave more than the range available to Beethoven on the pianos of earlier manufacture.

The extension in length and tonal range are the outward attributes of the inner grandeur of conception, a fullness of development, a complexity of detail, which characterize the last period of Beethoven's creative life, to which the "Hammerklavier" Sonata belongs.

Contemporary critics mistook this vastness of design and multiplicity of ideas for a confusion in Beethoven's mind in his last years. The picture of the master, almost totally deaf, untidy in his dress, unable to organize his daily life, anxious over his financial insecurity, was projected by such critics onto the music of Beethoven's last period, and the conclusion was drawn that it was the music of the decline. More astute commentators saw the beginning of the new era in this music as yet so strange. They argued that deafness itself might have led to greater concentration on fundamental problems of style, and that Beethoven's indifference to the social necessities of life was easily explained by his preoccupation with loftier tasks. On the other hand, Brahms denied that there is any departure from the established forms in the music of Beethoven's last period, and that, to the contrary, Beethoven was never more rigorous in his adherence to the fundamentals of the science of music as in these titanic creations.

It is quite understandable why some of Beethoven's critics demurred his novel usages. They seemed whimsical, avoidable, unnecessary. Why, for instance, leave the unresolved leading tone before going into C minor in the bridge passage in the recapitulation of the first movement? Why shift the octave progression in the left hand at the return of the Scherzo, instead of reproducing the passage as it was played the first time, and so as to avoid the grating **semitones**? Hans von Bülow (1830–94), an enlightened musician and a great respecter of Beethoven even when there is a suspicion of a slip of the pen, accepts these caprices of the master, but rebels at the superposition, in the thirty-eighth bar from the end of the "Hammerklavier" Sonata, of the passing F and G over the minor third, E-flat and G-flat in the left hand, claiming that the resulting effect is barbarous. His proposed emendation of F and G in the right hand to F-sharp and G-sharp would indeed eliminate the acoustical unpleasantness, were it not thematically a monstrosity.

Semitone. A half tone; the smallest interval in the Western scale.

The "Hammerklavier" Sonata offers as many stumbling blocks to the pianist. Difficult inner trills, uncomfortable crossings of hands at a very close range, so that the fingers collide on a single key, chords demanding unnatural extension, all these usages are doubtful inducements to frequent performances. Besides, the contrapuntal technique of writing, reaching its culmination in the *Grand Fugue* of the finale, presents additional difficulties, necessitating the subtlest possible use of dynamics in order to "orchestrate" the several voices.

This fugue of the finale embodies formal devices that are exceedingly difficult to bring out in an effective manner. In it the subject is presented in a variety of transformations, following the Bach tradition, namely in augmentation (played twice as slowly), inversion (playing ascending notes in descending, and vice versa), crab motion (playing the theme backward), and inverted crab motion (which is tantamount to reading the music upside down). The application of the term "crab" to retrograde progression is derived from the mistaken notion that crabs walk backward.

At the climactic point of the fugue, all these forms are combined in triple counterpoint, the fugue being in three voices, and are further telescoped in a stretto. But Beethoven's tempestuous temperament animates all this artifice, turning it into a medium of personal expression. The abstract architecture of fugal style gives way to a new conception, a Romantic fugue.

In the first three movements, the "Hammerklavier" Sonata follows the Classical model, with such modifications and extensions as are foreordained in Beethoven's earlier works. The first movement is in sonata form, with two contrasting subjects, a vigorous principal theme, and a lyrical subsidiary. But between the two themes, there is a wealth of material that is far from episodic. The development section of the movement contains a fugato on the rhythm of the principal vigorous subject. A meaningful interlude in quickly changing moods, dramatized by explosive rhythmic power, serves as a bridge to the final fugue. When the fugue has run its impetuous course, the conclusion is brief and assertive.

THE FELICITOUS FELIX MENDELSSOHN
(1809–47)

THE SPIRIT OF GERMAN MUSICAL ROMANTICISM is embodied in Felix Mendelssohn (1809–47) to the point of textbook clarity. His life harmonized beautifully with the Zeitgeist of the Romantic century, but he was spared personal anguish. He was born into a prosperous family: his father was a banker, his grandfather a philosopher. The ugly specter of anti-Semitism did not touch him with its black wings, for his parents became converted to Christianity long before he was born. Apart from his great gifts as a musician, he was endowed with a fine intellect, a scholarly disposition, linguistic ability, and a distinctive talent for landscape painting. Unlike most composers, he possessed great social charm and perfect manners in company. He was the darling of the Continent. He was beloved in England, where he traveled often, and he was the favorite composer of Queen Victoria. He was happy in his marriage. He was free from the besetting demon of the majority of creative men and women, that of overweening ambition. He never nurtured personal animosities. He was a friend of everyone he knew in his profession. His given name, Felix, spelled felicity. Fate that governs the lives of musicians could not, it seems, tolerate the existence of such an untroubled career. Mendelssohn died at the age of thirty-eight.

Mendelssohn was a true Romantic. His music is evocative; it flows as a facile narrative; it appeals directly to the heart. Its mastery is impeccable; nothing imperils the smooth progress of his melodies, harmonies, and rhythms. He excelled in instrumental music. His **symphonies** and **chamber music** are masterpieces of Romantic art. One should not seek profound manifestations of musical philosophy in these works, but one will never fail to find in them a true artistic sentiment, beautifully expressed.

Symphony. An orchestral composition in from three to five distinct movements or divisions, each with its own theme(s) and development. **Chamber music.** Vocal or instrumental music suitable for performance in a room or small hall.

Mendelssohn received his first piano lessons from his mother and also studied violin, foreign languages, and painting. His most important teacher in his early youth was Carl Friedrich Zelter (1758–1832), an influential figure in the Berlin musical world, who understood the magnitude of Mendelssohn's talent and in 1821 took him to Weimar and introduced him to Goethe, who took considerable interest in the boy after hearing him play.

Mendelssohn had another world besides his native country, and that other world was England. He loved England, and he loved London, even the London fog. "That smoky nest is fated to be now and ever my favorite residence," he wrote to his sister Fanny from sunny Naples. He wrote from London amusingly:

London is the most formidable and the most complicated monster on the face of the earth. In the whole of the last six months in Berlin I have not seen so many contrasts and so many varieties as in these three days. Just walk with me from my home down Regent Street; see the splendid broad avenue filled on both sides with pillared halls, unfortunately enveloped in fog. See the shops with signs as high as a man's head, and the omnibuses on which human beings tower up into the air. . . . See how a long row of coaches is left behind, stalled by some elegant equipage ahead; see how a horse rears, because the rider has some acquaintance in the house . . . and the thick John Bulls, each with two pretty and slender daughters on his arm. Oh, those daughters! But there is no danger from that quarter. The only danger is at the street corners and crossings, and I often say to myself to be careful and not to get run over in the general confusion.

England paid him back with adulation almost surpassing that accorded to Handel and Haydn, for whom London was also a second world. Every concert Mendelssohn played in London from his young days was a great social ceremony. One of the lengthiest articles in the 1879–89 Grove's *Dictionary of Music and Musicians* is devoted to Mendelssohn, in which a worshipfully meticulous account is given of his daily activities, visits, and sayings. Mendelssohn profoundly influenced the development of English music in nineteenth-century England, and the great vogue of English **oratorios** was developed from the success of Mendelssohn's choral works.

Oratorio (It.). An extended multi-movement composition for vocal solos and chorus accompanied by orchestra or organ.

Mendelssohn was not only a precocious musician, both in performing and in composition, but what is perhaps without a parallel in music history is the extraordinary perfection of his works written during adolescence. He played in public for the first time at the age of nine, and wrote a remarkable **octet** at the age of sixteen. At seventeen, he composed the **Overture** to Shakespeare's *A Midsummer Night's Dream*, an extraordinary manifestation of his artistic maturity, showing a mastery of form equal to that of the remaining numbers of the work, which were composed fifteen years later. He proved his great

Octet. A composition for eight voices or instruments.
Overture. A musical introduction to an opera, oratorio, etc.

musicianship when he conducted Bach's *St. Matthew Passion* in the Berlin Singakademie on March 11, 1829, an event that gave an impulse to the revival of Bach's vocal music.

Professional music historians are apt to place Mendelssohn below the ranks of his great contemporaries Schumann, Chopin, and Liszt. George Bernard Shaw, writing in 1889, gave an impartial but keen appraisal:

> Mendelssohn, though he expressed himself in music with touching tenderness and refinement, and sometimes with a nobility and pure fire that makes us forget all his kid glove gentility, his conventional sentimentality, and his despicable oratorio mongering, was not in the foremost rank of great composers. He was more intelligent than Schumann, as Tennyson is more intelligent than Browning; he is, indeed, the great composer of the century for all those to whom Tennyson is the great poet of the century.

The innate gift of music is an instinct, akin to the natural gift of language. Mythology may be closer to truth than musicology in that some men, women, and children are endowed with a divine spark of tonal imagination. Of all musicians known to history, Mendelssohn possessed the instinct of music in its purest form. Not even Mozart as a child had his genius developed to a perfection found in Mendelssohn's earliest works. A number of his string symphonies, written during his adolescent years, later came to light, revealing an extraordinary mastery of musical technique. This is not to say that the quality of Mendelssohn's music is comparable to Mozart's; rather, his art was an example of perfection that appears to be attained without gradual learning.

There were no tempestuous outbursts of drama or tragedy in Mendelssohn's symphonies, chamber music, piano compositions, or songs. His works could serve as a manual of proper composition of his time; his **modulations** were wonderfully predictable in their tonal fusion. His melodies were born on the wings of song; his **counterpoint** was never obtrusive; his orchestration was euphonious in its colorful harmony. Yet the very perfection of Mendelssohn's musical canon was the cause of the gradual decline of his popularity among musicians of the succeeding sesquicentenary. His music became associated with the spirit of Biedermeier: too facile, too fulsome in its *Gemütlichkeit* (good-naturedness).

Mendelssohn did not create disciples of his imitators; he could only attract epigones. But in performance by orchestras and instrumentalists, his music is ever alive; his symphonies, notably the "Scotch" and "Italian," maintain their smiling flow; his *Songs Without Words* are favorites of amateur and professional pianists alike. The popularity of his Violin **Concerto** remains undiminished among students and virtuosos. His trios and other chamber music are radiant in their communal cohesion. In sum, Mendelssohn was the musical personification of German romanticism.

Modulation. Passage from one key into another.
Counterpoint. Polyphonic composition; the combination of two or more simultaneous melodies.

Concerto (It.). An extended multi-movement composition for a solo instrument, usually with orchestra accompaniment and using (modified) sonata form.

Symphony No. 3 in A Minor *(*Scottish*), Op. 56 (1830–42)*

The Third Symphony in A Minor is known as the *Scottish* Symphony, inspired by Mendelssohn's journey to Scotland in 1829. Some elements of Scottish songs are discernible in the finale of the symphony. Mendelssohn himself conducted its first performance on March 3, 1842, with the Gewandhaus Orchestra in Leipzig.

The *Scottish* Symphony is in four traditional movements. The first movement, Andante con moto, followed by allegro un poco agitato, is typical of Mendelssohn's style: Romantic, smoothly flowing, melodious, and harmonious. The second movement, Vivace non troppo, is written in the manner of a scherzo: agile, propulsive, and energetic. There follows the

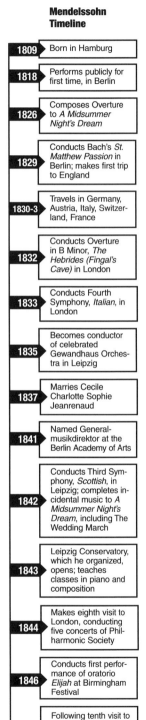

slow third movement, Adagio, in which a languorous theme undergoes numerous transformations while the rhythm is increasingly complex. The last movement is Allegro vivacissimo. It is syncopated and songful by turns. The coda, allegro maestoso assai, is in A major, homonymous of the *Scottish* Symphony's main tonality, A minor.

Symphony No. 4 in A Major (Italian), Op. 90 (1833)

Mendelssohn's Fourth Symphony is known as the *Italian*, perhaps because its composition followed his Italian journey in 1831. Mendelssohn completed it in 1833 in Berlin, and conducted its first performance in London with the Philharmonic Society, to which the score is dedicated, on May 13, 1833. At the same concert he appeared as soloist in a Mozart piano concerto, scoring a double triumph with London music lovers as composer and pianist.

For some reason Mendelssohn was not satisfied with the work and revised the score in 1837. Its Italian quality has been questioned by critics. In fact, Schumann mistook Mendelssohn's *Scottish* Symphony for the *Italian* and wrote exuberantly about the wrong work that the music might well provide an aesthetic substitute for actual travel in Italy. Thus musical geography can be confounded even in a most sensitive listener's mind, and misty Scotland can play the role of sunny Italy.

The *Italian* Symphony is in the traditional four movements. The first movement, Allegro vivace, in 6/8 time, starts energetically with an impulsive rhythmic subject in A major in the violins. The contrasting theme, more leisurely than the first, appears in the woodwinds, in E major. A vigorous development follows, leading to a comprehensive recapitulation in which the second theme is taken over by the strings.

The second movement, Andante con moto, in 4/4 time, is an elegiac interlude in D minor. Some commentators have suggested that the stately procession of the melody represents a march of pilgrims in Rome, providing a clue to the Italian associations of the work.

The third movement, in A major, 3/4 time, is marked Con moto moderato, and has the character of a symphony **minuet**. There is a brief middle section corresponding to a trio; the principal part then returns in a different instrumentation.

The last movement is entitled **Saltarello: Presto**, emphatically confirming the Italian derivation of the symphony. The *saltarello* ("leaping dance") is similar in spirit to the **tarantella**. It may have been inspired by Mendelssohn's sojourn in Rome during Carnival. "I was driving along the avenue," Mendelssohn wrote, "when I was suddenly pelted by a shower of sugar confectionery. I looked up and saw that they were thrown at me by a group of young ladies. I took off my hat and bowed, and they proceeded to pelt me even more determinedly." This scene may well be regarded as the stimulus for the colorful finale of the *Italian* Symphony.

Minuetto (It.), **minuet**. An early French dance form.

Saltarella, -o (It.). An Italian dance in 3/4 or 6/8 time.
Presto (It.). Fast, rapid; faster than "allegro."
Tarantella (It.). A southern Italian dance; also, an instrumental piece in a very rapid tempo and bold and brilliant style.

Overture to A Midsummer Night's Dream (1826)

Mendelssohn was an assiduous reader of Shakespeare in the excellent German translations by the playwright Johann Schlegel and the playwright and author Ludwig Tieck, which are regarded by Shakespearean scholars as the nearest approach to the essence of Shakespeare in any foreign language. Mendelssohn was only seventeen when he wrote the Overture to *A Midsummer Night's Dream*. The overture, Allegro di molto, in E major, in 2/2 time, opens with a progression of four long chords in the woodwind instruments, which somehow imparts an authentic Shakespearean flavor, redolent of fable, mystery, and wonderment. The action is then taken over by the strings, followed by "fairy music" in E minor. There are several allusions to the characters of the play; it is also said that the quick descending passages in the cellos were suggested to the boy composer by the buzzing of a large fly in the Mendelssohn family garden in Berlin.

Seventeen years later, at the command of King Friedrich Wilhelm IV of Prussia, Mendelssohn wrote additional music for the play, scored for solo voices, small orchestra, and chorus. He conducted the music at the king's palace in Potsdam on October 14, 1843. Several themes were taken from materials already found in the overture.

By far the most celebrated number in the score is the "Wedding March" in Act IV, which has since bestowed musical blessings on millions of married couples all over the world. It was in England that the Wedding March began to be used to accompany the bridal procession; the first such use of the work was for the marriage of Tom Daniel and Dorothy Carew at St. Peter's Church, Tiverton, on June 2, 1847. It became particularly fashionable, however, when it was played at the wedding of the princess royal to the crown prince of Prussia, the future Emperor Friedrich III, held at Windsor Castle in 1858.

Overture in B Minor, The Hebrides (Fingal's Cave), Op. 26 (1832)

Mendelssohn's overture *The Hebrides (Fingal's Cave)* was written under the impression of his visit, in 1829, to the island of Staffa, in Scotland. Fingal's Cave, the island's chief attraction, is 227 feet long and 42 feet wide. Mendelssohn wrote to his sister: "You will understand how the sight of the Hebrides affected me from the following," and he jotted down a few measures of his future overture. For some reason, after this spontaneous inspiration, Mendelssohn waited a long time before completing the score. He presented the manuscript to the Philharmonic Society of London at Covent Garden, which gave its first performance there on May 14, 1832.

The key of B minor seems to be peculiarly fitting to the tone painting of a dark cave in a northern climate. The contrasting theme is set in the relative key of D major, bringing light and the air of the open sea into the music. Formally, *Fin-*

gal's Cave is a paragon of structural solidity. The instrumentation is remarkable; the rolling passages in the low strings give a vivid illustration of stormy turbulence of wind and water. Yet Mendelssohn himself commented that the elaborate development section smelled more of counterpoint than of seagulls and saltwater fish.

Capriccio brillant *for Piano and Orchestra,*
Op. 22 (1832)

Mendelssohn composed the *Capriccio brillant* during his second visit to London, in 1832, when he was twenty-three years old. The score was completed on May 18, 1832, and Mendelssohn played it with an orchestra for the first time in London a week later. The work starts with a slow introduction in B major for piano solo. The principal theme is played with the light accompaniment of strings and, later, woodwinds. The main movement, Allegro con fuoco, introduces a lively subject in the solo piano part, which, in the process of development, appears in many keys, major and minor. The movement is sustained with unabated vivacity, and the ending is in minor, a procedure that is the reverse of the common practice of concluding a minor-key composition in a major key.

Overture to Ruy Blas *in C Minor, Op. 95*
(1839)

The music of Mendelssohn is lacking in all artifice and pretension. He composed, to use a German expression, "as a bird sings." There is no evidence in his manuscripts of any hesitancy in the transference of musical ideas to their final realization. Such technical facility often bespeaks mediocrity. But Mendelssohn was never mediocre. He imparted congenial expression to the human quality in music. He gave to music lovers a sentiment, an emotion, an aesthetic object which fitted perfectly into the artistic trends of the time. He contributed to the general musical repertory a number of perennial favorites, among them *Songs Without Words*, cherished by five generations of piano teachers, and the euphonious Wedding March.

No more romantic subject could be imagined than that of Victor Hugo's play *Ruy Blas*, purportedly a historical drama from the reign of Charles III of Spain (1716–88). In it, a Spanish nobleman removed from the royal court through the intrigues of the Queen is determined to avenge himself. He introduces his personable valet, named Ruy Blas, to the Queen as his cousin and contrives an assignation between them. But just as the ploy is about to come to fruition, Ruy Blas, a faithful subject of the Queen, refuses to go through with the iniquitous scheme, kills his master, and poisons himself.

Mendelssohn was asked to contribute incidental music for a performance of *Ruy Blas* at the Leipzig Municipal Theater, as a benefit for widows of deceased members of the theater orchestra. He was reluctant to comply, because he found the subject of Hugo's play distasteful, but an earnest appeal by interested parties to his eleemosynary feelings overcame his scruples. Working at great speed, he wrote an overture in three days, and conducted it on March 8, 1839. He intended to call the score *Overture to the Dramatic Fund,* with reference to the purpose of the commission of the work. It was only after his death that it was published under the title *Ruy Blas*, and an opus number was assigned to it.

The music of the overture is unrelated to the action of *Ruy Blas*, but it is dramatic in quality and can be fitted to any operatic subject. It has its usual share of melodramatic suspense portrayed in the ominous murmurations of the massed violins and in the solemn fanfares in the wind section of the orchestra. The cellos sing with ingratiating lyricism. The contrasts are expertly drawn, and the overture concludes in brilliant sonorities.

Concerto in E Minor for Violin and Orchestra, Op. 64 (1844)

Mendelssohn composed his Violin Concerto in 1844 for the famous violinist Ferdinand David, who gave its first performance in Leipzig on March 13, 1845. The concerto is in Mendelssohn's favorite key of E minor, a tonality that lends itself naturally to the disposition of the violin strings. It is in three movements. The first, Allegro molto appassionato in E minor, in 2/2 time, opens with a decisive beat, and the solo violin enters immediately. The theme is ingratiatingly euphonious, and is developed in decorative passage work. The orchestra enhances it in full sonority. The second theme is presented softly in the woodwinds. The violin is given a brilliant **cadenza**; there are cascades and **roulades** outlining the harmonic scheme. The ending summarizes the various thematic ingredients.

The second movement, Andante, evolves without pause from the first. It is in the bright key of C major. Considerable animation is encountered in the middle part of the movement, and then the original melody is returned.

The third and last movement opens with a brief introduction, allegretto non troppo, in the basic key of E minor, in 4/4 time. The key is then changed to E major in the principal section of the movement, Allegro molto vivace. There is a great deal of activity in the wind instruments, imparting the sense of a pastoral landscape. The form is that of a rondo with variations, with elements of **sonata**. The finale reaches the level of **fortissimo**, and the dash toward a logical and dynamically rich ending has the feeling of inevitability.

Cadenza (It.). An elaborate passage played or improvised by the solo instrument at the end of the first or last movement of a concerto.

Roulade (Fr.). A grace consisting of a move from one principal melody tone to another; a vocal or instrumental flourish.

Sonata (It.). An instrumental composition usually for a solo instrument or chamber ensemble, in 3 or 4 movements, connected by key, contrasted in theme, tempo, meter, and mood.

Fortissimo (It.). Extremely loud.

Octet in E-flat Major, Op. 20 (1825)

Child prodigies of the piano and violin are fairly common, but youthful composers are rare. Mozart and Schubert were marvels of precocious creative genius. Though Mendelssohn can-

Octet in E-flat Major, Op. 20

not be compared to them in sheer greatness, his technical facility in composition at a very early age was even more phe-
nomenal. He seems to have achieved a mastery of
counterpoint, harmony, and orchestration intuitively, for there
are no signs of hesitancy in the manuscripts of his boyhood.

Among his discarded juvenilia there are several full-fledged symphonies and operas. He was only seventeen when he wrote the remarkable Overture to *A Midsummer Night's Dream*. Still earlier, at sixteen, he composed his first explicitly **polyphonic** work, the Octet for Strings. In a marginal note, Mendelssohn specifies that the piece "must be played in true symphonic style." Indeed, the octet is a symphony in miniature, which can be performed by a full string orchestra without impairing its chamber music quality.

The octet adheres to the classical form of four movements. The first, Allegro moderato, ma con fuoco, in 4/4 time, opens in media res, with a strong statement based on the three notes of the tonic of E-flat major, the principal key of the work. There is a considerable amount of thematic deployment before the appearance of a contrasting subject in the **dominant**. Numerous ancillary motives become the substance of momentary variations and fleeting canonic configurations. A rhythmic episode in palpitating syncopated patterns introduces a dramatic element. In the recapitulation, the first theme is treated in full, while the second, in the tonic, as required by the conventions of sonata form, is compressed without congestion.

The second movement, Andante, in 6/8, is set in C minor. It begins mysteriously with naked open fifths in the lower strings; the **mediant** in the violas subsequently completes the **tonic** triad. A sudden transition to D-flat major follows. The emotional tonus is intensified. There are characteristic modulating sequences, Neapolitan cadences, and **chromatic** ascensions that are to become the hallmarks of Mendelssohn's mature style. New melodic materials are added. A rhythmic precipitation of syncopated passages in rapid sixteenth-notes leads to a coda in C minor.

The third movement, Allegro leggierissimo, in G minor, 2/4 time, is a **scherzo**. This scherzo must be played "pianissimo and staccato," Mendelssohn specifies in the score. The

Polyphonic. Consisting of two or more independently treated melodies; contrapuntal; capable of producing 2 or more tones at the same time, as the piano, harp, violin, xylophone.

Dominant. The fifth tone in the major or minor scales; a chord based on that tone.

Mediant. The third degree of the scale.
Tonic. The keynote of a scale; the triad on the keynote (tonic chord).
Chromatic. Relating to tones foreign to a given key (scale) or chord; opposed to diatonic.
Scherzo (It.). An instrumental piece of a light, piquant, humorous character.

injunction is imperative in order to achieve the requisite lightness indicated in the tempo mark of the movement. In writing this scherzo, Mendelssohn was inspired by the final stanza in the "Walpurgis Night" in Goethe's *Faust*. It is interesting to note that Goethe introduces this stanza with the words, "Orchestra, pianissimo":

> Clouds above and mist below
> Form an airy ocean,
> Through the leaves soft zephyrs blow,
> Starting a commotion.

Trill. The even and rapid alternation of two tones which are a major or minor second apart.

Tremolo (It.). A quivering, fluttering, in singing; an unsteady tone.

Alla breve (It.). In modern music, two beats per measure with the half note carrying the beat; also called "cut time."

Luminous plumes of melodic vapors rise from the music. Gentle undulations with light **trills** and swift **tremolos** limn the tonal picture of fairyland. Goethe was still living when Mendelssohn wrote the scherzo, which provides a perfect illustration for his romantic verse.

The last movement, Presto, in E-flat major, in **alla breve** (2/2) time, is a brilliant polyphonic study. A fugal theme arises from the deep register of the cellos, spreading to the violas and the violins in orderly procession. Gradually the entire ensemble becomes engaged. A series of modulatory sequences leads to a climax, which is followed by a détente. The fugal section is recalled, and the octet concludes with a concise coda.

THE PARADOXICAL RICHARD WAGNER
(1813–83)

LORD BEAVERBROOK, NO OPERA BUFF, was induced to attend a performance of *Tristan und Isolde*. "This Wagner," he inquired after sitting through the opera, "was he a clean-living man?" The answer should have been in the negative. By all accepted moral standards, Richard Wagner (1813–83) was not a clean-living man, in his relationships with women, in his financial transactions, or in his friendships. He stole Liszt's daughter from his friend, the champion of his music Hans von Bülow, while the latter was busy rehearsing *Tristan und Isolde*. When she bore Wagner's daughter, he named her Isolde. (In 1911 Isolde sued her own mother for a share in Wagner's royalties as Wagner's natural daughter, but the German tribunal ruled that inasmuch as her mother was still sharing von Bülow's bed and board at the time of conception, Wagner's paternity could not be legally proved.)

But Wagner was also a genius, the greatest creative artist of the nineteenth century, according to Thomas Mann, not merely as a composer but as a thinker who by the sheer power of his novel ideas revolutionized the concept of opera as **music drama**. Great revolutionaries in art have usually advanced by depicting contemporary life rather than sanctified subjects of mythology and ancient history. Wagner made his revolution by delving further into the symbolic world of the past. He called his art the "music of the future," and in this he propounded his greatest paradox. His critics accepted him at his word. It was the music of the future that they opposed.

Music drama. The original description of opera as it evolved in Florence early in the seventeenth century

The very vagueness of Wagner's stories as told in his music dramas allowed for varied interpretations of their meaning. George Bernard Shaw, who like Wagner loved paradox, proffered the most astonishing of these interpretations. Because Wagner was briefly engaged in the revolutionary movement of 1848, Shaw suggested that the struggle of the gods in *The Ring of the Nibelung* was a symbolic characterization of the revolutionists who had once been Wagner's comrades in arms. Some ardent Wagnerites believe that the texts, or **librettos**, that he wrote for his music dramas are as great from the literary standpoint as the music itself, but this opinion was discredited when professional literary critics dissected Wagner's bombastic jargon, arranged in curious syntax and overladen with strange neologisms.

Libretto (It.). A "booklet"; the words of an opera, oratorio, etc.

From the beginning of his career, Wagner became the center of tremendous controversy. He acquired fanatical followers who regarded him as the liberator of art from the shackles of tradition. From the other side of the barricade, he was the target of ridicule and denunciation. Cartoonists exercised their wit, showing Wagner in the process of conducting the siege of Paris during the Franco-Prussian war with a battery of musical guns. An American cartoon, entitled "Music of the Future," showed an orchestra supplemented by braying donkeys and a row of cats whose tails are pulled by a special operator. At the conductor's feet, a discarded **score** bears the inscription "Wagner—Not To Be Played Much Until 1995."

A tide of Wagnerophobia rose among musicians in the second quarter of the twentieth century as a reaction against turgid romanticism in general, but Wagner came back with a vengeance with another shift of popular taste, and was enthroned once more as an irresistible magician of musical color and theatrical drama. It remains true, however, that no contemporary composer chose to imitate Wagner. Stravinsky dismissed Wagner's era as "a lamentable chapter in music history."

Wagner's first significant opera was *Rienzi* (1840), inspired by Edward Bulwer-Lytton's historical novel of the same name dealing with the last Roman tribune Cola Rienzi, who flourished, and perished, in fourteenth-century Rome. In *Tannhäuser*, written in 1845, Wagner entered the domain of mythology, which was to remain the foundation of his music dramas. Tannhäuser was a real personage, a minstrel who flourished in the thirteenth century. Among medieval legends surrounding his name was a religious fantasy of his intimate association with Venus, his penitence, and his redemption. The Paris première of *Tannhäuser* was one of the great debacles in music history. The newspapers were full of bitter invective. Rossini remarked, "Wagner has some good moments but also bad quarter hours." One musician emerging from the theater was heard to remark, "Well, anyway, I have survived!" Wagner voluntarily withdrew the opera, and no further performances of *Tannhäuser* were given in Paris for some time.

Tannhäuser was followed by *Lohengrin*. The action takes place in and around the royal castle in Antwerp in the tenth century; Lohengrin, a knight of the Holy Grail, arrives in a boat drawn by a swan, to claim the hand of Elsa, the king's ward. She violates his injunction not to ask who he is, and Lohengrin is compelled to depart. The **prelude** to the third act of *Lohengrin* is a brilliant symphonic piece. It is followed in the opera by the famous wedding march, actually the Bridal Cho-

Score. A systematic arrangement of the vocal or instrumental parts of a composition on separate staves one above the other.

Prelude. A musical introduction to a composition or drama.

rus. Millions of happy couples (and some unhappy ones) have been led to the altar to the strains of the *Lohengrin* wedding march, in stiff competition with the even more celebrated matrimonial piece by Mendelssohn. (A reputable statistical survey indicates that marriages performed to Mendelssohn's music are usually durable, while those sped to marital bliss by Wagner are likely to end in divorce.)

Lohengrin was scheduled for performance in Dresden, but in the meantime Wagner had become embroiled in a revolutionary movement in Saxony during the turbulent year 1848. The production of *Lohengrin* was canceled, and printed announcements were posted bearing Wagner's likeness, ordering his arrest as a fugitive from justice. Wagner went into temporary exile in Switzerland, and it was Franz Liszt, his comrade-in-arms in "the music of the future," who brought out the opera for the first time in 1850.

The *Mastersingers of Nuremberg* (*Die Meistersinger von Nürnberg*, 1868) is an exception among Wagner's operas, for it has a distinct element of comedy. Yet, as in Wagner's previous operas, it has a historical foundation. Set in sixteenth-century Nuremberg, the story deals with a singing contest instituted by a guild of mastersingers. The principal contenders are Walther von Stolzing and the clerk Beckmesser. The latter was given by Wagner some pedantic traits of the celebrated anti-Wagnerian critic Eduard Hanslick; in fact, the part was assigned to a character named Hans Lick in Wagner's early sketches of the libretto.

In *The Ring of the Nibelung*, by Wagner's description a "festival play for three days and a preliminary evening," the center of contention is the magical ring of gold, coveted by gods, dwarfs, giants, and heroes. "The Ride of the Valkyries" from the second opera, *The Valkyries*, is the most celebrated symphonic episode in the entire tetralogy, representing the horsewomen of the mountains carrying slain heroes to their shrine, Valhalla. In the third music drama, *Siegfried*, Wagner projects his hero as a victor who obtains the coveted ring of the Nibelung and penetrates the magic fire surrounding his destined bride, Brünnhilde, one of the Valkyries. Siegfried himself is fated to be slain in the last opera of the tetralogy, *Twilight of the Gods*, in which Valhalla itself is consumed by flames.

Wagner's role in music history is immense. Not only did he create works of great beauty and tremendous brilliance, but he generated an entirely new concept of the art of music, exercising an influence on generations of composers all over the globe. Wagner had two great epigones: Anton Bruckner, who was called "the Wagner of the symphony," because his music embodied Wagner's harmony in lengthy symphonic works; and Richard Strauss, whom the German conductor and composer Hans von Bülow (1830–94) called Richard the Second (Wagner being Richard the First). Strauss accepted the Wagnerian idea of continuous melody, and expanded Wagnerian harmonies to the utmost limit of complexity in his symphonic poems, using leading motifs and vivid programmatic descriptions of the scenes portrayed in his music. (For this, Strauss was the recipient of invectives almost as violent as those hurled against Wagner himself.) Even Rimsky-Korsakov, far as he stood from Wagner's ideas of musical composition, reflected the spirit of *Parsifal* in his own religious opera, *The Legend of the City of Kitezh*. Arnold Schoenberg's first significant work, *Verklärte Nacht*, is Wagnerian in its color. When Wagner rejected traditional opera, he did so in the conviction that such an artificial form could not serve as a basis for true dramatic expression. In its place he gave the world a new form and new techniques.

In the domain of melody, harmony, and **orchestration**, Wagner's art was as revolutionary as was his total artwork on the stage. He introduced the idea of an endless melody, a continuous flow of **diatonic** and **chromatic** tones; the tonality became fluid and uncertain, producing an impression of unat-

Orchestration. The art of writing music for performance by an orchestra; the science of combining, in an effective manner, the instruments constituting the orchestra.

Diatonic. Employing the tones of the standard major or minor scale.

Chromatic. Relating to tones foreign to a given key (scale) or chord; opposed to diatonic.

tainability, so that the listener accustomed to classical modulatory schemes could not easily feel the direction toward the **tonic**. The prelude to *Tristan and Isolde* is a classic example of such fluidity of harmonic elements. The use of long unresolved dominant-ninth chords and the dramatic **tremolos** of **diminished-seventh chords** contributed to this state of musical uncertainty, which disturbed critics and audiences alike. But Wagnerian harmony also became the foundation of the new method of composition that adopted a free flow of modulatory progressions. Without Wagner, the chromatic idioms of the twentieth century could not exist.

Tonic. The keynote of a scale; the triad on the keynote (tonic chord).

Tremolo (It.). A quivering, fluttering, in singing; an unsteady tone.

Diminished-seventh chord. A chord consisting of three conjunct minor thirds, outlining a diminished seventh between the top and bottom notes.

Rienzi: *Overture (1840)*

Wagner took the subject of *Rienzi* from Edward Bulwer-Lytton's well-known historical romance, which Wagner read in the German translation. There was some social significance in the story. Rienzi was the last of Rome's popular tribunes, defender of the poor against the overbearing nobles. The happy ending is made possible when the nobles submit to the will of the people. The music of the opera contains some early Wagnerisms, which the *Gazette musicale de Paris* of April 11, 1869, described as Wagner's "trademarks." But in the main it is still conventional opera, not unlike Meyerbeer's, with **arias**, ensembles, and **choruses**, designed to give the singers an opportunity to exhibit their talents to best advantage.

Aria (It.). An air, song, tune, melody.

Chorus. A company of singers; a composition sung by several singers; also, the refrain of a song.

    He completed the overture on October 23, 1840. The opera itself was practically ready by the time the overture was composed. The fact that the overture (literally, "opening") should be composed after the main body of the opera is completed is no more strange than that the table of contents should be compiled after the book is finished. An overture is commonly a musical table of contents, including the most important musical paragraphs from the opera, with the vocal arias and choruses arranged for orchestral instruments.

Overture to
Rienzi
der Letzte der Tribunen

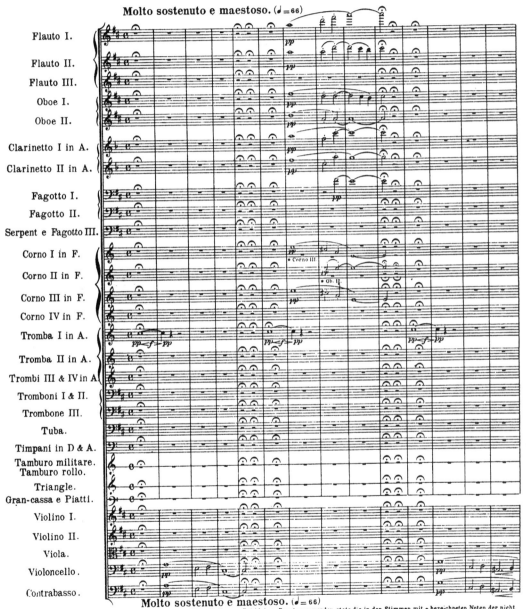

NB. Zugleich für vereinfachte Besetzung, eingerichtet von Fritz Hoffmann. Bei kleiner Besetzung werden stets die in den Stimmen mit • bezeichneten Noten der nicht vorhandenen Instrumente gespielt.

NB. *Adapted for smaller Orchestras by Fritz Hoffmann. With small orchestras, the notes representing the absent instruments (indicated by • in the parts) must be always played.*

Recitative. Declamatory singing, free in tempo and rhythm.

Chorale. A hymn tune of the German Protestant Church, or one similar in style.

Allegro (It.). Lively, brisk, rapid.

Fortissimo (It.). Extremely loud.

Sonata (It.). An instrumental composition usually for a solo instrument or chamber ensemble, in three or four movements, connected by key, contrasted in theme, tempo, meter, and mood.

The overture, in 4/4, in D major, begins with a trumpet call, which in the opera serves as a summons to arms against the nobles. After some **recitative** in the low strings and a brief **chorale** in the wind instruments, the violins, supported by the cellos, enter with the principal theme taken from Rienzi's prayer in the fifth act. Incidentally, there has been a controversy as to whether the gruppetto (turn or trill) of the theme should be played from above (D, E, D, C sharp, D), or from below (D, C sharp, D, E, D). No less a person than von Bülow instructed his players to take the turn from below, which is wrong, as he himself admitted a few years later. The theme grows in sonority and is soon taken up by the powerful ensemble of wood and brass. The violent brush-strokes in the strings are easily recognized as early Wagnerisms. Another trumpet call is sounded, and the orchestra begins the rapid movement, **Allegro** energico, on the theme of the chorus, "Gegrüsst sei hoher Tag" ("Greet the great day"), ending with the brass proclaiming the motto of the battle.

The orchestra continues in **fortissimo**. The brasses proclaim a martial theme. There is a transition to a calmer mood, and the cellos round off a falling cadence, of the type that the *Gazette musicale de Paris* called Wagner's trademark. The first violins now take up the principal theme of Rienzi's prayer, played nearly three times as fast as in the beginning of the overture. This, and the leaping accompaniment in a quickstep tempo, changes the character of the theme entirely. The brass has a sonorous interlude, and the full orchestra plays a new marching theme in A major. After a series of vigorous climaxes, the section concludes with the battle cry in the brass.

The now familiar trumpet call prepares for the recapitulation of the Allegro theme, this time to be played "a little more vivaciously." Again there is the battle cry in the brass, and the joyful marching theme returns in the key of the overture, D major. This return of a theme which previously was heard in the dominant key of A major indicates the **sonata form**, common to most classical overtures. The section marked molto più stretto is a coda (literally, "tail"). Here successive climaxes are reached by chromatic ascension toward the keynote, D. The overture ends with ten full D major chords, and one final D in unison.

Tannhäuser: *Overture and Bacchanal*

Tannhäuser was no mythical personage. There lived in the thirteenth century a minnesinger named Tanhuser, who wrote poems. He also went to the Holy Land as a Crusader. In folktales he has been made into a legendary knight who comes to Venusberg or, in terms of actual geography, Hörselberg in Thuringia, and meets the German counterpart of Venus in a mountain cavern. He remains with Venus but, after some time, recalls his higher ideals, and goes to Rome to beg forgiveness from the pope. He is told that forgiveness for the sin of consorting with a pagan goddess is as impossible as the flowering of a bare rod. But Tannhäuser's rod does blossom forth, and he now knows that he can die in peace. The aria "Dich, teure Halle," known also as "Elisabeth's Greeting," opens the second act of *Tannhäuser*, in which Elisabeth apostrophizes the Hall of Song in the Wartburg Castle, happy at Tannhäuser's return from his pagan adventures.

Such is the folk legend, which was used by several German poets before Wagner. In his brochure *Drei Operndichtungen* (*Three Librettos*), published in Leipzig in 1852, Wagner relates the story of his writing of *Tannhäuser*. The deciding moment came when Wagner thought of connecting the Tannhäuser story with another story, that of a "singers' competition" at Wartburg. Hence the full title of the opera, *Tannhäuser und der Sängerkrieg auf Wartburg* (*Tannhäuser and the Contest of Song at the Wartburg*).

Although Wagner called *Tannhäuser* a "romantic opera" rather than "music drama," it was a harbinger of the Wagnerian

Wagner Timeline

1813	Born in Leipzig
1832	Piano sonata is published
1832-34	Composes two operas, *Die Hochzeit* and *Die Feen*
1834	Becomes music director of a theater company in Magdeburg
1836	Leads premiere of opera *Das Liebesverbot* [Forbidden Love] in Magdeburg; marries actress Christine Wilhelmine (Minna) Planer
1837-39	Serves as music director of Königsberg town theater, then as music director of theater in Riga
1839	Arrives in Paris, subsists by making piano arrangements and writing articles for the *Gazette musicale*
1842	*Rienzi* is premiered in Dresden
1843	Conducts first performance of *Der fliegende Holländer* (*The Flying Dutchman*) in Dresden; named second Hofkapellmeister the following year
1845	Conducts first performance of *Tannhäuser* in Dresden
1848-49	Active as revolutionary; order is issued for his arrest, causing him to leave Dresden
1850	Liszt conducts *Lohengrin* in Weimar
1851	Expounds upon his radical theories of music in *Oper und Drama*
1852	Completes work on libretto for *Der Ring des Nibelungen*

(continued)

era. He wrote the text himself, establishing a unity of music and drama that became the foundation of his aesthetics. The characteristic Wagnerian idiom is here clearly recognizable, with its triadic expansion, melodic chromaticism, and opulent orchestration. *Tannhäuser* opened Wagner's opera cycle based on Germanic folklore, and in it he clearly outlined the importance of stage setting. He describes the events that led him to the composition of *Tannhäuser* in the following words:

> My third trip to Dresden took me through the valleys of Thuringia, from where one can see Wartburg towering above. How near was that sight to my heart! Yet, strangely enough, it was not until seven years later that I visited Wartburg for the first time, and it was from Wartburg that I cast the last glance at the German soil, which I had trod with heartfelt joy, and which I had to abandon as an outlaw, a refugee.

The reference to his status as an outlaw is explained by the fact that Wagner went into exile as a participant in the Dresden Revolution of 1848. As late as 1852, he was talked about in Germany as "that red revolutionary." When the question of a production of *Tannhäuser* at the Munich Opera House came up, an article in the press suggested that "the proper place for the Orpheus who, during the May revolt in Dresden, raised barricades with his lyre, is not the Munich Opera House, but prison."

Wagner's idea of *Tannhäuser* was far from pietistic. He describes his state of mind during the composition of the opera in vivid prose:

> How silly are the critics who, amidst their wanton living, have suddenly become spiritual, and who impute to my Tannhäuser a specifically Christian, impotently celestial-

ized tendency. . . . I was in a state of highly sensuous agitation which brought my blood and my nervous system to the point of feverish excitement when I conceived and carried out the composition of the music. . . . From this high state my eager vision became aware of a Woman; the Woman for whom the Flying Dutchman hankered from the sea-depths of his misery; the Woman who showed Tannhäuser the way to Heaven, and the one who brought Lohengrin from the sunlit heights down to the warm breast of the earth.

Wagner himself conducted the first performance of *Tannhäuser* at the Dresden Opera on October 19, 1845. The first performance of the overture as a concert piece was given at the Gewandhaus in Leipzig on February 12, 1846, with Mendelssohn conducting it from manuscript. Wagner provided a description of the overture. Briefly summarized, it appears as follows:

> The chant of the pilgrims is heard; it draws near, swelling into a mighty torrent of sound, and passes finally away. Magic sights and sounds emerge at night; a rosy mist fills the air. Shouts of exultation assail the ears, followed by a voluptuous dance. The seductive powers of Venus attract the senses, and she herself appears before Tannhäuser. After a night of revelry, the chant of the pilgrims is heard again, winning salvation for Tannhäuser. The songs of pagan worship are joined with the hymns of God. Spiritual devotion and sensuous passion, God and nature, unite in a kiss of hallowed love.

It is difficult to imagine that the music of *Tannhäuser*, which impresses the modern listener as a charmingly innocuous score, full of mellifluous harmonies and melodious sequences,

**Wagner Timeline
(cont.)**

1882 — Completes *Parsifal* in Palermo; it is performed at Bayreuth Festival

1883 — Dies in Vienna; interred in garden of Wahnfried

Overture to

Tannhäuser

und der Sängerkrieg auf Wartburg

should ever have impressed anyone as unusual and strange. Yet the critic of *The Times* of London wrote the following incredible lines in 1855:

> So much incessant noise, so uninterrupted and singular an exhibition of pure **cacophony**, was never heard before. And, all this is intended to describe the delight and fascinations which lured the unwary to the secret abode of the goddess of beauty. We sincerely hope that no execution, however superb, will ever make such senseless discords pass, in England, for manifestation of art and genius.

Cacophony. A raucous conglomeration of sound.

The enlarged version of the orchestral Bacchanale was added to the score for the Paris performance of March 13, 1861, a performance that made history because of the hostile manifestations in the audience, which forced the withdrawal of the opera after the third performance. The Paris humor periodical, *Charivari*, printed a cartoon representing a young woman playing the piano, and her mother sitting in a chair in the same room. "You are playing wrong notes," says the mother. "But, Maman, I am playing *Tannhäuser*," the young lady replies. "Oh, that's different," remarks Maman.

The fiasco of *Tannhäuser* in Paris in 1861 made history. "*Tannhäuser* has passed by, and the 'music of the future' was no more," wrote a French music critic. "Imagine a Hindu god with seven arms and three heads enthroned in a Greek temple: this is the emblem of the incongruous opera of Herr Wagner. His score is nothing but musical chaos. The unintelligible is its ideal. It is a mystic art proudly dying of inanition in a vacuum." The famous French writer Prosper Mérimée, the author of the original story of Bizet's *Carmen*, contributed to the chorus of condemnation for Wagner's opera. "*Tannhäuser* was a colossal bore," he wrote. "I believe that I could write something similar tomorrow, inspired by my cat walking on the piano keyboard."

Tristan and Isolde: *Prelude and Liebestod*

Wagner was fascinated by Nordic legends of gods and godlike men and women. He wrote his own texts, often using peculiar neologisms and forming compound nouns to express an idea containing two related concepts. From the words *Liebe* ("love") and *Tod* ("death") he coined *Liebestod* (love-death). For *Tristan and Isolde*, Wagner took the subject from an old Cornish legend, in which Tristan is sent by the king to bring his, the king's, bride, Isolde, to his side. But a love potion inflames both Tristan and Isolde with mutual love. Tristan dies of the wounds inflicted on him by the king's henchmen and Isolde follows him in death, which becomes the supreme fulfillment of their love, Liebestod. The first performance of *Tristan and Isolde* was given in Munich on June 10, 1865, with Hans von Bülow as the conductor. It was then that Wagner became infatuated with von Bülow's wife, Cosima, a daughter of Liszt, whom he married after her divorce. He named their daughter, who was born premaritally of this union, Isolde.

The opening phrase of the prelude, marked "slow and languorously," is famous. It is intoned by the cellos, and consists of an ascending sixth followed by chromatically falling notes. The resulting theme is the leading motive for the love potion. It is echoed by the oboes in ascending chromatics, symbolic of yearning. The entire prelude is evolved from these initial figures, depicting voluptuous love as only Wagner could incarnate it in music. Through the prelude and Liebestod, tidal waves rise and fall, swelling to fortissimo and receding to **pianissimo**.

Pianissimo (It.). Very soft.

This new chromatic music was unacceptable to the musical establishment. *Tristan and Isolde* was particularly irritating to listeners who were accustomed to an Italian type of opera, in which the arias and the recitatives were clearly delineated. Eduard Hanslick, the venomous anti-Wagnerite, wrote that the prelude to *Tristan and Isolde* reminded him of an old Italian

Tristan und Isolde
Prelude and Liebestod

(Prelude and Love-Death / Vorspiel und Isoldens Liebestod)

painting of a martyr whose intestines were slowly unwound from his body on a reel. A German professor of music denounced the opera as "modern cat music, which can be produced by hitting black keys and white keys of the piano keyboard at random."

In America, too, the anti-Wagnerian tide threw up a lot of angry words. John Sullivan Dwight, the editor of *Dwight's Journal of Music*, declared *Tristan and Isolde* to be "the very extreme of the modern extravagance and willfulness in the spasmodic strife to be original in music. In its expression, its reiterated, restless, fruitless yearning and monotonous chromatic wail, we find it simply dreary and unprofitable."

For modernists, on the other hand, the prelude was a prophetic vision of atonality. Alban Berg inserted the opening measures of the prelude in his atonal *Lyric Suite*. But Debussy, whose attitude toward Wagner was ambivalent, made fun of the famous opening in his whimsical "Golliwog's Cakewalk" from Children's Corner. After quoting the ascending minor sixth and the descending chromatic notes in the same key and in the same rhythmic pattern as in the Prelude, he followed it with a group of derisively sounding chords. He added insult to injury by marking the passage *avec une grande émotion* ("with great emotion").

The Mastersingers of Nuremberg: *Prelude*

The Mastersingers of Nuremberg was performed for the first time in its entirety in Munich on June 21, 1868. Wagner wrote the score to his own libretto, as he did in most of his operas. The central character of the opera, the mastersinger Hans Sachs, a cobbler by trade, was an actual historical figure. In the opera he arranges a competition for the best song composed and sung by one of the town citizens, and the prize is the hand of Eva, the daughter of a local goldsmith. The winner is

Overture to
Die Meistersinger von Nürnberg

Walther, who sings a song about love in springtime. His chief rival is Beckmesser, an envious town clerk without talent, who loses out in the end.

Wagner wrote the prelude (or overture) in 1862. The opera was performed for the first time in its entirety in Munich on June 21, 1868. The prelude opens with a magnificent marching tune in C major, the theme of the guild of the mastersingers. The second theme is Walther's prize-winning song; it is introduced by the flute, and imitated by the oboe and the clarinet. The fanfares of the march return. A development follows, in which the principal themes are ingeniously elaborated. Particularly remarkable is the interlude for woodwinds, in the manner of a **scherzo**. As the music progresses, the **polyphonic** network achieves a triumph of technical mastery. The overture ends in a glorious display of C major sonorities.

Scherzo (It.). A joke, jest; an instrumental piece of a light, piquant, humorous character. **Polyphonic.** Consisting of two or more independently treated melodies; contrapuntal; capable of producing two or more tones at the same time, as the piano, harp, violin, xylophone.

The Ring of the Nibelung—The Valkyries: *Act I; Act III, Ride of the Valkyries*

Few musicians of Wagner's time could remain neutral when confronted with his music. Many were fanatically worshipful; others were repelled. Tchaikovsky wrote to his friend the Russian composer Sergei Taneyev in 1877,

> I heard *The Valkyries*. If indeed Wagner is destined to be regarded as the greatest figure in music of our time, one may well despair of the future. Can it be that his operas represent the last word in composition? Can it be that this pretentious, pompous, and uninspired trash will be the delight of the coming generations? If so, it will be terrible.

Anti-Wagnerian literature is rich in invective:

> Being a Communist, Herr Wagner is desirous of forcing the arts into fellowship with his political and social prin-

ciples. In his music the true bases of harmony are cast away for a reckless, wild, extravagant, and demagogic cacophony, the symbol of profligate libertinage! This man, this Wagner, this author of *Tannhäuser*, *Lohengrin*, and so many other hideous things, this preacher of the Music of the Future, was born to feed spiders with flies, not to make happy the heart of man with beautiful melody and harmony. Who are the men that go about as his apostles? Men like Liszt—madmen, enemies of music to the knife, who, conscious of their impotence, revenge themselves by endeavoring to annihilate it. These musicians of young Germany are maggots that quicken from corruption.

The foregoing tirade appeared in *The Musical World of London*, on June 30, 1855. As a matter of fact, calling Wagner a Communist was not entirely without foundation. Wagner was involved in the revolutionary agitation in Dresden in 1848, the year of the *Communist Manifesto* of Karl Marx, and he was forced to flee; the police posted announcements, with Wagner's likeness, ordering his arrest.

Some of the most brilliant articles inveighing against Wagner belong to the famous Vienna critic Eduard Hanslick, a master of degrading metaphor. Here is his description of Wagner's method of composition: "A little motive begins, but before it is allowed to develop into a real melody it is twisted, broken, raised and lowered through incessant **modulations** and **enharmonic** shifts, with scrupulous avoidance of all closing cadences, like a boneless tonal mollusk, self-restoring and swimming into the horizonless sea."

Modulation. Passage from one key into another.
Enharmonic. Differing in notation but alike in sound.

Wagner could well afford to look down on his detractors with a smile of worldly success. He had had his share of trials and tribulations. He had spent a month in a debtors' prison in Paris; he had untold troubles with women. But sometimes his greatest disasters turned into triumphs by default. The fiasco of *Tannhäuser* in Paris became a *scandale du siècle.*

The compensation for these misfortunes was ample. Wagner found a fairy-tale prince in the person of the youthful King Ludwig II of Bavaria, who became his ardent admirer. It was Ludwig who, before he went completely insane, laid the foundation for a festival theater in Bayreuth, which became the home of the famed Wagner Festival.

Wagner's supreme achievement was *The Ring of the Nibelung*, "a stage festival play for three days and a preliminary evening," according to Wagner's own description. It may be regarded therefore either as a tetralogy or a trilogy with a prelude. The "preliminary evening" is *Das Rheingold* (*The Rhine Gold*), which serves as a prologue to the trilogy that followed: *Die Walküre* (*The Valkyrie*), *Siegfried*, and *Götterdämmerung* (*The Twilight of the Gods*). The prologue outlines the struggle among the gods, the heroes, and the mortals. Wotan, the lord of the gods, plans the building of Valhalla. For its defense Wotan begets nine Valkyries, powerful horsewomen who ride in the clouds. Wotan also procreates earthlings, among them Siegmund and Sieglinde, whose fate unfolds in *The Valkyries*.

The introduction to *The Valkyries* depicts a storm in the forest, with a main motive ominously sounded in the low strings. As the curtain rises, Siegmund, exhausted from wandering, stumbles into the hut of Hunding, the husband of Sieglinde. Siegmund and Sieglinde do not know that they are brother and sister. The leading motive of their love is one of the most impassioned melodies Wagner ever wrote. At Sieglinde's instigation Siegmund draws the magic sword which Wotan had left deeply sunk in a tree trunk. Hunding appears, and they engage in a fight. But Wotan intervenes and breaks Siegmund's sword in two with his spear, which allows Hunding to kill Siegmund.

The third act opens with the celebrated symphonic episode, Ride of the Valkyries. Brünnhilde, Wotan's favorite Valkyrie, gives the news that Sieglinde is to bear a son by Sieg-

Prelude to
Parsifal

*) An jedem Pulte nur der erste Spieler.

land, where it came into the possession of the knights of the Round Table at King Arthur's court.

Stories of the origin of the Holy Grail were not confined to the Last Supper or the Crucifixion. According to one version, the Holy Grail was a fragment of a crown that sixty thousand angels made for Lucifer. The archangel Michael struck it from Lucifer's head, and when it fell to the ground a part of it became the Grail. The symbolism of a sacred vessel characterizes many folktales. Often a vase is a token of victory. Cups given to winners at sports events are the mundane descendants of the Grail. The etymology of the word itself is not clear. It has been explained as an altered form of *sang real* ("royal blood"), or *sangraal*. Another derivation is from the Provençal word *grial*, "vessel," with the vowels transposed (not an uncommon philological phenomenon), resulting in the spelling *grail*.

In writing *Parsifal*, Wagner followed the epic romance *Parzival* by the German minnesinger Wolfram von Eschenbach, changing the spelling to Parsifal on the assumption that the name came from the Arabic words fal parsi ("pure fool"). In the romantic hagiography of the Middle Ages, only "a pure fool made wise through pity" can be qualified to become the keeper of the Grail. Wagner was long fascinated with the figure of Wolfram, who appears in *Tannhäuser* and sings the famous invocation to the Evening Star, Venus.

There are three acts in *Parsifal*. The knights of the Holy Grail congregate in Monsalvat, in Spanish Galicia. Amfortas, the keeper of the Grail, suffers from a mysterious wound that can be healed only by the touch of the sacred spear with which Christ's side was pierced on the Cross. Parsifal is apprehended for killing a wild swan, and is expelled. In the second act Parsifal wanders into the domain of the sinister magus, Klingsor, in Moorish Spain. Seductive "flower girls" surround Parsifal, and the floweriest girl of them all, the lascivious Kundry, implants a penetrating kiss on Parsifal's inexperienced lips.

Being a "pure fool," Parsifal recoils in horror. It is suddenly revealed to him that the wound of Amfortas must have been the punishment for his surrender to Kundry's blandishments, and that the sacred spear must be in Klingsor's possession. In the most pregnantly succinct line ever uttered in any opera, he exclaims, "Amfortas! The wound!" Klingsor appears and, furious that his stratagem in corrupting and thus neutralizing "the pure fool" has failed, hurls the spear at him, but it remains suspended in a spiritual magnetic field generated by Parsifal's mystical halo of goodness. Parsifal seizes the spear and makes the sign of the Cross with the scabbard. Thereupon Klingsor's unholy realm dissolves in ruins.

In the third act Parsifal returns to the kingdom of the Grail carrying the spear and heals Amfortas with its touch. The Holy Grail is then revealed to him and he holds it aloft. He is anointed as the king of the Holy Grail. Kundry, who was condemned to perdition for having mocked at Christ, is baptized by Parsifal, but she can no longer receive the charisma of redemption and falls lifeless on the ground, as the Holy Grail shines above in mystical light.

The dramatic action in *Parsifal*, as in other Wagner music dramas, is guided by a system of leading **motives**, serving as identification tags for the characters of the stage, symbolic inanimate objects, and abstract ideas. Incidentally, the term "**leitmotiv**" was never used by Wagner himself, who preferred the designation *Grundthema* ("basic theme"). For a private performance of the prelude to the opera, given for Ludwig II, Wagner provided a commentary on the symbolic meaning of the music. The opening motive is that of Love, which is identified also with the Last Supper. Wagner quotes the words of Christ: "Take, eat; this is my body. . . . Drink ye all; this is my blood, which is shed for many for the remission of sins." The theme is a throbbing musical phrase, in a gently **syncopated** rhythm, outlined melodically by an ascending major triad followed by a conjunct upper **tetrachord**.

The second cardinal motive is that of the Holy Grail, melodically encompassing the interval of an octave from the

Motive. A short phrase or figure used in development or imitation.

Leitmotiv (Ger.). Leading motive; any striking musical motive (theme, phrase) characterizing one of the actors in a drama or an idea, emotion, or situation.

Syncopation. Shifting of accents from strong beat to weak beat or between beats.
Tetrachord. The interval of a perfect fourth; the four scale-tones contained in a perfect fourth.

dominant to the dominant. The ending of the phrase is an ancient formula of Saxon liturgy, known as the "Dresden Amen," and it appears also in Mendelssohn's *Reformation* Symphony. There can be no question of Wagner's borrowing either from Mendelssohn or from liturgy. An ending of this nature is a natural cadence in a chorale.

Tempo (It.). Rate of speed, movement; time, measure.

A change of **tempo** leads to the announcement of the important theme of faith, a strong unambiguous utterance in the modal configurations of medieval chants. The motive appears four times in succession, in unprepared modulations by minor thirds, Wagner's favorite formula, much in evidence also in *Tristan and Isolde*. Analytically, it is significant that the successive tonics in such modulations by minor thirds form a chord of the diminished seventh, the *accorde di stupefazione* of Italian opera composers, used at melodramatic climaxes to depict sinister supernatural agencies and so instill *stupefazione* in the listeners.

Appoggiatura (It.). "Leaning" note; a grace note that takes the accent and part of the time value of the following principal note.

Wagner never quite shook off such old-fashioned theatrical effects in his harmonic scheme. Thus Kundry's motive in *Parsifal* consists of a rapid descending passage along the tonal lines of a diminished-seventh chords sensitized by expressive **appoggiaturas**. Klingsor's motive is also derived from the "chord of stupefaction." The music of the Good Friday Spell is taken from the symphonic portion of the third act of *Parsifal*, in which Parsifal, arriving in Monsalvat on Good Friday to be anointed, surveys the pastoral scene of the land. The themes of Parsifal, the Holy Grail, and faith are blended in an enfilade of euphony in this music. The Wagnerian principle of endless melody receives here its finest realization. It is an apotheosis of redemptive Christianity.

Siegfried Idyll

Wagner planned his own life as if it were a heroic music drama. He placed himself above the common standards of nineteenth-century morality. Never in his writings or in his conversation did he show any evidence of regret about his ways with loyal friends and trusting women. He had no compunctions in luring away Liszt's daughter Cosima from her husband, Hans von Bülow, while the latter was ardently rehearsing *Tristan und Isolde*. When a daughter was born to Wagner and Cosima, still Bülow's wife, Wagner named her Isolde.

In June 1869 Cosima bore Wagner a son. "Ein Sohn ist da! Der musste Siegfried heissen!" ("A son is here! He must be called Siegfried!") Wagner proudly wrote in a dedicatory poem to Cosima. She obtained her divorce from von Bülow shortly after Siegfried's birth. Wagner and Cosima were finally married in August 1870. For Cosima's thirty-third birthday, on Christmas Eve, 1870 (Wagner was twenty-four years her senior), Wagner arranged a performance of his "symphonic birthday greeting" entitled "A Tribschen Idyll"—Tribschen was the name of Wagner's villa near Lucerne, Switzerland, where he stayed with Cosima—"with birdsong and orange sunrise, offered to his Cosima by her Richard." The work subsequently became known as *Siegfried Idyll*, in sentimental allusion to Wagner's baby son, and also to the hero of the third opera in the *Ring* tetralogy, which he was composing at the time, and which provided most of the thematic materials for the *Idyll*.

Wagner organized the rehearsals for a surprise performance of *Siegfried Idyll* in great secrecy in a Lucerne hotel. Early in the morning of Christmas Day, 1870, the musicians were assembled at Tribschen, on the stairs leading to Cosima's room. Wagner conducted standing at the top, with the orchestra men occupying the steps, and the first performance was played at seven-thirty in the morning. Several more performances were given during the day.

The themes of *Siegfried Idyll* derive mainly from the love duet between Siegfried and Brünnhilde in the closing scene of the opera, except for a lullaby, "Schlaf, mein Kind," which is a folk song. The tonality, E major, is the Siegfried key in *The Ring*.

The orchestration is economical, comprising, besides the strings, one flute, one oboe, two clarinets, one bassoon, and two horns. The musical texture is lucid and transparent. *Siegfried Idyll* is perhaps the most truly Romantic piece written by Wagner, and one of his few purely orchestral compositions. *Siegfried Idyll* is one of the most tender musical expressions in all instrumental literature. Even the most violent critics of Wagner could scarcely call it loud or inharmonious.

JOHANNES BRAHMS
(1833–97)
The Third B of Music

I knew that someday soon someone would suddenly appear as the greatest expression of our time in an ideal manner, one who would develop his mastery not by gradual unfolding, but suddenly, like Minerva springing from Jupiter's head in full armor. And he has come, a young blood, at whose cradle Graces and Heroes kept their vigil. His name is Johannes Brahms.

In these words, in an article entitled "New Paths," Robert Schumann introduced to the world the twenty-year-old Brahms. He gave a vivid description of Brahms the pianist:

Sitting at the piano, he began to discover wondrous regions. We were carried deeper and deeper into enchanted circles. There was genius in his playing that made an orchestra out of the piano, with plaintive and jubilant voices. There were **sonatas**, or rather veiled symphonies, songs whose poetry is understood without knowing the words. And then, it seemed, he united all these in a roaring torrent rushing toward a waterfall, with a rainbow in the waters streaming downward accompanied by butterflies and nightingales.

Sonata (It.). An instrumental composition usually for a solo instrument or chamber ensemble, in three or four movements, connected by key, contrasted in theme, tempo, meter, and mood.

Johannes Brahms (1833–97) appeared on the musical horizon at the height of the German Romantic movement. At that time, romanticism was something more than the word connotes today. It was imagination run free in luxuriant fantasy, in which the borderline between fancy and reality was adjustable according to the intensity of emotion. Schumann was a great Romantic musician, and he believed that Brahms belonged to the same exciting company.

But there was a great difference between Schumann and Brahms. Schumann wrote programmatic music, in which the written notes reflected passing moods, with fanciful titles to express these moods. Brahms, on the other hand, wrote absolute music. The titles of his works merely designate the form—symphony, sonata, **rhapsody**, **intermezzo**—without any hints as to their emotional content. Only in his expression marks did Brahms lift the veil from his inner feelings, as for instance in the indication "Con intimissimo sentimento"—with the most intimate sentiment.

Rhapsody, rapsodie (Fr.). An instrumental fantasia on folk songs or on motives taken from primitive national music.

Intermezzo (It.). A light musical entertainment alternating with the acts of the early Italian tragedies; incidental music; a short movement connecting the main divisions of a symphony.

And so Brahms became the bearer of the classical tradition, the third B in the august company of Bach and Beethoven. The man who gave him this proud title was Hans von Bülow, the great conductor, pianist, and wit extraordinary. There was symbolism in his famous pronouncement. His favorite key, von Bülow explained, was that of Beethoven's

Eroica Symphony, with three flats in the key signature for E-flat major. In German, flats in general are sometimes called B's. The three B's of the *Eroica* were to the conductor Hans von Bülow the three great musical names: Bach, Beethoven, and Brahms. He elaborated the point when he called the first symphony of Brahms the "Tenth Symphony," an artistic successor to Beethoven's nine symphonies.

Brahms spent his youth in Hamburg, a bustling port that stimulated practical energy rather than flights of imagination. His father was a professional player on flute, violin, and horn, but played the most unromantic instrument in the Hamburg Philharmonic, the double bass. Brahms studied piano, and appeared in public at the age of fourteen. He began to compose with circumspection, and published his early works under assumed names. His first professional position was as a choral director and piano teacher. He also directed a ladies' choir, consisting of his students and their friends, for which he drew up a humorous set of rules, with a recurrent admonition: "The members of the ladies' choir must be present, that is to say, they shall arrive punctually at the appointed time."

The name of Brahms gradually became known outside his native city. He received invitations to appear as pianist-composer and conductor elsewhere in Germany and then in Vienna, which eventually became his hometown. Devoted to his parents and to his youthful memories, he paid several visits to Hamburg. He learned that his father was not doing very well in his profession, and he left a note for him: "Father, music is the best consolation. When in need, read carefully your score of Handel's *Saul*, and you will be comforted." In that score, Brahms had left several banknotes of high denomination.

With his friends, Brahms was charming and sentimental, but with unwanted admirers and ambitious composers he was often gruff. There are many stories illustrating these contradictory qualities in his character. Once Brahms was walking in the countryside near Vienna, when a gentleman approached

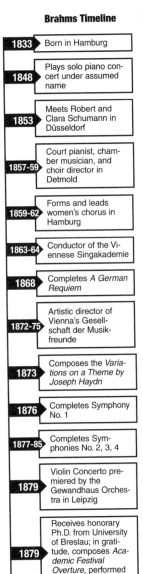

Brahms Timeline

1833	Born in Hamburg
1848	Plays solo piano concert under assumed name
1853	Meets Robert and Clara Schumann in Düsseldorf
1857-59	Court pianist, chamber musician, and choir director in Detmold
1859-62	Forms and leads women's chorus in Hamburg
1863-64	Conductor of the Viennese Singakademie
1868	Completes *A German Requiem*
1872-75	Artistic director of Vienna's Gesellschaft der Musikfreunde
1873	Composes the *Variations on a Theme by Joseph Haydn*
1876	Completes Symphony No. 1
1877-85	Completes Symphonies No. 2, 3, 4
1879	Violin Concerto premiered by the Gewandhaus Orchestra in Leipzig
1879	Receives honorary Ph.D. from University of Breslau; in gratitude, composes *Academic Festival Overture*, performed there in 1881
1881	Soloist at premiere of the Piano Concerto No. 2 in Budapest
1896	Composes *Four Serious Songs*
1897	Dies in Vienna

him and, with many flattering words, asked for his autograph. "Oh, you probably want my brother, the composer," said Brahms. "Just wait here, and he will be back soon from the village." Then Brahms continued his walk in peace. When a social snob accosted Brahms at a summer concert in a Vienna park, Brahms whispered to him: "Please be silent! They are playing my piece!" The snob stopped conversation at once, and after the number was over, he became effusive in his compliments. But the piece was a march by a popular composer, Gungl. Brahms was quick at double-edged repartee. Once a musical friend sharply criticized an instrumental work written by a local German duke. Brahms cautioned him: "Be careful in your judgment—one never knows who is the real composer of the duke's piece."

Impatient with ambitious and arrogant colleagues, Brahms admired works by his contemporaries even from an entirely different camp, stylistically speaking. He went to many performances of *Carmen* in Vienna and inscribed a few notes of the "Blue Danube Waltz" on a fan belonging to Strauss's wife Adele with the following inscription: "Unfortunately, not by me." But he said of the Swiss-German composer Joachim Raff, who enjoyed great fame at the time, that only Raff's pupils should be subjected to the hearing of his symphonies as a punishment for their foolhardy decision to study with him.

Earnestness of purpose and stateliness of form distinguish the music of Brahms, but there is also a mildness, a musical loving-kindness, and pervading sentiment that imparts a feeling of intimacy. And there is also variety. Brahms is the composer of the ingratiating Lullaby, but he also wrote the fiery Hungarian Dances. Those infatuated with the sensuous charm of French music are apt to reject Brahms. When fire exits were placed in the new Symphony Hall in Boston in 1900, the quip made the rounds that these should have been marked "Exit in Case of Brahms." But Brahms survived that particular fire, and when a famous orchestra opens its season, as likely as not, it is a symphony of Brahms that resounds over the musical portals. This "Entrance in Case of Brahms" demonstrates that audiences as well as performers have long accepted Brahms as a legitimate successor to Bach and Beethoven in the triad of "the three B's of music."

ORCHESTRAL MUSIC

Symphony No. 1 in C Minor, Op. 68 (1855–76)

Brahms undertook the composition of a symphony at the age of twenty, but abandoned it when he felt unequal to the task. Portions of the work found their way into his First Piano **Concerto**. It was not until he reached the age of forty that he completed a symphony started in his late twenties. This time he carried it out, and the completed work was the great Symphony in C minor. It was first performed in Karlsruhe on November 4, 1876, with Otto Dessoff conducting the orchestra from manuscript. A few days later, Brahms himself conducted the work in Mannheim.

> **Concerto** (It.). An extended multi-movement composition for a solo instrument, usually with orchestra accompaniment and using (modified) sonata form.

Once more, the conductor Hans von Bülow launched a winged phrase when he described the First Symphony of Brahms as the Tenth Symphony, the rightful successor to Beethoven's nine symphonies. There are some parallels in the lives of Beethoven and Brahms. Both were born in North Germany: Beethoven in Bonn, Brahms in Hamburg. Both went to Vienna to live, to write music, and to die. Both were symphonists of universal expression; yet their inspiration was nurtured on the melodic and rhythmic patterns of Central European folk songs.

Much musicological rhetoric has been expended on the origin of the noble horn melody that appears out of nowhere with such splendid illumination in the last movement of the First Symphony of Brahms. Some attempted to trace it to the

Symphony No. 1

in C Minor, Op. 68

chimes of Westminster Abbey in London. The solution of the riddle is found in the published correspondence between Brahms and Clara Schumann. Vacationing in the Austrian Alps, Brahms sent a postcard to Clara, dated September 12, 1868, in which he jotted down the C-major horn theme note for note, just as it appears in the symphony. "The Alpine horn blew this today," he inscribed. And he set this salutation to the tune: "Hoch auf'm Berg, tief im Tal, grüss' ich dich viel tausendmal" ("High on the hill, deep in the vale, I greet you many thousand times"). The presence of F-sharp in this bland C-major tune is easily explained, for it corresponds to the eleventh **overtone** of C in the natural harmonic series as sounded on an Alpine horn, bugle, or shepherd's pipe.

Overtone. Harmonic tone.

The First Symphony enjoyed excellent success in Europe, but for some strange reason it ran into a storm of critical abuse in America. A Boston critic delivered himself of this curious dictum: "Johannes Brahms is a modern of the moderns, and his C-Minor Symphony is a remarkable expression of the inner life of this anxious, introverted age." Another American critic declared that the work was "mathematical music evolved with difficulty from an unimaginative brain." Philip Hale, the cultured annotator of the Boston Symphony concerts, described the symphony as "the apotheosis of arrogance."

The symphony is in four movements arranged in the classical order: fast, slow, neither fast nor slow, fast. The first movement, un poco sostenuto, in C minor, is set in 6/8 time. Romantic German analysts are wont to describe the opening as the "music of destiny," and the slowly rising melody of the violins as an arduous effort to escape the gravity pull of the tonic **pedal point** in the double basses and the double bassoon. However that might be, the ensuing **Allegro** tears itself free of the shackles of destiny. Musical motion becomes more fluid and is constantly refreshed by rhythmic cross-currents. The relentless syncopated rhythms create a sense of tension,

Pedal point. A tone sustained in one part to harmonies executed in the other parts.
Allegro (It.). Lively, brisk, rapid.

Dominant. The fifth tone in the major or minor scales; a chord based on that tone.

Recapitulation. A return of the initial section of a movement in sonata form.

Andante (It.). Going, moving; moderately slow tempo.

Mediant. The third degree of the scale.

Scherzo (It.). A joke, jest; an instrumental piece of a light, piquant, humorous character.

Oboe (Ger.). An orchestral instrument with very reedy and penetrating though mild tone.

Adagio (It.). Slow, leisurely; a slow movement.

Chromatic. Relating to tones foreign to a given key (scale) or chord; opposed to diatonic.

Canon. Musical imitation in which two or more parts take up, in succession, the given subject note for note; the strictest form of musical imitation.

Cadence. Rhythm; also, the close or ending of a phrase, section, or movement.

until the protracted stand on the **dominant** signals the advent of the **recapitulation**. A magisterial coda follows, and the movement concludes in resonant C major.

The second movement, **Andante** sostenuto, is in E major, in 3/4 time. Its opening theme is one of Brahms's finest melodic inspirations. Here rhythmic prosody has a natural ring, and the harmonies, with their constant lowering of the **mediant**, suggest a crepuscular mood. The movement is an eclogue of poetic modalities.

The third movement, Un poco allegretto e grazioso, in A-flat major, in 2/4 time, is a bucolic **scherzo**. The clarinet sets the pastoral tone, which the **oboe** echoes. In the graceful trio, the wind instruments and the strings engage in a genial dialogue.

The finale is in C minor, in 4/4 time. An introductory **adagio** creates a somber mood in a **chromatically** embroidered chorale. The tempo is gradually accelerated to Più andante. It is here that the horn solo makes its clarion call, the melody Brahms heard in the Alps. It is echoed by the flute in the high register; a **canonic** development ensues, leading to a grandiloquent peroration, allegro non troppo ma con brio. The Alpine horn tune is recalled momentarily; an insistent drumroll presages the return to the major tonic of the symphony. After a chorale-like episode there is a coda saturated with sonorous energy. Although the final **cadence** is plagal, the concluding series of C-major chords provides full satisfaction to classically attuned ears.

Symphony No. 2 in D Major, Op. 73 (1877)

George Bernard Shaw, writing when Brahms was not yet canonized as the third great B of music, said bluntly: "Brahms is enjoyable when he merely tries to be pleasant or naively sentimental, and insufferably tedious when he tries to be profound." Brahms's followers were derisively labeled "Brahmins," so as to give full measure of dignity, and perhaps stuffiness, to their ideals.

Strangest of all, Brahms himself was convinced that his music brought little cheer to the world. Even with regard to his Second Symphony, conceived in the pleasant surroundings of rural Germany in the summer of 1877, and permeated with pastoral lightness, he wrote to his publisher: "I have never written anything quite so sad. The score should be printed with black edges." He repeated the same estimate in almost identical words in another letter. If it was a joke, then indeed Brahms must have been a sorry humorist. It is more plausible to suggest that Brahms was not the impulsive genius type, that the source of his inspiration was more like an evenly flowing river than a geyser, and that he himself failed to realize the lighter side of his genius. Also, it is quite possible that in making this estimate of his symphony, he thought chiefly of the adagio, which is indeed profoundly meditative, if not hopelessly sad.

Clara Schumann, who was a critical friend, wrote this in her diary after Brahms played some of the work for her: "Johannes came this evening, and played the first movement of his second symphony in D major, and it delighted me. . . . Also, he played some of the last movement, which gave me great joy. This symphony will bring him more success than the first, and its genius, and marvelous workmanship will impress the musicians, too."

The Second Symphony was completed in only a few months, which was remarkable, considering that it took Brahms fully fifteen years to compose the First Symphony. He was anxious to hear it performed, but there were obstacles. Finally, a performance was announced in Vienna, but the copyist could not finish the orchestral parts in time, which resulted in a three-week postponement. The symphony was eventually played by the Vienna Philharmonic on December 30, 1877, under Hans Richter. Brahms himself conducted it later in

Leipzig, but was dissatisfied with the reception. Three days after that performance, he wrote to his publisher and asked him whether the first movement should be rewritten. Characteristically, he inquired whether, in the publisher's opinion, the new movement should not rather be in a minor key. However, the doubts soon abated, and there was no more thought of rewriting.

The symphony opens in 3/4 time, in the key of D major. After an opening bar in the cellos and basses, with a figure of three notes, the tonic, the leading tone, and again the tonic, the horns play the theme. The woodwinds answer it. The horns restate the theme in the supertonic, and once more, the woodwinds give an answer. The entire statement is symmetrical, each of the four periods having four bars. This grouping of bars in twos and fours remains characteristic for the entire movement. The violins and violas play a transitional episode. There is a kettledrum beat, and the opening three-note figure is heard, which appears to be of no incidental significance. Then the violins introduce a new theme of a light character, which is immediately imitated by the flute, and then more insistently, in overlapping rhythms. Cross-accents signal a further increase in tension, but it is suddenly discharged by light passages in the woodwinds. Then the cellos and violas proclaim an emotional subject in minor, which is repeated by the woodwinds. An energetic development follows, with **syncopated** figures. Syncopation is now stabilized in a dash-dot figure, against which the rest of the orchestra leads in groups of ascending three notes, on the main beats. There is a climax, and a cascade of violins brings the music to a calmer level.

The violas and second violins play the emotional theme in a major key, while the flute weaves a counterpoint in triplet figurations. Then the woodwinds take over the theme, while the violins furnish the triplet counterpoint. This is the end of the **exposition**, and the beginning of the development. The function of the development is to make a review of all the

Syncopation. Shifting of accents from strong beat to weak beat or between beats.

Exposition. The opening of a sonata movement, in which the principal themes are presented for the first time.

themes presented in the exposition, using different keys, changed **intervals**, and new **tone-color**. We hear the horn theme, and the three-note figure of the opening bar of the symphony, which latter is here extended into a sequence. The flutes repeat the horn theme, and the three-note progressions overlap in canonic imitation. The long-silent trombones join the orchestra. The rhythmic tension grows, with numerous cross-accents underlying the feeling of unrest. Fragments of the horn theme assume apocalyptic proportions, as proclaimed by the woodwinds and the brass, with the support of percussion. The light theme of the beginning now appears in minor, **fortissimo**. There are Beethoven-like transitions from darkness to light and, characteristically, fortissimo is associated with the minor keys, pianissimo with major. The climax is reached, and the flute and clarinet drop in a descending scale, to prepare for the recapitulation.

Interval. The difference in pitch between two tones.
Tone-color. Quality of tone; timbre.

Fortissimo (It.). Extremely loud.

In the recapitulation, the horn theme is given to the oboes. The emotional cello-viola theme is now in B minor, the relative key of the tonic. It is repeated in the woodwinds. As in the exposition, the rhythms thicken, the syncopated figures appear, and, once more, a cascade of notes falls to bring the music to a quieter range. The woodwinds now play the original cello-viola theme in a major key, and this time it is the viola that furnishes the triplet counterpoint. The roles are exchanged once more, so that the cellos and violas are assigned their original theme, with the flute playing the counterpoint. The music grows more tenuous, and there is a feeling of approaching conclusion. The horn theme reappears in a dynamic outburst and the light theme of the beginning is inconspicuously recalled. The violins play a cadential form of the horn theme, while the lower strings move importantly in three-note figures. The woodwinds flash the dancing motive, against plucked strings. The mood is now serene, the horns begin their theme, but leave it unfinished. A full chord completes the movement.

Beginning the second movement, the cellos present a long, meaningful subject, in a slow falling cadential figure, with the counterpoint of the bassoons, surging against the cellos. The violins take up the theme, but play only the first four bars. The wind instruments follow with an interlude, in which a characteristic seesawing fragment of the theme is developed in the horn, oboes, and flutes. The cellos and basses imitate the swaying figure. There is a lull, and the woodwinds play a graceful interlude, in 12/8, gently moving forward, in slow syncopated figures. The strings develop this rhythm, but soon the main beat asserts itself over the syncopated progressions. The pace of the movement doubles. Parallel to this rhythmic acceleration, there is a dynamic expansion, until a climax is reached

The thematic elements now include the initial motive, the three-note figure, and the rhythmic figurations in double time. The principal theme is played by the strings, and then taken up by the wind instruments, solo and in groups. Its faithful counterpoint accompanies the theme. There are variations, and the second portion of the theme, not heard since its initial appearance, is now given in full by the violins. After a short episode, this section of the theme is sounded in a modified form, against the rapid figurations of the violins. The theme is quoted here and there, and the quiet ending is now near. The surging scale of the contrapuntal figure is heard to the last, seconded by the muffled kettledrums. The final chord is in B major, the key of the movement.

The third movement is full of rural grace. It is in G major, 3/4 time, and the **accent** on the last beat gives it a quasi-Slavic tang. The slow dance tune, in woodwinds, is accompanied by plucked cellos. Suddenly, the tempo changes to presto, in 2/4. This is simply a variation of the dance theme, using the same intervals, and the characteristic accent on the **upbeat**. A new modification of the theme appears in a vigorous section in C major, but here the tune is not only altered rhythmically, but also inverted, so that the thematic interdependence is hardly noticeable. The movement slackens, with the fatuous lights

Accent. A stress.

Upbeat. The raising of the hand in beating time; an unaccented part of a measure.

still flickering on the pointed cross-accents in the woodwinds. Then the original tempo returns, with slight variations of the theme. Soon, only the tail end remains of the theme, and there is a half-cadence. The tempo is now a rapid 3/8, another remote variation of the inverted theme. It passes quickly in alternations of strings and woodwinds. Finally, the original theme returns in a new key of F-sharp major. But a modulation to the original G major is easily effected. There is a moment of silence, and the movement ends quietly.

The fourth movement is a typical fast finale. It is in the key of the symphony, D major, in cut (2/2) time. The restless theme is sounded in unison by the strings. The woodwinds join for the second section of the subject. After a brief lull, the entire orchestra plays the opening bars, but the rest of the theme is modified melodically as well as rhythmically. Again there is a slackening, brightened up by rapid **arpeggios** in the clarinet, and a new theme appears in the dominant key. It passes from the strings to the woodwinds, and soon develops into an energetic rhythmic episode, marked by strong syncopation. There are running scales, in thirds, in the woodwinds. The syncopation spreads to the entire orchestra. Then the original theme comes back, appearing in various keys. The tempo subsides; there is an episode, marked tranquillo, in **triplet** figures, ultimately traceable to the intervals of the opening subject.

The tranquil episode is developed, with the indication, sempre più tranquillo. The movement is still in triplets. Then the falling fourths, characteristic of the second section of the theme, appear in doubly slow tempo, that is, in the **augmentation**. The recapitulation is announced by the strings in unison, identical with the beginning. But immediately after this identification, the recapitulation deviates from the course of the exposition, and the orchestration is new. Then the second theme appears in the tonic. Again we hear the running thirds, the syncopated chords. The trombones enter significantly, and then the kettledrums, presaging the climax. The coda is long and brilliant.

Arpeggio (It.). Playing the tones of a chord in rapid, even succession.

Triplet. A group of three equal notes performed in the time of two of like value in the established rhythm

Augmentation. Doubling (or increasing) the time value of the notes of a theme or motive, often in imitative counterpoint.

Symphony No. 3 in F Major, Op. 90 (1883)

Brahms completed the Third Symphony in the summer of 1883, shortly after the death of Wagner, his great rival in musical aesthetics. To Brahms and to the "Brahmins," this symphony was a reassertion of the Classical faith. The symphony was performed for the first time at a Vienna Philharmonic Society concert on December 2, 1883, under the direction of Hans Richter. Eduard Hanslick, the powerful Vienna critic, declared that the Third Symphony was superior to the first two, "the most compact in form, the clearest in the details, and the most plastic in the leading themes."

There were several attempts by Brahms's friends to affix a durable subtitle to this symphony. Both Hanslick and Richter suggested "Eroica," but admitted that the parallel with Beethoven's Third was not complete: the heroic element lacked defiance and tragedy. Clara Schumann thought the best name would be "Forest Idyll," and even wrote a tentative program to fit the description. Finally, Max Kalbeck, the author of the most worshipfully detailed biography of Brahms, declared that the symphony was inspired by the sight of the statue of Germania at Rüdesheim. Though it is true that Brahms believed in the great destiny of the German race, particularly its North German branch, it can be questioned whether he needed a statue of stone for musical inspiration.

After Brahms conducted the Third Symphony in Berlin on January 16, 1884, Carl Lachmund, one of the last American pupils of Liszt, wrote enthusiastically from Berlin to *Freund's Weekly*:

> Brahms has been visiting Berlin. He came to conduct his new symphony. I can hardly find words to express the high praise it deserves. Everything is expressed in a clear and concise form. Though the themes are fine, the beauty of the work lies more in the development. Brahms

Symphony No. 3

in F Major, Op. 90

has a wonderful gift for developing manifold beauties out of his motives or short themes, and in this respect he strongly resembles Beethoven. The symphony, on the whole, may be termed pastoral, though the last movement is decidedly heroic. The third movement is especially charming, and had to be repeated at the rehearsal as well as at the concert.

It is an interesting fact that Brahms did not think it prejudicial to repeat a movement of the symphony. When Hans Richter did exactly that at the first performance in London, on May 12, 1884, an English critic complained bitterly:

> Is it really necessary to inform Herr Richter that the four movements of a symphony constitute an organism, and that to make one part of that organism twice as long as it was designed by the author is to destroy the harmony of the whole? If we should be informed that similar abuses have been practiced at Vienna in the presence and with the tacit consent of Brahms himself, such a fact would only prove that where personal vanity comes into play, a grave German composer is as open to temptation as a French soubrette.

J. S. Shedlock, an English critic of some eminence, coupled Brahms with Antonín Dvořák (1841–1904) as preservers of the classical tradition against Wagner's newfangled theories of art. He termed the Third Symphony "a noble and earnest work" and its production in England "an event of no small importance."

The first American performance of Brahms's Third Symphony took place at one of Van der Stucken's Novelty Concerts in New York, on October 24, 1884. Shortly afterward, on November 8, 1884, it was given by the Boston Symphony Orchestra. The American critics were as receptive to Brahms as their English and German colleagues. The *Boston Evening Transcript* wrote:

> Now that Wagner is dead, there is no composer in the world from whom a new work in one of the larger musical forms is looked for with such deep interest. Brahms stands almost alone today as a composer who, although wholly modern in spirit and style, seems to feel that nothing impels him to relinquish the traditional musical forms, and to strike out into a wholly new path. The time has fully come for the people who are fond of talking about Brahms's brains, to think well what they are saying. Thank heaven, the man has brains, an article of which no one can have too much.

But there was some dissension. The *Boston Traveller* wrote:

> Brahms occupies a position in music similar to that held by mathematics in the common curriculum of study. To the majority of students who sincerely desire to cultivate music from an art standpoint, Brahms represents a school of composition abstract and cold. He often forgets beauty of sound in an absorbing earnestness of form; the characteristics of his intelligence prevent his music taking hold upon our sympathies.

The *New York Evening Post*, which had always hewn to the Wagnerian line, condemned the new symphony unequivocally: "If this Symphony is to be accepted as evidence, Brahms has said his last word in music. There is nothing of striking originality in the whole work. Repeated hearing is not likely to reveal hidden beauties as everything in it seems clear and superficial." The *Musical Gazette* of Boston made the common reproach of too much science:

The Symphony is of course dignified in character, but, like the great mass of the composer's music, it is painfully dry, deliberate and ungenial. Its themes are brief according to the method of Brahms, and he no sooner evolves four bars of melody than he sets to work to develop it, and keeps it aggravatingly meandering through labored counterpoint and twisted rhythm. . . . We yearn for more tune in Brahms, even at the loss of something of his persistent masterly development. There is something else in music besides mere science.

Ten years later, Edgar Stillman Kelley, then a young composer and a critic for the *San Francisco Examiner*, roundly condemned the Third Symphony, and all of Brahms, in his column of May 9, 1894:

After the weary, dreary hours spent in listening to the works of Brahms I am lost in wonder at the amount of devotion accorded him and the floods of enthusiasm with which he is overwhelmed. I try to console myself that this last light of the classic school exerts a valuable conservative influence at a time when music, if it were allowed to follow in the lines marked out by Wagner, would soon fall into utter disintegration. But no! Mistaking Brahms's unbeauty for a new line of thought, his followers amuse themselves with seeking in what a variety of means they, too, can twist and torture a series of commonplace tones and chords.

All these stirrings, pro and con, throw an interesting light on the status of music at the time when Wagner's school of composition was naturally opposed to the classical tradition. In our day, the acceptance or nonacceptance of Brahms is submerged in the larger question of postclassical heritage in music. By a curious twist of music history, Brahms is now classified not with the classicists, but with the Romantic composers of the nineteenth century. The tendency of present-day classicists is to go further back in search of true classical art. In new music Brahms is not an influence, but to every musician he nonetheless remains a constant companion.

Symphony No. 4 in E Minor, Op. 98 (1884–85)

Brahms wrote his Fourth Symphony in 1884–85, under the fresh impression of his fourth trip to Italy, where he was an observant student of Roman antiquities. It is also known that at the time he was reading the Greek classics in a translation. The Fourth Symphony may not have been directly conditioned by Brahms's interest in classical art, but a certain congeniality of inspiration, a certain austerity of expression may have been the result of these classical leanings.

At the time of composition of the Fourth Symphony, Brahms was in his early fifties. After an ardent youth and formative middle age, Brahms had now reached the philosophical period of his life. He was serene, secure in the knowledge of his own powers, working systematically and evenly. He had recently grown a flowing beard. When his friend Joseph Widmann saw him bearded for the first time, he found in Brahms's appearance "a symbol of perfect maturity of his powers." During Brahms's travels in Italy, he invariably attracted attention in the streets, in the railway carriage, in the museums. To the Italians he was a picture of genius, but he was more often taken for a sculptor or a university professor than a musician. Brahms himself derived a great deal of amusement from the fact that a school book of geography used his photograph as an illustration of a perfect type of the Caucasian race.

The Fourth Symphony is indeed a symbol of perfect maturity of Brahms's genius. Hans von Bülow, the friend and interpreter of Brahms's orchestral music, referred to it

Symphony No. 4

in E Minor, Op. 98

reverently as the Thirteenth Symphony, taking Beethoven's nine symphonies into the count, and continuing with Brahms's four. "No. 4 is colossal," wrote von Bülow, "It breathes inexhaustible energy from A to Z."

Brahms himself had no such reverence for his music. He jocularly called the Fourth Symphony the "Waltz and Polka affair," the waltz being the last movement, and the polka the third. But he liked it better than any other of his works. He also liked to conduct the Fourth, although he was no match for von Bülow in the art of orchestral conducting. For the first performance, which took place at Meiningen on October 25, 1885, Bülow prepared the symphony at painstaking rehearsals, but let Brahms conduct the concert. Richard Strauss, who was assistant conductor at Meiningen at the time, tells that Brahms, as conductor, made no great impression, but "one did hear the music." Brahms subsequently went on tour with the orchestra as guest conductor of his symphony, and precipitated a minor quarrel with von Bülow when he agreed to conduct a second performance at Frankfurt.

Unlike Wagner, Brahms was never the target of criticism as an innovator. But he was often accused of being overscientific. It was said that Brahms's themes, at least in symphonic and **chamber music**, were derived from the development, which was formed in his mind first. The triumph of Brahms as a scientist of music comes in the last movement of the Fourth. It is a **Passacaglia**, variations over a continuously repeating motive, never departing from the key of the symphony, E minor, and representing a numerically perfect concatenation of thirty-two periods of eight bars each, up to the coda. The theme, an eight-note motto, one note to a bar, is derived from the bass of the **chaconne** from Bach's Cantata No. 150.

Elisabeth von Herzogenberg, a friend of Brahms and herself a fine musician, was dismayed by the technical complexity of the last movement when she played it in a piano arrange-

Chamber music. Vocal or instrumental music suitable for performance in a room or small hall.

Passacaglia (It.). An old Italian dance in stately movement on a ground base of four measures.

Chaconne (Fr.). A Spanish dance; an instrumental set of variations over a ground bass, not over eight measures long and in slow 3/4 time.

ment. "It is more for the lens of a microscope," she wrote to Brahms, "for the erudite and the scientific than for an average music lover." But when she heard it in the orchestra she forgot her misgivings: "The movement might as well be three times as long, and the audience would have enjoyed it, even without knowledge and understanding of passacaglia and such things as that."

Not every listener was as understanding as Elisabeth von Herzogenberg. Hugo Wolf, at that time a young Wagnerian, wrote with bitter irony about Brahms's ***Krebsgang*** ("crab walk," a technical term for retrograde imitation where the melody is read from right to left): "Art to compose without inspiration has surely found in Brahms its chief protagonist. Like the Lord himself, Brahms knows the trick of making something out of nothing." Yet Brahms was not an anti-Wagnerian. In the Third Symphony, written shortly after Wagner died, there is a distinct musical reference to Wagner's Venusberg music from *Tannhäuser*. In the Fourth Symphony, the second subject of the first movement comes, without purpose or quotation, amazingly close to Hunding's leading motive in *The Valkyries*, particularly in its rhythmical formula.

Brahms had the heart of a genial peasant and loved the countryside of Austria. His lighter symphonic movements reflected the peasant side of his creative talent. Elisabeth von Herzogenberg gave a description of the scherzo of the fourth movement, to which Brahms jocularly referred as a polka: "What a sweep in your scherzo! It seems as if you wrote it down holding your breath, or in one sustained breath. One has a feeling of growing bigger and stronger listening to it." However, there is "science" in this movement, too, or at least great adroitness in handling the simple theme in different keys, and also in the inverted form.

Shortly before his death, Brahms attended a performance of his Fourth Symphony by the Vienna Philharmonic Society. Racked by cancer, emaciated and weak, he responded to the

Krebsgang (Ger.). Literally, "crab walk"; a retrograde motion of a given theme or passage.

applause of the audience after each movement. Florence May, the English pianist who lived many years in Germany and Austria, described the scene:

> Tears ran down his cheeks as Brahms stood, shrunken in form, with lined countenance, strained expression, white hair hanging lank; and through the audience there was a feeling as of a stifled sob, for each knew that they were saying farewell. Another outburst of applause, and yet another; one more acknowledgment from the Master, and Brahms and Vienna had parted forever.

Concerto for Piano and Orchestra No. 1 in D Minor, Op. 15 (1854–58)

Schumann wrote in his diary after young Brahms showed him his first compositions: "Brahms came in today: a genius." He followed this private endorsement with an enthusiastic article in which he welcomed Brahms as a new great force in music. To Brahms, this accolade was the guiding event in his career. Brahms inherited the spirit of Schumann's romanticism, which found its expression in the gentility of mood, the euphony of harmony, the fluidity of rhythm, and the dynamic quality of his music, still preserving a strict classical attitude toward the formal aspects of composition. To him, music was human thought expressed in tones. Each of his instrumental works seems to represent a musical syllogism, in which themes are premises, and deductions are made according to unchallengeable laws of musical esthetics.

Brahms was a classicist in a Romantic century. To Eduard Hanslick, he was the paragon of the "beautiful in music." But to critics seeking sensuous enjoyment from the sounds of music, his Romantic classicism lacked emotion and artistic humanity. It is amazing to read the reviews of Brahms at the height of his inventive powers and fame, that described his music as strained, unnatural, unimaginative, pedantic, fragmentary, disjointed, cold, tiresome, dry, morbid, even unintelligible! George Bernard Shaw, whose first profession was that of a music critic, wrote disdainfully: "Brahms takes an essentially commonplace theme; gives it a strange air by dressing it in the most elaborate and far-fetched harmonies; keeps his countenance severely; and finds that a good many wiseacres are ready to guarantee him as deep as Wagner, and the true heir of Beethoven."

The battle of rival aesthetic codes that raged in the nineteenth century between the followers of Brahmsian classicism and Wagnerian romanticism has long subsided. Brahms has been firmly established as a master craftsman. Despite the many misguided prophecies of his inevitable decline, his music remains a mainstay in concert programs today.

Brahms wrote two piano concertos, separated by an interval of twenty years. The first, in D minor, was the by-product of a two-piano sonata turned symphony that Brahms planned to write in 1854, when he was twenty-one years old. Some materials from this sonata-symphony went into the initial two movements of the concerto. This early work also incorporated a scherzo originally destined for the decomposed symphony, but for some reason Brahms did not transplant the scherzo into the concerto, which would have been a fourth movement.

Despite the synthetic origin of the concerto, it holds together remarkably well as a self-consistent composition. The only sign of its heterogeneous origin is the relatively unvirtuosic appearance of the solo piano part. The tragic character of the opening of the concerto and of the second movement, Adagio, is explained by the circumstance that Brahms wrote them under the impression of Schumann's attempting suicide by jumping into the Rhine River from a bridge.

The first movement of the concerto, Maestoso, retains its original symphonic grandeur. The principal theme introduced by the orchestra is built on large vaulting intervals. The dramatic character of this subject is enhanced by abrupt trochaic endings of each member of the musical phrase, over a sustained **pedal point**. It brings a Romantic response from the piano part. There is a great deal of thematic deployment. The songful second subject, in F major, presented by the piano solo, has a distinct Schumannesque quality in its narrative, balladlike exposition. There follows a protracted development. The recapitulation is classically outlined, and the ending is in rousing fortissimo.

Pedal point. A tone sustained in one part to harmonies executed in other parts, usually a bass tone, tonic and/or dominant.

The second movement, Adagio, in D major, in 6/4 time, was originally subtitled by Brahms with the Latin words carved over the doorway of the Benedictine monastery at Kanzheim in the novel *Kater Murr* by E. T. A. Hoffmann: "Benedictus, qui venit in nomine Domini." The slow movement is meant to be a portrait of Clara Schumann, as Brahms told her in a letter. The main theme appears in the muted violins, with the piano providing artful counterpoint. After an elegiac interlude, there is a quiet ending.

The third and last movement is a brilliant rondo, Allegro non troppo, in D minor, in 2/4 time. This is the only movement in the concerto that was written independently from the material of the incomplete symphony. The rondo assumes the form of variations with some interesting rhythmic translocations. A piano **cadenza** leads to a brilliant ending in D major.

Cadenza (It.). An elaborate passage played or improvised by the solo instrument at the end of the first or last movements of a concerto.

The first performance of the concerto was given, from manuscript, in Hannover on January 22, 1859. Brahms himself was the soloist, and his friend the famous violinist Joseph Joachim conducted the orchestra. The Hannover correspondent of the important German music periodical *Signale für die musikalische Welt* reported that each movement was applauded and that the "young artist was tumultuously recalled at the end of the concert." But when five days later Brahms played the concerto with the prestigious Gewandhaus Orchestra in Leipzig, the same periodical described the concerto as "unhealthy" and proceeded to take it to pieces:

One can hardly speak of organic development and logical elaboration. Like infusoria, seen in a drop of water through a microscope, the musical ideas, barely born, devour each other, and vanish. One must absorb this unfermented mass, and as a dessert, swallow a dose of shrieking dissonances and cacophonous sounds.

Serenade No. 2 in A Major, Op. 16 (1858–59)

Contrapuntal. Pertaining to the art or practice of composition with two or more simultaneous melodies.

The **contrapuntal** complexity, the depth of musical expression, the somewhat haughty academicism of Brahms's last period are not in evidence in the music written during his youthful years. His Serenade in A major belongs to this early period. It was sketched when Brahms was in his middle twenties, and was slightly revised in his early forties. The result is a relatively simple work with a superinduced technical elaboration.

Serenade. An instrumental composition imitating in style an "evening song," sung by a lover before his lady's window.

The **Serenade** is interesting first of all because it is scored for an orchestra without violins. This imparts a certain somber quality to the tone color; it also enhances its Romantic character. In the absence of the violins, the horns and the woodwinds assume a greater importance. Romantic devices inaugurated by Weber, fanfarelike progressions of instruments in pairs, lend special color to the music. In the first movement, the clarity of the principal theme is contrasted with the chromatic meanderings of the second subject. A new group of melodic motifs introduces dancelike rhythms. These thematic ingredients enter a skillful contrapuntal game in the development section. The original subjects return in an almost orthodox recapitulation.

The ensuing scherzo is cast in the key of C major. Its rhythmic pattern is determined by the presence of off-beat accents that overlap the metrical divisions in a characteristically Brahmsian cross-rhythm. The slow movement, Adagio ma non troppo, in A minor, opens as a gentle **barcarole**. The smooth flow of the music is, however, interrupted by dramatic epi-

Barcarole (Ger.). A vocal or instrumental piece imitating the song of the Venetian gondoliers.

sodes in diminished-seventh harmonies, recalling similar passages of the First Symphony. The musical motion is doubled in frequency, creating a contrapuntal network of considerable complexity. Modulations carry the music far afield along the cycle of keys, before coming to rest on the major tonic.

The next movement is marked Quasi minuetto, implying a departure from the parent form of the classical **minuet**. Its tonal pattern is simple, and the expressive chromaticisms of subsidiary melodies do not transgress the basic tonality. The final **Rondo** signals the resumption of simple harmonic procedures of Brahms's youngest days. Again there are fanfare-like figures; the propulsive rhythm carries the movement along with but a few reflective moments of lyrical recollection. The movement concludes on an optimistic proclamation of musical romanticism.

Minuetto (It.), **minuet**. An early French dance form.

Rondo (It.). An instrumental piece in which the leading theme is repeated, alternating with the others.

Variations on a Theme by Joseph Haydn, Op. 56A (1873)

The title may well be misapplied. The theme itself, originally called "St. Anthony Chorale," was used by Haydn in one of his so-called Zittau Divertimentos, but in all probability it was a traditional hymn of unknown provenance. Indeed, these **divertimentos**, or *Feldpartiten* (suites for wind band) are now considered spurious. Whatever the source of the theme itself, Variations represents a development of great significance in the career of Brahms as a symphonic composer. It was written in 1873, prior to the composition of his First Symphony, but it embodies the distinctive traits of his symphonic style. The orchestral treatment in the Variations preserves the main features of the "Zittauer divertimenti," with an emphasis on wind instruments, as in band arrangements.

Divertimento (It.), divertissement (Fr.). A light and easy piece of instrumental music.

There are eight variations and a finale. Analytically, the variations are of the "characteristic" type, stemming from Beethoven's example, rather than from the formal "ornamental" variations of the Baroque and Rococo. Each variation possesses a distinctive character in its modality, dynamic distribution of instrumental timbres, and individual rhythmic patterns. The theme, Andante, is in B-flat major, as in Haydn's original score. It is brought out by the woodwind instruments, with the lower strings providing a discreet accompaniment in **pizzicato**. All odd-numbered variations are in B-flat major; all even-numbered variations are in B-flat minor, with the exception of variation 6, which is in B-flat major, as is the finale.

Pizzicato (It.). Pinched; plucked with the finger; a direction to play notes by plucking the strings.

Variation 1, Poco più animato, is distinguished by a typically Brahmsian combination of four notes against six notes in a bar of 2/4, which imparts to the music a sense of stimulating fluidity. Variation 2, Più **vivace**, is marked by a punctuating syncopation of the principal rhythmic pattern of the subject. Variation 3, Con moto, is a pastoral eclogue, with delicate crewel-work in the contrapuntal background, dolce e legato. Variation 4, Andante con moto, in 3/8, is a locus classicus of invertible counterpoint in the twelfth, with the countersubject appearing in the low register and then transposed an octave and a fifth higher, without a change in the theme itself. The perturbations resulting from this polyphonic **salto** mortale are stupendous, for **consonances** become **dissonances** and vice-versa—but Brahms was a supreme master of this sort of thing.

Vivace (It.). Lively, animated, brisk.

Salto (It.). Leap; skip or cut.
Consonance. A combination of two or more tones, harmonious and pleasing, requiring no further progression to make it satisfactory.
Dissonance. A combination of two or more tones requiring resolution.
Sforzando, sforzato (It.). A direction to perform the tone or chord with special stress, or marked and sudden emphasis.
Presto (It.). Fast, rapid; faster than "allegro."

Variation 5, Vivace, in 6/8 time, is a scherzo in a fine filigree texture, in which passages in pianissimo are vitalized by recurrent puffs of off-beat **sforzando**. Variation 6, Vivace, in 2/4 time, is an incisive instrumental movement, opening in throbbing pianissimo and reaching fortissimo at the climax. Variation 7, Grazioso, in 6/8 time, is a gentle barcarole. The cross-accents result in a rhythmic interference in the implied dual meter of 3/4 and 6/8, imparting to the movement a Spanish character. Variation 8, **Presto** non troppo, in B-flat minor, has the sonority of Romantic precipitation that Brahms favored in the rapid movements of his symphonies. A pause separates this variation from the Finale, which is the longest part of the entire set. Its form is that of a passacaglia, with a short theme of five bars in the ground bass recurring eighteen times in succession, while a cornucopia of florid counterpoint descends upon it from the upper voices. The principal theme returns in the coda, and the Variations conclude in a blaze of B-flat major chords.

Concerto for Violin and Orchestra in D Major, Op. 77 (1878)

The Violin Concerto belongs in the symphonic period of Brahms. It was composed in 1878, a year after the Second Symphony, and it is written in the same key of D major. But apart from this there are no thematic points of contact between the two works. The Violin Concerto was written for the violinist Joseph Joachim, a great friend of Brahms's and a famous virtuoso. Brahms had some trouble with the organization of the concerto. He planned originally to write four movements, including a scherzo, but was dissatisfied with the result, and eliminated the extra movement. Joachim made all kinds of suggestions for the improvement of the violin part, but Brahms proved to be uncommonly reluctant to make changes, and followed Joachim's advice only in technical matters of bowings, accents, rests, etc.

Joachim played the first performance, with Brahms himself conducting, at a Gewandhaus concert in Leipzig on January 1, 1879. Reports of the quality of performance differ. Florence May, in her Brahms biography, wrote: "Joachim played with a love and devotion which brought home to us in every bar the direct or indirect share he has had in the work." But Max Kalbeck, the author of the voluminous life of Brahms, was critical of Joachim and found his performance even technically inadequate. Brahms himself was enthusiastic. "Joachim played my concerto more and more magnificently with each rehearsal," he wrote to a friend. "The cadenza produced such an effect that the audience applauded right through the coda." An amusing episode brought snickers to the listeners. Brahms, never a careful dresser, forgot to fasten his unbuttoned suspenders and, semaphoring the orchestra in large gestures of his short meaty arms, he had to fight the downward movement of his trousers, and his shirt showed under the waistcoat.

The concerto eventually became a standard work of the violin repertory, but there were skeptical voices in Germany and elsewhere about the enormous difficulties of the work. A famous quip had it that the Brahms Concerto was not for violin and orchestra, but against the violin.

The first movement, Allegro non troppo, in D major, in 3/4 time, opens with a broad subject in the low register of the orchestra, establishing at once a Brahmsian mood of declarative elegance. A contrasting subject, dynamically tense and sharply syncopated, in D minor, is introduced and developed. After a very long orchestral introduction the violin solo comes in with a cadenzalike passage. It assumes the role of an exterior decorator (not unlike the style of Beethoven's Violin Concerto), beautifying the thematic developments in the orchestra with florid ornamentation. When it finally takes over the main theme, it does so in a grand manner, in the high treble, with **double stops**. A cozy waltzlike theme introduces the warm environment of Viennese gemütlichkeit. The recapitulation is maintained in vigorous tones. There is a formidable cadenza, composed by Joachim for the first performance, and the movement comes to a satisfying close.

The second movement, Adagio, in F major, in 2/4 time, is bucolic. The oboe announces an elegiac subject. The violin solo elaborates the theme in countless variations. There is a contrasting middle section, and the pastoral mood returns for a soft ending. The Finale: Allegro giocoso ma non troppo vivace, is a rondo with melodic material suggesting a festive Gypsy tune. There is a constant interplay between the soloist

Double stop. In violin playing, to stop two strings together, thus obtaining two-part harmony.

and orchestra; the solo part here reaches the height of virtu-osity. It provides a fitting ending to a nobly conceived but mundanely effective work.

Academic Festival Overture, *Op. 80 (1880)*

There is no other composer to whom the title of doctor would apply as perfectly as to Brahms. But he had to wait for his doc-tor's degree until his fame made it imperative for a German university to award him an honorary title. It was the University of Breslau that gave Brahms the honorary doctoral degree on March 11, 1879, and it is quite certain that far from adding to Brahms's stature by this honor, the Breslau University added to its own academic standing by its act.

The Latin wording of the degree described Brahms as "Artis musicae severioris in Germania nunc princeps." The translation is best made from the last word to the first to ren-der the Latin word order more intelligible: "The first now in Germany in serious musical art." The word "severioris" liter-ally means "more severe, stronger," the inference being that Brahms was the greatest German composer in the severe polyphonic style. Some critics belonging to Wagner's circle discerned in this work an implied condemnation of opera. Brahms never wrote any works for the stage, and the phrasing of the degree seemed to recommend his abstention from the less "severe" art of the theater.

The Breslau University faculty made it plain to Brahms that, in lieu of a doctoral thesis, they expected from him a "doc-toral symphony" or, at the very least, a festive song. Brahms replied with professorial humor that he would be glad to come to Breslau and to take part in a doctoral banquet and some ninepin games. Breslau University finally got a musical doctoral thesis from Brahms: the *Academic Festival Overture*, Op. 80. Some of Breslau's professors thought the title was too dry and academic, and suggested *Viadrina*, which was the Latinized name of Breslau University, with reference to the river Oder (in Latin, Viadua), on which Breslau is situated. But Brahms decided to stick to the original name.

He spoke of the overture as a "potpourri on students' songs à la Suppé," but then he was notoriously irreverent to his own music. Max Kalbeck, Brahms's Boswell, whose four-volume biography of the master sets all records for minuteness and detail, finds in the *Academic Festival Overture* more than a token of appreciation for an honor. He believes it is an ode to the spirit of freedom, comradeship, and joy of living of the old German universities. He finds in the opening theme of the overture a double reminiscence of the Rákóczy March (the Hungarian "Marseillaise" of 1848) and the Paris Entrance March of 1813, symbolizing the emergence of the spirit of liberation from the armies of military conquest and from the oppressive reaction in post-Napoleonic Europe. The concluding song, "Gaudeamus Igitur," was indeed a symbol of students' rebellion against the police surveillance in German universities.

Four student songs are used in the *Academic Festival Overture*, apart from original thematic material. The first song, "Wir hatten gebauet ein stattliches Haus" ("We had built a stately house"), makes its appearance, after a long drumroll, in the brass, softly, as if from afar. This theme is in the key of C major, suggesting the famous horn theme of the First Symphony, which is also in C major. The second song is "Der Landesvater," in the key of E major. If the C-minor opening of the overture is regarded as the first theme, and the C-major song as the second theme, then "Der Landesvater" may be construed as a second movement, an Andante. The third movement in all of Brahms's four symphonies is a Viennese scherzo. In the *Academic Festival Overture*, the scherzo effect is provided by the "Fuchslied" ("Fox Song"), introduced, appropriately enough, by the laughing bassoons. This song is a hazing song for a freshman, who is asked impertinent questions about his family, and then is given a pipe too strong for a freshman's lungs. It is in quick polka time; it is bandied about from the bassoons to the oboes, from the basses to the flutes, from the violins to the brass, and further appears in various combinations of these instruments, until it is finally sounded by the whole orchestra. If the symphonic interpretation of the overture is valid, then the concluding song, "Gaudeamus Igitur," is the finale. This finale parallels the coda of Beethoven's Fifth Symphony, with which it has the key, C major, in common.

The orchestration of the *Academic Festival Overture* is interesting. Brahms accords in it more place to percussion instruments than in any of his other symphonic works, and adds metal sonorities of the cymbals and the triangle which are somehow alien to the accepted picture of Brahms as the greatest composer in the "severe type of musical art." But then, Brahms's intention was not to justify his doctorate, but rather to assert his consanguinity with the German student body, with a perceptible undertone of self-mockery.

Brahms went to Breslau to conduct the overture himself, and the first performance took place at the university on January 4, 1881. Other performances followed immediately, and very soon, the *Academic Festival Overture* became an orchestral favorite the world over. The *Overture* may not be the revelation of Brahms at his greatest, but it is an expression of his less solemn and, paradoxically, less professorial self.

OTHER WORKS

Intermezzos for Piano (1871–78)

Brahms used to write piano pieces in batches, several at a time. In writing these pieces, he often was influenced by the anticipated opinion of his two women friends, both eminent pianists, Clara Schumann and Elisabeth von Herzogenberg. Clara Schumann was seventy-four years old at the time Brahms sent her his last batch of Four Piano Pieces, Op. 119.

The Intermezzo Op. 76, no. 3, is one of the shortest pieces Brahms ever wrote. It is in A-flat major, and comprises only thirty bars. There are two musical subjects, alternating in simple succession, without a trace of development: a, b, a, b. The first subject is characteristically syncopated; the second is in gently moving triplets. Huneker describes this intermezzo in his impressionistic language as a "tender wreath of moonbeams and love." Edwin Evans all but gives up the task of analysis: "Too ethereal for description in the terms of everyday employment." But he does comment upon the form: "Notwithstanding its shortness, it is divided into two portions, which are practically a repeat of one another. But the repetition only seems to respond to the listener's longing to hear the lovely strain again, and in doing so to make it even more charming than before."

The Intermezzo Op. 76, no. 4, is remarkable for the use Brahms makes of tonality. The key signature is in two flats, and the opening bar is the dominant seventh of B-flat major. But having implied the principal key by aural harmony and visual time signature, Brahms shuns the tonic in a most deliberate manner. He veers momentarily toward G minor, in a deceptive cadence, as it were, and then proceeds enharmonically to remote keys, farther and farther away from the tonic. It is only in the second section that the tonic makes its appearance in the pedal, and even then as the bass of the minor **subdominant**. Clear and unadulterated B-flat major appears for the first time only in the last two bars. This deceptive procedure is characteristic of Brahms; other instances of similar avoidance of the tonic are found in the second movement of the First Clarinet Sonata, where the tonic triad does not appear until the twenty-second bar, and in the Second Rhapsody for Piano, Op. 79, in which the principal key of G minor does not appear until the eleventh bar. The Intermezzo Op. 76, no. 4, is thus the extreme instance of Brahms's tonofugal idiosyncrasy, for here the tonic **triad** is not reached until the very last bars.

The Intermezzo Op. 116, no. 4, is an adagio in the clearly

Subdominant. The tone below the dominant in a diatonic scale; the fourth degree.

Triad. A "three-tone" chord composed of a given tone (the root), with its third and fifth in ascending order in the scale.

expressed key of E major. The first section is marked by a wavy motion in triplets on the first beat. This rhythmic accentuation is intensified in the second section, where the movement is in sixteenth notes. But the upbeat is always free from the accentuating waves. The piece is thus a study in acceleration and retardation, secured not by the actual increase and decrease of tempo, but by the quicker rate of motion in a given metrical unit. Harmonically and melodically, the important effect is that of the upward resolution of the augmented triad in the opening phrase.

The Intermezzo Op. 118, no. 6, is in E-flat minor. In this intermezzo Brahms delights in long **appoggiaturas**, projected upon the harmony notes at close range, so that a sensation of acute discord is created. Brahms applied this method consciously. Writing to Clara Schumann about another piece similarly constructed (Intermezzo in B Minor, Op. 119, no. 1), he confesses: "It teems with discord. These may be all right and quite explicable, but you may not perhaps like them," and adds with a touch of Brahmsian humor, "and if so, I might wish that they were less right and more pleasing to you." Apart from the conscious use of discord, the Intermezzo in E-flat Minor is extremely pure in its form, which is ternary. The middle section is in the relative key of G-flat minor, and is distinguished by quick pulsating rhythms, in thirty-second notes. Edwin Evans, in his extraordinary handbooks to Brahms's complete works, comprising altogether 1,581 pages in four volumes, has this to say about this intermezzo: "This is a movement portraying the utmost grief and passion. . . . There is no bending of the form to his will; nothing (except maybe a highly refined pianism) to point particularly to Brahms." The pianism is indeed quite extraordinary, almost acrobatic, in that Brahms makes the left hand cross the right in light arpeggios, at times in the identical register, to the point of collision and coincidence.

The Intermezzo Op. 119, no. 2, is another instance of Brahms's tonofugal harmony. Ostensibly the piece is in E minor,

Appoggiatura (It.). "Leaning" note; a grace note that takes the accent and part of the time value of the following principal note.

Toccata (It.). A composition for organ or harpsichord (piano), free and bold in style.

with a middle section in E major. But the E-minor triad never appears at all, and when the final cadence seems to lead to the tonic, it is the major tonic of the middle section that provides the resolution. The movement is **toccata**-like with both hands alternating in quick groups of two notes. The second section is, rather unexpectedly, a Viennese waltz, as charming as any by Brahms. The concluding section is almost an exact repetition of the first, and the ending is in E major.

Three Rhapsodies for Piano—Nos. 1 and 2, Op. 79 (1880); No. 3, Op. 119 (1892)

On a concert tour, Brahms stopped at Leipzig one day in 1879, and called on his dear friends, the von Herzogenbergs, to play for them his two newly composed piano pieces. Heinrich von Herzogenberg was a plodding composer of sorts, but his wife, Elisabeth, was an excellent and intelligent pianist, the type of German woman of taste that inspires the great among German men of genius. Brahms maintained with her an epistolary *amitié amoureuse* typical of his relations with women.

The original titles of the two Op. 79 pieces were Capriccio: Presto agitato and Capriccio: Molto passionato. Brahms decided to rename them, and asked Frau von Herzogenberg what she thought of "rhapsody" for a title. He also added playfully that he could not possibly improve on the dedication, which was made to her. She replied, after an outburst of gratitude and admiration, that she felt the simpler title Klavierstücke (Piano Pieces), would suit the pieces better, and that the music did not conform to the general idea of a rhapsody, but she quickly admitted that "rhapsody" was the best of the descriptive titles.

"This B-minor Rhapsody," James Huneker wrote in the preface to the selected edition of Brahms's piano works, "sounds as if its composer were trying to make a harsh pragmatic statement; in it there is more intellectual acrimoniousness than rhapsody. . . . Acrid as the patina on antique metal, this first rhapsody is for the head rather than for the heart." This judgment, coinciding in part with that of Frau von Herzogenberg, is puzzling: the musical analysis would tend to show that the First Rhapsody is much more "human" than the second. It is in perfect three-part form; the main section, which is repeated in full in the third part of the piece, is tonally clear, and the modulations take place only after the fundamental key is established. There is a touch of humor in the lyric D-minor phrase, which is a quotation from Grieg's theme in "The Death of Ase" from the *Peer Gynt* Suite, No. 1. Brahms no doubt intended it as an amortization of the melody loan Grieg had made for his Piano Concerto from Brahms's E-flat Minor Scherzo, Op. 4.

Huneker liked the Second Rhapsody as much as he disliked the first: "A wonderful, glorious, bracing tone-picture, in which Brahms, the philosopher, burns the boats of his old age and becomes for the time a youthful Faust in search of a sensation. A hurricane of emotion that is barely stilled at the end, this Rhapsody reminds me of the bardic recital of some old border ballad. . . . It is an epic in miniature." In the same letter in which Elisabeth von Herzogenberg suggested the title Klavierstücke, she gave a vivid account of a "G-minor night," which she spent trying to recall the music of Brahms's Second Rhapsody before she received the manuscript: "a night like that is terrible to live through, and the Almighty, if he is at all musical, should show us mercy. Scraps of the glorious music pursue you, and you vainly try to put them together. Then suddenly, a phrase breaks through the fog, then another.... In despair, you count one hundred to fall asleep, but sleep eludes you." Indeed, the Second Rhapsody is hard to remember from a single hearing: in fact, the key of the "G-minor night" does not appear until the eleventh bar and, even then, only as the minor subdominant of the key of D major.

The last rhapsody is the fourth piece of the Four Piano

Pieces, Op. 119, and is the last original piano piece that Brahms composed. He wrote arrangements and piano exercises, but the inspiration for the piano as a medium of Romantic self-expression was gone. He composed this last rhapsody in 1892, the year of the death of Frau Elisabeth von Herzogenberg.

Sonata for Piano and Clarinet (or Viola) No. 1 in F Minor, Op. 120, No. 1 (1894)

The register of the clarinet practically coincides with that of the viola. The lowest note of the viola is C, an octave below the middle C, and the lowest note of the clarinet in B flat for which Brahms's sonatas are written is D. It is, therefore, possible to play on the viola a part written for the clarinet. But in discussing Brahms's sonatas for viola and piano it should not be forgotten that they were originally intended for the clarinet, and that the viola was a second thought, and is indicated on the title page in parentheses.

Brahms composed the two Clarinet Sonatas, Op. 120, in the summer of 1894 at Ischl. He gave the first performance of the sonatas in Vienna on January 7, 1895, playing the piano part. He was sixty-one years old and at the height of his fame. With his famous beard, he looked like a venerable professor, or a celebrated artist, but these sonatas were to be his last important instrumental works: he died in Vienna on April 3, 1897. Despite Brahms's absolute recognition in the musical world, the two clarinet sonatas were not accepted by the critics with uniform kindness. Otto Floersheim wrote after the Berlin performance in October 1895:

> The compositions themselves were grievously disappointing, at least for those who anticipated much of anything from the Johannes Brahms of today. Brahms is completely *ausgeschrieben*; these two sonatas prove it beyond the shadow of a doubt. The first one in F minor is

the less unimportant of the two, and is in four movements, of which the slow one in A flat is the most, and the first movement the least disappointing.

The English critics were much more deferential to the great Brahms. When the clarinet sonatas were performed in London in June, 1895, the reviewer of the *London Atheneum* wrote:

> With regard to the merits of the work, definite judgment must be reserved, for Brahms does not write carelessly and should not be hastily criticized. But there need be no hesitation in saying that the sonatas are well worthy of his reputation as the most gifted representative of classical music. They are noteworthy for freshness and geniality, and do not in the least smell of the lamp.

The clarinet sonatas were given the first American performance in Boston by Arthur Foote, the American composer, and Pourtau, the clarinetist of the Boston Symphony Orchestra, on November 25, 1895. Wrote Philip Hale in the *Boston Journal*, referring retrospectively to the Leipzig performance of January 27, 1895:

> Dr. Johannes Brahms, pianist—and what a pianist! one of ten thumbs—appeared with the clarinetist, Richard Mühlfeld of Meiningen, at a chamber concert in the Gewandhaus, Leipzig, and they then played two new sonatas for clarinet and piano. Neither of the sonatas made much of an impression, and in the conventional notices of the concert, yawns were heard between the lines.

Then turning to the occasion, Hale went on:

> The first movement is priggish; it is entitled passionate, but here Brahms's imagination dropped. The second

movement has more color, and is at least suggestive of the mood. The third movement promises something at first, but after a few measures, it is nothing but notes, notes, notes. The finale is drearily academic. What an absurd theme is that given first to the clarinet! Not even Mr. Pourtau could make anything out of the gurgle, gurgle. It is idle now to inquire into the cause of Brahms's late passion for the clarinet, or to ask whether the upper tones of this instrument blend readily with the tones of a piano, even when the pianist has an agreeable touch. It is only necessary to regret that in this sonata Brahms gives an example of premature senility.

Speaking analytically, the two Sonatas for Clarinet (or viola), Op. 120, are representative of Brahms's last period, which includes the Fourth Symphony and the intermezzos and rhapsodies for piano. Brahms's harmonic style is here characterized by a spirit of free **modulation**. The First Clarinet Sonata gives many instances of this modulatory technique. The first movement, Allegro appassionato, in 3/4 time, is in the key of the sonata, F minor, but almost immediately a G flat is introduced, which confutes the impression of the principal key. However, F minor is explicitly shown in the first subject. In the development section there are instantaneous shifts toward the sharp keys, and the return to the principal key is effected by **enharmonic** change. This procedure of clockwise modulation over the entire cycle of scales when the principal key is in flats, as in this movement, and the converse procedure by modulating counterclockwise when the principal key is in sharps as in the Fourth Symphony, is characteristic of Brahms's harmonic technique.

Modulation. Passage from one key into another.

Enharmonic. Differing in notation but alike in sound.

WEBSITES/BIBLIOGRAPHY/ DISCOGRAPHY

In compiling this list, it is impossible to be exhaustive or complete. All nineteen of these composers have generated mountains of literature and recordings; some pieces can be heard on fifty or more different CDs! It is also difficult if not impossible to recommend one recording as being "better" than all others. For this reason, the following lists give a selective sampling of books and CDs on each composer and composition covered in this book. The websites chosen give the reader an idea of what is available and indicate links to other sites that currently exist. Keep in mind that websites come and go; a good search engine will help you locate these and future sites quickly.

J. S. BACH

Websites

http://www.jsbach.org/

J. S. Bach home page. An extensive biography, tour of Bach's life in Germany, catalog of his works, bibliography, recommended recordings, and other Bach resources on the Web.

http://www.basistech.com/bach/

J. S. Bach newsgroup. The Frequently Asked Questions (FAQ) resource for the newsgroup is alt.music.j-s-bach.

http://www.jsbach.net/bcs/index.html

Bach Central Station. Links to sites covering all aspects of Bach's life and work.

Books

Boyd, Malcolm. *Bach* (The Master Musicians). NY: Schirmer Books, 1997.

_____. *Bach: The Brandenburg Concertos*. NY: Cambridge, 1993.

_____, ed. *J. S. Bach, Oxford Companion of Music*. NY: Oxford, 1999.

Butt, John. *The Cambridge Companion to Bach*. NY: Cambridge, 1997.

_____. *Bach: Mass in B Minor*. NY: Cambridge, 1991.

David, Hans T., Arthur Mendel, and Christoph Wolff, eds. *The New Bach Reader: A Life of Johann Sebastian Bach in Letters and Documents*. NY: Norton, 1999.

Stauffer, George. *Bach, the Mass in B Minor: The Great Catholic Mass* (Monuments of Western Music). NY: Schirmer Books, 1996.

Wolff, Christoph, Eugene Helm, and Ernest Warburton. *The New Grove Bach Family* (The New Grove). NY: Norton 1997.

Recordings

INSTRUMENTAL WORKS

Chaconne in D Minor for Unaccompanied Violin; from Partita No. 2, BWV 1004 (1720)

> Julian Bream, guitar EMI Classics 55123

> C. Booth, harpsichord, Olympia 437

Orchestral Suite No. 3 in D Major, BWV 1068 (c. 1729–31)

> Berlin Academy of Early Music, Harmonia Mundi 901578

> Berlin Philharmonic (von Karajan, conductor), Deutsche Grammophon 453001-2

> Bach Festival Orchestra (Menuhin, conductor), Royal Classics 6481

Concerto No. 1 in C Minor for Two Harpsichords, BWV 1060 (1729)

> Hamburg Philharmonic; Frantz and Eschenbach, piano soloists, Deutsche Grammophon 415665-2

ORGAN WORKS

Toccata, Adagio, and Fugue in C Major, BWV 564 (c. 1708–17)

> E. Power Biggs, Sony Masterworks 42644

> M. Murray, Telarc 80127

Passacaglia in C Minor, BWV 582 (c. 1708–17)

> Anthony Newman, Helicon Classics 1010

> Karl Richter, London Classic 455291-2

Ricercare à Six from *The Musical Offering*, BWV 1079 (1747) (orchestration by Anton Webern)

> Leipzig Bach Collegium, Capriccio 10 032

RELIGIOUS WORKS

Cantata No. 51 "Jauchzet Gott in Allen Landen" (date unknown)

> Stuttgart Bach Collegium, Novalis 150029

> American Bach Soloists, Koch International Classics 7138

Cantata No. 53, "Schlage Doch" (date unknown)

> Zagreb Solisti, Vanguard Classics 2-64

Cantata No. 158, "Der Friede Sei Mit Dir" (date unknown)

> Monteverdi Choir, Teldec 93687

> Leonhardt Consort, Teldec 2292-42633

The Passion of Our Lord According to St. Matthew, BWV 244 (1727)

English Baroque Soloists/Monteverdi Choir, Archiv 427648-2

Berlin Philharmonic (von Karajan, conductor), et al., Deutsche Grammophon 419789-2

Philharmonia Orchestra (Klemperer, conductor) EMI Classics 63058

Chicago Symphony (Solti, conductor), et al., London 42177-2

GEORGE FRIDERIC HANDEL

Websites

http://www.intr.net/bleissa/handel/home.html

> Handel home page. Information and links on the composers.

http://www.intr.net/bleissa/ahs/

> American Handel Society. Scholarly site with links.

Books

Burrows, Donald. *Handel*. NY: Schirmer Books, 1995.

_____. *Handel's Messiah*. NY: Cambridge, 1991.

_____, ed. *Cambridge Companion to Handel*. NY: Cambridge, 1998.

Dean, Winton. *Handel's Dramatic Oratorios and Masques*. NY: Oxford, 1959.

_____, and John Merrill Knapp. *Handel's Operas, 1704–1726* (revised edition). NY: Oxford, 1995.

_____, with Anthony Hicks. *The New Grove Handel*. NY: Norton, 1997.

LaRue, C. Steven. *Handel and His Singers: The Creation of the Royal Academy Operas, 1720–1728*. NY: Oxford, 1995.

Mann, Aflred. *Handel: The Orchestral Music*. NY: Schirmer Books, 1997.

Recordings

INSTRUMENTAL MUSIC

Overture to *Agrippina* (1709)

> Academy of St. Martin in the Fields (Silito, conductor) Capriccio 10 420

The Faithful Shepherd (1712; rev. 1734)

> London Philharmonic (Beecham, conductor) Dutton 8018

Water Music (1717)

> New York Philharmonic (Boulez, conductor) Sony 38480

> Academy of Ancient Music (Hogwood, conductor) L'Oiseau–Lyre 40059-2

Concerto Grosso No. 12 in G Major (1739)

> Budapest Strings, Naxos 8.553028

> Vienna Concentus Musicus, Teldec 95500-2

FRANZ JOSEPH HAYDN

Websites

http://home.wxs.nl/~cmr/haydn/index.htm

CMR Music Services Haydn home page.

http://w3.rz-berlin.mpg.de/cmp/haydnj.html

CMP Haydn home page. Biography, links, and bibliography.

Books

Larsen, Jens Peter. *The New Grove Haydn*. NY: Norton, 1997.

Rosen, Charles. *The Classical Style: Haydn, Mozart, Beethoven*. NY: Norton, 1997.

Sisman, Elaine, ed. *Haydn and His World* (Bard Music Festival Series). Princeton, NJ: Princeton U. Press, 1997.

Recordings

SYMPHONIES

Symphony No. 88 in G Major (1787)

Berlin Philharmonic (Furtwangler, conductor), Deutsche Grammophon 447439-2

Columbia Symphony (Walter, conductor), Sony Classical 66485

Symphony No. 92 in G Major ("Oxford") (1789)

Cleveland Orchestra (Szell, conductor), Sony Classical 46322

Symphony No. 95 in C Minor (1791)

New York Philharmonic (Bernstein, conductor), Sony Classical 47553

Symphony No. 99 in E-flat Major (1793)

Philharmonia Orchestra (Slatkin, conductor), RCA Red Seal 0902-68425-2

Symphony No. 104 in D Major ("London") (1795)

Royal Concertgebouw Orchestra (Harnoncourt, conductor), Teldec 2292-43526-2

Pittsburgh Symphony (Previn, conductor), EMI Classics 65178

CONCERTOS

Concerto for Violoncello in C Major (c. 1765)

English Chamber Orchestra (Barenboim, conductor), Jacqueline Du Pre (cello), EMI Classics 4780

Academy of St. Martin in the Fields (Brown, conductor), Mstislav Rostropovich (cello), EMI Classics 49305

Concerto for Violoncello in D Major (1783)

English Chamber Orchestra (Garcia, conductor), Yo-Yo Ma (cello), Sony 44562

Concerto for Trumpet in E-flat Major (1796)

English Chamber Orchestra (Leppard, conductor), Wynton Marsalis (trumpet), Sony Classical 57497

Academy of St. Martin in the Fields (Marriner, conductor), Alan Stringer (trumpet), London 430633-2

Symphonie Concertante in B-flat Major (1792)

Vienna Concentus Musicus (Harnoncourt, conductor), Teldec 2292-44196-2

OTHER WORKS

The Seven Last Words of Christ (1795–96)

Juilliard String Quartet, et al., Sony Classical 44914

The Seasons (1799–1801)

St. Paul Chamber Orchestra, Minnesota Chorale, Koch International 7065

Vienna Symphony, A. Schoenberg Choir, Teldec 2292-42699-2

WOLFGANG AMADEUS MOZART

Websites

http://www.frontiernet.net/~sboerner/mozart/

The Mozart Project website.

http://www.mhrcc.org/mozart/mozart.html

Links, bibliography, biography, and more.

Books

Clive, Peter. *Mozart and His Circle*. New Haven: Yale U. Press, 1993.

Dimond, Peter. *A Mozart Diary: A Chronological Reconstruction of the Composer's Life, 1761–1791*. Westport, CT: Greenwood, 1997.

Landon, H. C. Robbins. *Mozart: The Golden Years*. NY: Schirmer Books, 1989.

_____. *Mozart and Vienna*. NY: Schirmer Books, 1991.

Sadie, Stanley. *The New Grove Mozart*. NY: Norton, 1983.

Solomon, Maynard. *Mozart: A Life*. NY: HarperCollins, 1995.

Recordings

ORCHESTRAL MUSIC

Symphony No. 25 in G Minor, K. 183 (1773)

Vienna Philharmonic (Bernstein, conductor), Deutsche Grammophon 429221-2

Symphony No. 32 in G Major, K. 318 (1779)

Berlin Philharmonic (von Karajan, conductor), Deutsche Grammophon 429668-2

Symphony No. 36 in C Major, K. 425 ("Linz") (1783)

Berlin Philharmonic (Abbado, conductor), Sony Classical 66859

Symphony No. 38 in D Major, K. 504 ("Prague") (1787)

Vienna Philharmonic (Walter, conductor), Sony Classsical 64474

Symphony No. 39 in E-flat Major, K. 543 (1788)

Royal Concertgebouw Orchestra (Harnoncourt, conductor), Teldec 9031-77596-2

Symphony No. 40 in G Minor, K. 550 (1788)

Chicago Symphony (Levine, conductor) RCA 09026-61397-2

Overture to *Der Schauspieldirektor*, K. 486 (1786)

Calgary Philharmonic (Bernardi, conductor), CBC 5149

Overture to *The Marriage of Figaro*, K. 492 (1786)

New York Philharmonic (Bernstein, conductor), Sony Classical 47601

CONCERTOS

Concerto No. 5 for Violin in A Major, K. 219 (1775)

Jascha Heifetz (violin), Memories 3007/8

Concerto for Three Pianos in F Major, K. 242 (1776)

London Philharmonic, Ashkenazy, Barenboim, and Ts'ong (piano), London 421577-2

Concerto for Flute and Harp in C Major, K. 299 (1778)

Chamber Orchestra of Europe, James Galway (flute), RCA Red Seal 7861-2

Concerto for Piano No. 24 in C Minor, K. 491 (1786)

RCA Victor Orchestra (Krips, conductor), Arthur Rubinstein (piano), RCA Gold Seal 7968-2

Concerto for Piano No. 25 in C Major, K. 503 (1786)

English Chamber Orchestra, Murray Perahia (piano and conductor), Sony 37267

Concerto for Piano No. 27 in B-flat Major, K. 595 (1791)

Philadelphia Orchestra (Ormandy, conductor), Rudolf Serkin (piano), Sony Odyssey 42533

Concerto for Clarinet in A Major, K. 622 (1791)

Academy of St. Martin in the Fields (Marriner, conductor), J. Brymer (clarinet), Philips 416483-2

Sinfonia Concertante for Violin and Viola in E-flat Major, K. 364/320d (1779)

Orpheus Chamber Orchestra, Deutsche Grammophon 429784-2

CHAMBER MUSIC

String Quartet No. 15 in D Minor, K. 421 (1783)

Guarneri String Quartet, Philips 426240-2

String Quartet No. 17 in B-flat Major ("Hunt"), K. 458 (1784)

Budapest String Quartet, Enterprise 99300

String Quartet No. 19 in C Major ("Dissonant"), K. 465 (1785)

Melos String Quartet, Deutsche Grammophon 429818-2

"Eine kleine Nachtmusik" (Serenade in G Major), K. 525 (1787)

Vienna Philharmonic (von Karajan, conductor), EMI Classics 66388

LUDWIG VAN BEETHOVEN

Websites

http://www.geocities.com/Vienna/Strasse/2914/beethoven/

Beethoven Experience. Biography, pictures, and compositions.

http://www.music.sjsu.edu/Beethoven/index/home_page.html

Beethoven Center. Course syllabi, journal, and general information from the American Beethoven Society.

Books

Grove, Sir George. *Beethoven's Nine Symphonies*. NY: Dover, 1962.

Kerman, Joseph, and Alan Tyson. *The New Grove Beethoven*. NY: Norton, 1997.

Levy, David. *The Ninth Symphony*. NY: Schirmer Books, 1995.

Sipe, Thomas. *"Eroica" Symphony*. NY: Cambridge, 1998.

Solomon, Maynard. *Beethoven*, 2nd revised ed. NY: Schirmer Books, 1998.

Recordings

SYMPHONIES

Symphony No. 3 in E-flat Major (*Eroica*), Op. 55 (1804)

New York Philharmonic (Bernstein, conductor), Sony Classical 47514

Philadelphia Orchestra (Muti, conductor), EMI Classics 69783

Symphony No. 5 in C Minor, Op. 67 (1807–8)

Berlin Philharmonic (von Karajan, conductor), Deutsche Grammophon 419051-4

Symphony No. 7 in A Major, Op. 92 (1811–12)

Vienna Philharmonic (Furtwangler, conductor), EMI Classics 68903

Symphony No. 8 in F Major, Op. 93 (1812)

Boston Symphony (Koussevitzky, conductor), Pearl 9185

Symphony No. 9 in D Minor ("Choral"), Op. 125 (1822–24)

Vienna Philharmonic (Abbado, conductor), Deutsche Grammophon 419598-2

OVERTURES

The Creatures of Prometheus, Op. 43 (1801)

Leonore Overture No. 3, Op. 72a, No. 3 (1806)

Coriolanus Overture, Op. 62 (1807)

Egmont Overture, Op. 84 (1810)

Overture to *King Stephen*, Op. 117 (1812)

Overture to *The Consecration of the House*, Op. 124 (1822)

> All six works: Vienna Philharmonic (Bernstein, conductor), Deutsche Grammophon 423481-2

CONCERTOS

Piano Concerto No. 2 in B-flat Major, Op. 19 (1785; rev. 1794–95, 1798)

> Chicago Symphony (Levine, conductor), A. Brendel (piano), Philips 412787-2

Piano Concerto No. 3 in C Minor, Op. 37 (1800)

> Cleveland Orchestra (Ashkenazy, conductor and piano), London 433321-5

Romance in G for Violin and Orchestra, Op. 40 (1802)

> Scottish Chamber Orchestra (Laredo, conductor and violin), IMP Classics 977

Piano Concerto No. 4 in G Major, Op. 58 (1803–6)

> Royal Philharmonic (Previn, conductor), E. Ax (piano), RCA Silver Seal 60476-2

Piano Concerto No. 5 in E-flat Major ("Emperor"), Op. 73 (1809)

> Chicago Symphony (Reiner, conductor), Van Cliburn (piano), RCA Gold Seal 7943-2

Concerto in C Major for Violin, Cello, and Piano, Op. 56 (1804)

> Vienna Philharmonic, Camerata 25 CM 252

Violin Concerto in D Major, Op. 61 (1806)

> Isaac Stern, Sony Classical 66941

CHAMBER MUSIC

String Quartet No. 1 in F Major, Op. 18, No. 1 (1799–1800)

String Quartet No. 8 in E Minor ("Razumovsky" Quartets), Op. 59, No. 2 (1805–6)

String Quartet No.13 in B-flat Major, Op. 130 (1825–26)

String Quartet No. 14 in C-sharp Minor, Op. 131 (1825–26)

String Quartet No. 16 in F Major, Op. 135 (1826)

> Complete Recordings of the string quartets:
>
> Emerson String Quartet, Deutsche Grammophon 447075-2
>
> Guarneri String Quartet, RCA Red Seal 60456/57/58-2-RG

PIANO WORKS

Piano Sonata No. 14 in C-sharp Minor ("Moonlight"), Op. 27, No. 2 (1801)

> V. Horowitz, Sony Classical 53467
>
> A. Rubinstein, RCA Red Seal 5674-2

Piano Sonata No. 28 in A Major, Op. 101 (1816)

Vladimir Ashkenazy, London 452176-2

Piano Sonata No. 29 in B-flat Major ("Hammerklavier"), Op. 106 (1817–18)

A. Brendel, Philips 446093-2

G. Gould, Sony Classical 52645

FELIX MENDELSSOHN

Websites

http://utopia.knoware.nl/~jsmeets/m/mendelsb.htm

Links, biographical information, and more.

http://titan.iwu.edu/~mcooper/mendelssohns/

Mendelssohn at the millennium. Academic site.

Books

Todd, R. Larry. *Mendelssohn:* The Hebrides *and Other Overtures*. NY: Cambridge, 1993.

_____, ed. *Mendelssohn and His World*. Princeton, NJ: Princeton U. Press, 1991.

Vietrcik, Greg. *The Early Works of Felix Mendelssohn: A Study in the Romantic Sonata Style* (*Musicology*, Vol. 12). London: Gordon and Breach, 1993.

Recordings

Symphony No. 3 in A Minor, Op. 56 (*Scottish*) (1830–42)

Symphony No. 4, Op. 90 (*Italian*) (1833)

Both symphonies:

Lepizig Gewandhaus (Masur, conductor), Teldec 2292-43463-2

Berlin Philharmonic (Levine, conductor), Deutsche Grammophon 427670-2

Octet in E-flat Major, Op. 20 (1825)

Academy of St. Martin in the Fields Chamber Ensemble, Philips 420400-2

Overture to *A Midsummer Night's Dream* (1826, 1843)

Boston Symphony (Ozawa, conductor), Deutsche Grammophon 439897-2

Overture to *The Hebrides (Fingal's Cave)*, Op. 26 (1832)

Capriccio Brillant for Piano and Orchestra, Op. 22 (1832)

Philadelphia Orchestra (Ormandy, conductor), Ruold Serkin (piano), Sony Classical 48186

Overture to *Ruy Blas*, Op. 95 (1839)

Both overtures (and others by Mendelssohn):

Bamberg Symphony (Flor, conductor), RCA Red Seal 07863-57905-2

Concerto in E Minor for Violin and Orchestra, Op. 64 (1844)

Vienna State Opera Orchestra (Golschmann, conductor), M. Elman (violin), Vanguard Classics 8034

RICHARD WAGNER

Websites

http://www.geocities.com/Vienna/Strasse/2906/wagner.html

Wagner home page. "Beginner's guide" to the operas of Wagner.

http://www.zazz.com/wagner/index.shtml

Wagner on the Web. Links, FAQs, and bulletin board.

Books

Cord, William O. *An Introduction to Richard Wagner's* Der Ring des Nibelungen: *A Handbook*. Athens, OH: Ohio U. Press, 1995.

Deathridge, John, and Carl Dalhaus. *The New Grove Wagner*. NY: Norton, 1997.

Gutman, Robert W. Richard Wagner: *The Man, His Mind, and His Music*. NY: Harcourt, Brace, 1990.

Osborne, Charles. *The Complete Operas of Richard Wagner*. NY: Da Capo, 1993.

Spotts, Frederic. *Bayreuth: A History of the Wagner Festival*. New Haven: Yale U. Press, 1994.

Wagner, Richard. *Pilgrimage to Beethoven and Other Essays*. Lincoln: U. of Nebraska, 1994.

Recordings

Rienzi: Overture (1840)

Chicago Symphony (Reiner, conductor), Arlecchino 45

Cleveland Orchestra (Szell, conductor), Sony Classical 62403

Tannhäuser: Overture and Bacchanale (1842–45)

NBC Symphony (Toscanini, conductor), RCA Gold Seal 09026-60306-2

Twilight of the Gods (1848–52 and 1869–74): "Siegfried's Rhine Journey"

Both selections:

Berlin Philharmonic (Maazel, conductor), Telarc 80154

The Ring of the Nibelung—The Valkyries (1851–56): Act I; Act III, "Ride of the Valkyries"

Tristan and Isolde: Prelude and Liebestod (1856–59)

Royal Opera House, Covent Garden, Orchestra (Elder, conductor), Jane Eaglen, (soprano), Sony Classical 62032

Parsifal: Prelude to Act I (1865 and 1877–82)

New York Philharmonic (Mehta, conductor), Sony Classical 45749

The Mastersingers of Nuremberg: Prelude (1868)

Berlin Philharmonic (von Karajan, conductor), Deutsche Grammophon 439022-2

Siegfried Idyll (1870)

London Classical Players (Norrington, conductor), EMI Classics 55479

JOHANNES BRAHMS

Websites

http://www.mjq.net/brahms/

> Brahms home page.

http://www.island-of-freedom.com/BRAHMS.HTM

> Biography, links, and other information.

Books

Avins, Styra, ed. *Johannes Brahms: Life and Letters.* NY: Oxford University Press, 1997.

Botstein, Leon, ed. *The Complete Brahms*. NY: Norton, 1999.

Frisch, Walter. *Brahms: The Four Symphonies*. NY: Schirmer Books, 1996.

_____, ed. *Brahms and His World*. Princeton, NJ: Princeton U. Press, 1990.

MacDonald, Malcolm. *Brahms* (The Master Musicians). NY: Schirmer Books, 1993.

Musgrave, Michael. *The Cambridge Companion to Brahms*. NY: Cambridge, 1999.

Swafford, Jan. *Johannes Brahms: A Biography*. NY: Knopf, 1997.

Recordings

ORCHESTRAL MUSIC

Symphony No. 1 in C Minor, Op. 68 (1855–76)

Symphony No. 2 in D Major, Op. 73 (1877)

Symphony No. 3 in F Major, Op. 90 (1883)

Symphony No. 4 in E Minor, Op. 98 (1884–85)

> All four symphonies:
>
> Utah Sympohny (Abravanel, conductor), Vanguard Classics 1719
>
> Chicago Symphony (Barenboim, conductor), Erato 94817
>
> Houston Symphony (Eschenbach, conductor) Virgin Classics 61360

Concerto for Piano and Orchestra No. 1 in D Minor, Op. 15 (1854–58)

> Boston Symphony (Leinsdorf, conductor), Van Cliburn (piano), RCA Gold Seal 60357-2

Serenade No. 2 in A Major, Op. 16 (1858–59)

> New York Philharmonic (Bernstein, conductor), Sony Classical 47536

Variations on a Theme by Haydn, Op. 56A (1873)

> Philadelphia Orchestra (Ormandy, conductor), Sony Classical 63287

Concerto for Violin and Orchestra, in D Major, Op. 77 (1878)

> London Philharmonic (Tennstedt, conductor), Nigel Kennedy (violin), EMI Classics 54187

Academic Festival Overture, Op. 80 (1880)

> New York Philharmonic (Masur, conductor), Teldec 72291

OTHER WORKS

Intermezzos for Piano (1871–78)

Three Rhapsodies for Piano—Nos. 1 and 2, Op. 79 (1880); No. 3, Op. 119 (1892)

> Complete Piano Music:

> Martin Jones, Nimbus 1788

> Selections:

> Artur Rubinstein, RCA Gold Seal 09026-62592-2

Sonata for Piano and Clarinet (or Viola) No. 1 in F Minor, Op. 120 (1894)

> Pinchas Zuckerman, RCA Red Seal 09026-61276-2

PETER ILYICH TCHAIKOVSKY

Websites

http://www.geocities.com/Vienna/5648/

> The world of Tchaikovsky. Biography, links, picture gallery, and more.

Books

Kearney, Leslie. *Tchaikovsky and His World*. Princeton, NJ: Princeton U. Press, 1998.

Poznansky, Alexander. *Tchaikovsky: The Quest for the Inner Man*. NY: Schirmer Books, 1993.

_____. *Tchaikovsky's Last Days: A Documentary Study*. NY: Oxford, 1996.

Recordings

Symphony No. 4, Op. 36 (1877–78)

> Vienna Philharmonic (von Karajan, conductor), Deutsche Grammophon 439018-2

Symphony No. 5 in E Minor, Op. 64 (1888)

> Leipzig Gewandhaus (Masur, conductor), Teldec 18966 (also includes Symphonies 4 and 6)

Symphony No. 6 in B Minor, Op. 74 (*Pathétique*) (1893)

> London Symphony (Abbado, conductor), Deutsche Grammophon 437401-2 (also includes Symphonies 4 and 5)

Manfred Symphony, Op. 58 (1885)

> Academy of St. Martin in the Fields (Marriner, conductor), Capriccio 10 433

Piano Concerto No. 1 in B-flat Minor, Op. 23 (1875)

> New York Philharmonic (Bernstein, conductor), A. Watts (piano), Sony Classical 47630

Francesca da Rimini, Symphonic Fantasia, Op. 32 (1876)

> Chicago Symphony (Barrenboim, conductor), Deutsche Grammophon 44523-2

Variations on a Rococo Theme for Violoncello and Orchestra, Op. 33 (1877)

> Pittsburgh Symphony (Maazel, conductor), Yo-Yo Ma (cello), Sony Classical 48382

Violin Concerto in D Major, Op. 35 (1878)

> London Philharmonic (Barbirolli, conductor), J. Heifetz (violin), EMI Classics 64030

Overture "1812," Op. 49 (1880)

> Chicago Symphony (Abbado, conductor), Sony Classical 45939

NIKOLAI RIMSKY-KORSAKOV

Websites

http://www.geocities.com/Vienna/3606/

> Rimsky-Korsakov home page. Biography, works, and general information.

Books

Abraham, Gerald. *Rimsky-Korsakov: A Short Biography*. Ann Arbor, MI: AMS Press, 1975.

Rimsky-Korsakov, N. *My Musical Life*. Boston: Faber and Faber.

Seaman, Gerald R. *Nikolai Andreevich Rimsky-Korsakov, A Guide to Research*. NY: Garland, 1989.

Yastrebtsev, V. V. *Reminiscences of Rimsky-Korsakov*. Ed. and trans. Florence Jonas. NY: Columbia U. Press, 1985.

Recordings

Quintet for Piano, Flute, Clarinet, French Horn, and Bassoon (1876)

> Nash Ensemble, CRD 3409

The May Night (1829)

> Moscow Radio Orchestra & Radio Chorus (Golovanov, conductor), LYS 090/91

Capriccio espagnol, Op. 34 (1887)

> Berlin Philharmonic (Maazel, conductor), Deutsche Grammophon 449769-2

Symphonic Suite: *Scheherazade ("After 'A Thousand and One Nights'")*, Op. 35 (1888)

> New York Philharmonic (Bernstein, conductor), Sony Classical 47605

Le Coq d'Or (The Golden Cockerel): Introduction to the Wedding Procession) (1906–7)

> Philadelphia Orchestra (Ormandy, conductor), Sony Odyssey 39786

GUSTAV MAHLER

Websites

http://www.netaxs.com/~jgreshes/mahler/

> Mahler WWW site. Information, biography, and links.

http://www.visi.com/~mick/shrine.html

> Virtual shrine. Bulletin board for Mahler-philes.

Books

Carr, Jonathan. *Mahler: A Biography*. Woodstock, NY: Overlook Press, 1997.

Cooke, Deryck. *Gustav Mahler: An Introduction to His Music*, 2nd ed. NY: Cambridge, 1988.

de la Grange, Henry-Louis. *Gustav Mahler: Vienna: The Years of Challenge (1897–1904)*. NY: Oxford, 1995.

Mitchell, Donald. *Gustav Mahler: The Early Years*. Berkeley: U. of California Press, 1995.

_____, and Andrew Nicholson, eds. The Mahler Compendium. Clarendon: Oxford, 1999.

Recordings

SYMPHONIES

Symphony No. 1 in D Major (*Titan*) (1883–88)

   Berlin Philharmonic (Abbado, conductor), Deutsche Grammophon 431769-2

Symphony No. 4 in G Major (*Humoresque*) (1899–1901)

   Vienna Philharmonic (Walter, conductor), E. Schwarzkopf (soprano), Arkadia 767

Symphony No. 6 in A Minor ("Tragic") (1903–5)

   New York Philharmonic (Bernstein, conductor), Sony Classical 47581

VOCAL MUSIC

Songs of a Wayfarer (*Lieder eines fahrenden Gesellen*) (1883–85)

Songs on the Death of Children (*Kindertotenlieder*) (1901–4)

The Song of the Earth (*Das Lied von der Erde*) (1907–9)

   All three works:

   Halle Orchestra (Barbirolli, conductor), J. Baker (mezzo), EMI 62707

CLAUDE DEBUSSY

Websites

http://www.execpc.com/~mchadjin/debussy/

   Debussy page.

http://public.srce.hr/~fsupek/

   Musical impressions. In French and English; includes links, biography, and more.

Books

Nichols, Rogers. *The Life of Claude Debussy*. NY: Cambridge, 1998.

Parks, Richard S. *The Music of Claude Debussy*. New Haven: Yale U. Press, 1990.

Roberts, Paul. *Images: The Piano Music*. Seattle: Amadeus Press, 1996.

Recordings

Prélude à l'après-midi d'un faune (1892–94)

Pélléas et Mélisande (1893, 1898, 1901–2)

Lile National Orchestra (Deltour, conductor), Naxos 8.660047-9

Nocturnes (1892–99)

String Quartet, Op. 10 (1893)

Symphonic Suite: *La Mer* (1903–5)

Two Dances for Harp and String Orchestra (1903)

Los Angeles Chamber Orchestra (Schwarz, conductor), B. Allen (harp), EMI Classics 47520

Jeux (1912)

All three works:

Swiss Romande Orchestra (Ansermet, conductor), London 433711-2

Six epigraphes antiques (1914)

Katia and Marielle Labeque, Philips 289454771-2

RICHARD STRAUSS

Websites

http://people.unt.edu/~dmeek/rstrauss.html

Home page. Biography, links, and more.

Books

Boyden, Matthew. *Richard Strauss*. Boston: Northeastern U. Press, 1999.

Gilliam, Bryan. *Richard Strauss and His World*. Princeton, NJ: Princeton U. Press, 1992.

Kennedy, Michael. *Richard Strauss: Man, Music, Enigma*. NY: Cambridge, 1999.

_____. *Richard Strauss* (Master Musicians series). NY: Schirmer Books, 1996.

Williamson, John. *Strauss: Also Sprach Zarathustra*. NY: Cambridge, 1993.

Recordings

Don Juan, Op. 20 (1888–89)

Chicago Symphony (Barrenboim, conductor), Erato 2292-45625-2

Till Eulenspiegel's Merry Pranks, Op. 28 (1894–95)

New York Philharmonic (Bernstein, conductor), Sony Classical 47626

Thus Spake Zarathustra, Op. 30 (1895–96)

Berlin Philharmonic (von Karajan, conductor), Deutsche Grammophon 447441-2

Seattle Symphony (Schwarz, conductor), Delos 3052

Don Quixote, Op. 35 (1896–97)

Boston Symphony (Ozawa, conductor), Yo-Yo Ma (cello), Sony 39863

A Hero's Life, Op. 40 (1897–98)

Cleveland Orchestra (von Dohanyi, conductor), London 436444-2

Symphonia Domestica, Op. 53 (1902–3)

> Berlin Philharmonic (Furtwangler, conductor), Arabesque 6082

Salome (1903–5)

> Philadelphia Orchestra (Ormandy, conductor), Sony Classical 53511

Der Rosenkavalier (1909–10)

> Vienna Philharmonic/State Opera Chorus, London 425950-2

ARNOLD SCHOENBERG

Websites

http://www.primenet.com/~randols/schoenberg/schoenlinks.html

> Directory of information about Schoenberg, including links.

http://www.schoenberg.at/Default.htm

> Schoenberg Institute site (in English and German). Official site with general information.

Books

Bailey, Walter B. *Schoenberg Companion*. NY: Greenwood, 1998.

Frisch, Walter, ed. *Schoenberg and His World*. Princeton, NJ: Princeton U. Press, 1999.

Rosen, Charles. *Arnold Schoenberg*. Chicago: U. of Chicago Press, 1996.

Recordings

Transfigured Night, Op. 4 (1899)

> New York Philharmonic (Boulez, conductor), Sony Classical 48464

Gurre-Lieder (1900–1903 and 1910–11)

> Berlin Royal Symphony Orchestra, St. Hedwig's Cathedral Choir, Düsseldorf Municipal Choral Society, London 430321-2

Chamber Symphony No. 1, Op. 9 (1906)

> Chamber Orchestra of Europe (Holiger, conductor), Teldec 2292-46019-2

Pierrot lunaire, Op. 21 (1912)

> Contemporary Chamber Ensemble (Weisberg, conductor), Nonesuch 79237-2

Orchestration of Two Chorale Preludes by Bach (1922)

> Houston Symphony (Eschenbach, conductor), RCA Gold Seal 09026-68658-2

A Survivor from Warsaw, Op. 46 (1947)

> London Symphony Orchestra (Craft, conductor), Koch International Classics 7263

MAURICE RAVEL

Websites

http://www.paix.com/ravelpic.html

Biography of Ravel, plus the text of his essay "Recollections of My Lazy Childhood."

http://www.nycopera.com/education/ravel.html

NYC Opera biography. Short biographical sites.

Books

Burnett-James, David. *Ravel* (Illustrated Lives of the Composers). NY: Music Sales, 1988.

Larner, Gerald. *Maurice Ravel*. London: Phaidon, 1996.

Orenstein, Arbie. *Ravel: Man and Musician*. NY: Dover, 1991.

Recordings

ORCHESTRAL MUSIC

Alborada del gracioso (1908)

Valses nobles et sentimentales (1912)

Daphnis and Chloé: Suite #2 (1913)

Rapsodie espagnole (1919)

Le Tombeau de Couperin (1920)

La Valse (1920)

Orchestration of *Pictures at an Exhibition* by Modest Mussorgsky (1922)

New York Philharmonic (Bernstein, conductor), Sony Classical 47595

Boléro (1928)

All of these works:

Cleveland Orchestra (Boulez, conductor), Sony Classical 45842

Montreal Symphony (Dutoit, conductor), London 421458

French National Orchestra (Inbal, conductor), Denon 75001

WORKS FOR SOLO INSTRUMENT AND ORCHESTRA

Tzigane (1924)

Orchestra of Paris (Martinon, conductor) with I. Perlman (violin), EMI Classics 47725

Concerto for the Left Hand (1931)

Baltimore Symphony (Comissiona, conductor), L. Fleisher (piano), Vanguard Classics 4002

Concerto for Piano and Orchestra in G Major (1932)

Columbia Symphony (Bernstein, conductor and piano), Sony Classical 47571

CHAMBER MUSIC

String Quartet in F Major (1903)

Cleveland String Quartet, Telarc 80011

Sonatine (1905)

St. Louis Symphony (Slatkin, conductor), A. de Larrocha (piano), RCA Red Seal 09026-60985-2

Introduction and Allegro (1907)

Academy of St. Martin in the Fields, Chandos 8261

BÉLA BARTÓK

Websites

http://www.futurenet.co.uk/classicalnet/reference/composers/bartok.html

Short biography, discography, and sound files.

http://www.ultranet.com/~cwholl/bartok/timeline.html

Timeline of Bartók's life.

Books

Chalmers, Kenneth. *Bartók* (20th Century Composers). London: Phaidon, 1995.

Cooper, David. *Concerto for Orchestra*. NY: Cambridge, 1998.

Laki, Peter, ed. *Bartók and His World*. Princeton, NJ: Princeton U. Press, 1995.

Milne, Hamish. *Bartók* (Illustrated Lives of the Great Composers). NY: Music Sales, 1987.

Suchoff, Benjamin. *Concerto for Orchestra*. NY: Schirmer Books, 1995.

_____, ed. *Bartók's Essays*. Lincoln: U. of Nebraska Press, 1992.

Wilson, Paul. *The Music of Béla Bartók*. New Haven: Yale U. Press, 1992.

Recordings

Duke Bluebeard's Castle (1911, rev. 1912, 1918)

Berlin Philharmonic (Hatink, conductor), EMI Classics 56162

The Miraculous Mandarin: Suite (1918–19)

Minnesota Orchestra (Skrowaczewski, conductor), Vox Box 3015

Concerto for Piano and Orchestra No. 1 (1926)

Hungarian State Orchestra (Fischer, conductor), G. Sandor (piano), Sony Classical 45835

Concerto for Piano and Orchestra No. 2 (1930–31)

Budapest Symphony (Ligeti, conductor), J. Jando (piano), Naxos 8.5501771

Music for String Instruments, Percussion, and Celesta (1936)

Chicago Symphony (Boulez, conductor), Deutsche Grammophon 447747-2

Concerto for Violin No. 2 (1937–38)

Minneapolis Symphony (Dorati, conductor), Y. Menuhin (violin), Mercury 434350-2

Contrasts for Violin, Clarinet, and Piano (1938)

Benny Goodman (clarinet), Joseph Szigeti (violin), Béla Bartók (piano), Hungaroton 12326/31; reissued on Magic Talent 48047

Concerto for Two Pianos and Orchestra (1940)

New York Philharmonic (Bernstein, conductor), P. Entremont (piano), Sony Classical 47511

Concerto for Orchestra (1943)

>Philadelphia Orchestra (Ormandy, conductor), Sony Classical 48263

IGOR STRAVINSKY

Websites

http://www.island-of-freedom.com/STRAV.HTM

>Island of Freedom. Links and MIDI files.

http://www.geocities.com/Vienna/1807/strav.html

>Stravinsky page. Biography, works, and essays.

Books

Craft, Robert. *Chronicle of a Friendship*. Nashville: Vanderbilt U. Press, 1994.

Cross, Jonathan. *The Stravinsky Legacy*. NY: Cambridge, 1998.

Oliver, Michael. *Igor Stravinsky*. London: Phaidon, 1995.

Stravinsky, I. *An Autobiography*. NY: Norton, 1998 (reissue).

_____. *Memories and Commentaries*. Berkeley: U. of California Press, 1981.

_____, and Robert Craft. *Expositions and Developments*. Berkeley: U. of California Press, 1983.

Taruskin, Richard. *Stravinsky and the Russian Traditions*. Berkeley: U. of California Press, 1996.

Walsh, Stephen and Patrick. *The Music of Igor Stravinsky*. Oxford: Clarendon Press, 1993.

Recordings

The Nightingale (*Le Rossignol*) (1908–14)

>London Symphony (Craft, conductor), MusicMasters 01612-67184-2

The Firebird: Suite (1910, rev. 1919, 1945)

>Houston Symphony (Stokowski, conductor), EMI Classics 65207

The Rite of Spring (*Le Sacre du printemps*) (1911–13)

>Boston Symphony (Monteux, conductor), RCA Gold Seal 09026-61898-2

Petrushka (1919)

>New York Philharmonic (Mehta, conductor), Sony 358223

The Wedding (*Les Noces*) (1921–23)

>Swiss Romande Orchestra (Ansermet, conductor), London 443467-2

Octet for Wind Instruments (1923)

>Netherlands Wind Ensemble, Chandos 9488

Oedipus Rex (1927, rev. 1948)

>Saito Kenon Orchestra (Ozawa, conductor), Philips 438865-2

Concerto in D for Violin and Orchestra (1931)

>Chicago Symphony (Barenboim, conductor), I. Perlman (violin), Teldec 4059 98255 2

Perséphone for Narrator, Tenor, Chorus, and Orchestra (1933, rev. 1949)

> Orchestra of St. Lukes (Craft, conductor), MusicMasters 01612-67103-2

Jeu de Cartes (Card Game): Ballet in Three Deals (1935–37)

> Chicago Symphony (Solti, conductor), London 443775

Symphony in Three Movements (1942–45)

> Israel Philharmonic (Bernstein, conductor), Deutsche Grammophon 445338-2

Circus Polka (1942; arr. for orchestra, 1944)

> London Symphony (Tilson Thomas, conductor), RCA Red Seal 09026-68865-2

SERGEI PROKOFIEV

Websites

http://musicinfo.gold.ac.uk/music/prokofiev.html

> Prokofiev archive. Collection of archival materials at the University of London, established by Prokofiev's widow.

http://web.mit.edu/eniale/www/music/prok.html

> Elaine's Prokofiev page. Essays on the composer, with links.

Books

Gutman, David. *Sergei Prokofiev* (Illustrated Lives of the Great Composers). NY: Music Sales, 1992.

Minturn, Neil. *The Music of Sergei Prokofiev*. New Haven: Yale U. Press, 1997.

Prokofiev, S. *Soviet Diary 1927 and Other Writings*. Boston: Northeastern U. Press, 1992.

Samuel, Claude. *Prokofiev*. NY: Marion Boyars, 1999.

Recordings

ORCHESTRAL MUSIC

Sinfonietta, Op. 5/46 (1914, rev. 1929)

> Royal Scottish National Orchestra (Jarvi, conductor), Chandos 8442

Symphony No. 1 in D Major, Op. 25 (*Classical*) (1916–17)

> Berlin Philharmonic (von Karajan, conductor), Deutsche Grammophon 437253-2

Concerto No. 1 in D for Violin and Orchestra, Op. 19 (1916–17)

Concerto No. 3 in C Major for Piano and Orchestra, Op. 26 (1917–21)

> Moscow Philharmonic (Tchistiakov, conductor), E. Kissin (piano), RCA Red Seal 60051-2

Divertimento, Op. 43 (1925, 1929)

> Royal Scottish National Orchestra (Jarvi, conductor), Chandos 8728

Concerto No. 5 in G Major for Piano and Orchestra, Op. 55 (1932)

> Israel Philharmonic (Mehta, conductor), Y. Bronfman (piano), Sony Classical 52483

Concerto No. 2 in G Minor for Violin and Orchestra, Op. 63 (1935)

    Both works:

        Los Angeles Philharmonic (Salonen, conductor), C-L Lin (violin), Sony Classical 53969

        BBC Symphony (Rozhdestvensky, conductor), I. Perlman (violin), EMI Classics 47025

Symphonie Concertante in E Minor for Violoncello and Orchestra, Op. 125 (1952)

    Pittsburgh Symphony (Maazel, conductor), Yo-Yo Ma (cello), Sony Classical 48382

OTHER WORKS

The Fiery Angel (1919)

    Paris National Opera, Ades 141572

String Quartet No. 1, Op. 50 (1931)

    Emerson String Quartet, Deutsche Grammophon 431772-2

Peter and the Wolf (1936)

    Vienna State Opera Orchestra (Goossens, conductor), J. Ferrer (narrator), MCA Classics 2-9820

    Atlanta Symphony (Levi, conductor), P. Schickele (narrator), Telarc 80350

Cinderella (1946)

    London Symphony (Previn, conductor), EMI Classics 68604

DMITRI SHOSTAKOVICH

Websites

http://www.siue.edu/~aho/musov/dmitri.html

    Shostakovichiana. Articles, reviews, and commentary.

Usenet - alt.fan.shostakovich

    Chat about the controversial book *Testimony* and other issues surrounding Shostakovich's life.

Books

Fay, Laurel E. *Shostakovich: A Life*. NY: Oxford, 1999.

Ho, Allan B., and Dmitry Feofanov. *Shostavoich Reconsidered*. London: Toccata Press, 1999.

Shostakovich, D. *Testimony: The Memoirs of Dmitri Shostakovich*. Ed. Solomon Volkov. NY: Proscenium, 1999.

Wilson, Elizabeth. *Shostakovich: A Life Remembered*. Princeton, NJ: Princeton U. Press, 1995.

Recordings

ORCHESTRAL MUSIC

Symphony No. 1, Op. 10 (1924–25)

    Royal Philharmonic (Ashkenazy, conductor), London 425609-2

Symphony No. 5, Op. 47 (1937)

New York Philharmonic (Bernstein, conductor), Sony Classical 47615

Symphony No. 7, Op. 60 ("Leningrad") (1941)

NBC Symphony (Toscanini, conductor), RCA Gold Seal 60293-2

Symphony No. 10, Op. 93 (1953)

Cleveland Orchestra (von Dohnanyi, conductor), London 430844

Symphony No. 11, Op. 103 ("The Year 1905") (1957)

Houston Symphony (Stokowski, conductor), EMI Classics 65206

Concerto No. 1 for Piano, Trumpet, and Strings, Op. 35 (1933)

"Moscow Virtuosi," RCA Red Seal 60567-2

Concerto for Violin and Orchestra, Op. 77 (1947–48)

Russian State Symphony (Vedernikov, conductor), M. Fedotov (violin), Triton 17006

VOCAL WORKS

The Nose, Op. 15 (1927–28)

Not currently on disc.

Lady Macbeth of the District of Mtzensk, Op. 29 (1930–32)

London Philharmonic (Rostropovich, conductor), Ambrosian Opera Chorus, EMI Classics 49955

Song of the Forests: Oratorio for Children's Choir, Mixed Choir, Soloists, and Orchestra, Op. 81 (1940)

Moscow Philharmonic/State Boys' Choir/Yurlov Russian Choir, Russian Disc 11048

CHAMBER MUSIC

Quintet for Piano and String Quartet, Op. 57 (1940)

Moscow String Quartet, C. Orbelian (piano), Russian Disc 10031

String Quartets Nos. 4 (Op. 83, 1949) and 8 (Op. 110, 1960)

Kreutzer String Quartet, IMP 6600622

GLOSSARY

Absolute pitch. Ability to name instantly and without fail any note struck on the piano keyboard or played on an instrument. This is a rare, innate faculty, which appears in a musical child at a very early age, distinct from "relative pitch," common among all musicians, in which an interval is named in relation to a previously played note. Also known as "perfect pitch."

Accent. A stress.

Acciaccatura (It.) (äht-chäh-käh-toóräh). A note a second above, and struck with, the principal note and instantly released.

Adagio (It.) (äh-däh′jŏh). Slow, leisurely; a slow movement.

Ad libitum (Lat.) (ähd li′bi-tŭm). A direction signifying that the performer's preferred tempo or expression may be employed; that a vocal or instrumental part may be left out.

Alla breve (It.). In modern music, two beats per measure with the half note carrying the beat; also called "cut time."

Allegretto (It.) (ähl-lĕh-gret′tŏh). Quite lively; moderately fast.

Allegrissimo (It.) (ähl-lĕh-gris′sē-mŏh). Very rapidly.

Allegro (It.) (äh-lā′grŏh). Lively, brisk, rapid.

Alleluia. The Latin form of *Hallelujah!* (Praise the Lord!) as used in the Roman Catholic service.

Allemande (Fr.) (ähl-l′mahn′d), **allemanda** (It.) (ähl-lĕh-mähn′däh). A lively German dance in 3/4 time.

Andante (It.) (ähn-dähn′tĕh). Going, moving; moderately slow tempo.

Andantino (It.) (ähn-dähn-tē′nŏh). A little slower than andante, but often used as if meaning a little faster.

Antiphonal. Responsive, alternating.

Appoggiatura (It.) (ähp-pŏhd-jäh-too′räh). "Leaning" note; a grace note that takes the accent and part of the time value of the following principal note.

Arabesque. A type of fanciful pianoforte piece; ornamental passages accompanying or varying a theme.

Arco (It.). Bow. *Arco in giù*, down-bow; *arco in su*, up-bow.

Aria (It.) (ah′rē-äh). An air, song, tune, melody.

Aria da capo (It.). Three-part form of operatic aria: principal section with main theme; contrasting section with second theme and key change; elaborated repeat of principal section.

Arietta (It.) (ährē-et′täh), **ariette** (Fr.) (ah′rē-et'). A short air or song; a short aria.

Arpeggio (It.) (ar-ped′jŏh). Playing the tones of a chord in rapid, even succession.

Atonality. The absence of tonality; music in which the traditional tonal structures are abandoned and there is no key signature.

Attacca (It.). Begin what follows without pausing, or with a very short pause.

Augmentation. Doubling (or increasing) the time value of the notes of a theme or motive, often in imitative counterpoint.

Barcarole (Ger.). A vocal or instrumental piece imitating the song of the Venetian gondoliers.

Bel canto (It.) (bel kăhn'tŏh). The art of "beautiful song," as exemplified by eighteenth and nineteenth century Italian singers.

Binary. Dual; two-part.

Binary form. Movement founded on two principal themes, or divided into two distinct or contrasted sections.

Bitonality. Harmony in two different tonalities, as *C* major and *F* sharp major played simultaneously.

Bolero (Sp.). A Spanish national dance in 3/4 time and lively tempo (*allegretto*), the dancer accompanying his steps with castanets.

Bourrée (Fr.) (boo-rā'). A dance of French or Spanish origin in rapid tempo in 2/4 or 4/4 time.

Burlesque. A dramatic extravaganza, or farcical travesty of some serious subject, with more or less music.

Cacophony. A raucous conglomeration of sound.

Cadence. Rhythm; also, the close or ending of a phrase, section, or movement.

Cadenza (It.) (kăh-den'dzăh). An elaborate passage played or improvised by the solo instrument at the end of the first or last movement of a concerto.

Canon. Musical imitation in which two or more parts take up, in succession, the given subject note for note; the strictest form of musical imitation.

Cantabile (It.). "Singable"; in a singing or vocal style.

Cantata (It.) (kăhn-tah'tăh). A vocal work with instrumental accompaniment.

Canzonetta (It.), **canzonet.** A solo song or part-song; a brief instrumental piece.

Capriccio (It.). An instrumental piece of free form, distinguished by originality in harmony and rhythm; a caprice.

Castrato (It. (kăh-strah'tŏh). A castrated adult male singer with soprano or alto voice.

Celesta. Percussion instrument consisting of tuned steel bars connected to a keyboard.

Cembalo (It.) (chĕm'băh-lŏh). Harpsichord, pianoforte; in old times, a dulcimer.

Chaconne (Fr.) (shăh-kŏhn'). A Spanish dance; an instrumental set of variations over a ground bass, not over eight measures long and in slow 3/4 time.

Chamber music. Vocal or instrumental music suitable for performance in a room or small hall.

Chansonette (Fr.). A short song of a light nature.

Chorale (kŏh-rahl'). A hymn tune of the German Protestant Church, or one similar in style.

Chorus. A company of singers; a composition sung by several singers; also, the refrain of a song.

Chromatic. Relating to tones foreign to a given key (scale) or chord; opposed to diatonic.

Clavecin (Fr.). A harpsichord.

Coda (It.) (kŏh'dăh). A "tail"; hence, a passage ending a movement.

Con brio (It.). "With noise" and gusto; spiritedly.

Concertante (It.). A concert piece; a composition for two or more solo voices or instruments with accompaniment by orchestra or organ, in which each solo part is in turn brought into prominence; a composition for two or more unaccompanied solo instruments in orchestral music.

Concertino (It.). A small concerto, scored for a small ensemble; the group of soloists in a concerto grosso.

Concerto (It.) (kŏhn-chär′tŏh). An extended multi-movement composition for a solo instrument, usually with orchestra accompaniment and using (modified) sonata form.

Concerto grosso (It.) (kŏhn-chär′tŏh grô′sŏh). An instrumental composition employing a small group of solo instruments against a larger group.

Con forza (It.). With force, forcibly.

Consonance. A combination of two or more tones, harmonious and pleasing, requiring no further progression.

Contralto (It.) (kŏhn-trähl′tŏh). The deeper of the two main divisions of women's or boys' voices, the soprano being the higher; also called alto.

Contrapuntal. Pertaining to the art or practice of counterpoint.

Contrapuntist. One versed in the theory and practice of counterpoint.

Counterpoint. Polyphonic composition; the combination of two or more simultaneous melodies.

Countertenor. A male singer with an alto range.

Courante (Fr.) (koo-rähn′t), **coranto** (It.). An old French dance in 3/2 time.

Crescendo (It.) (krĕh-shen′dŏh). Swelling, increasing in loudness.

Da capo (It.). From the beginning.

Development. The working out or evolution (elaboration) of a theme by presenting it in varied melodic, harmonic, or rhythmic treatment.

Diatonic. Employing the tones of the standard major or minor scale.

Diminished-seventh chord. A chord consisting of three conjunct minor thirds, outlining a diminished seventh between the top and bottom notes.

Diminuendo (It.) (dē-mē-noo-en′dŏh). Diminishing in loudness.

Diminution. The repetition or imitation of a theme in notes of smaller time value.

Dissonance. A combination of two or more tones requiring resolution.

Divertimento (It.) (dë-vâr-tē-men′tŏh), **divertissement** (Fr.) (dē-vâr-tēs-mahn′). A light and easy piece of instrumental music.

Dodecaphonic. Using the technique of modern composition in which the basic theme contains twelve different notes.

Dolce (It.). Sweet, soft, suave; a sweet-toned organ stop.

Dolcissimo (It.). Very sweetly, softly.

Dominant. The fifth tone in the major or minor scale; a chord based on that tone.

Double stop. In violin playing, to stop two strings together, thus obtaining two-part harmony.

Duple time. Double time; the number of beats to the measure is divisible by two.

Eighth note. A note equal to one-half of the duration of a quarter note.

Embellishment. Also called a grace; a vocal or instrumental ornament not essential to the melody or harmony of a composition.

Enharmonic. Differing in notation but alike in sound.

Entr'acte (Fr.). A light instrumental composition or short ballet for performance between acts.

Exposition. The opening of a sonata movement, in which the principal themes are presented for the first time.

Falsetto. The highest of the vocal registers.

Fandango (Sp.). A lively dance in triple time, for two dancers of opposite sex, who accompany themselves with castanets or tambourine.

Fantasia (It.) (făhn-täh-zē′äh), **Fantasie** (Ger.) (făhn-tä-zē′). An improvisation; an instrumental piece with free imitation in the seventeenth to eighteenth centuries; a piece free in form and more or less fantastic in character.

Finale (It.) (fē-nah′lĕh). The last movement in a sonata or symphony.

Fioritura (It.) (fē-ŏh-**r**e-too′**r**äh). An ornamental turn, flourish, or phrase, introduced into a melody.

Flautando (It.). A direction in violin music to play near the fingerboard so as to produce a somewhat "fluty" tone.

Forlane (Fr.). A lively Italian dance in 6/8 or 6/4 time.

Forte (It.) (fôh**r**′tĕh). Loud, strong.

Fortissimo (It.) (fôh**r**-tis′sē-mŏh). Extremely loud.

Fugato (It.) (fŏŏ-gah′tŏh). "In fugue style"; a passage or movement consisting of fugal imitations not worked out as a regular fugue.

Fugue (fewg). Contrapuntal imitation wherein a theme proposed by one part is taken up equally and successively by all participating parts.

Gamelan. A typical Indonesian orchestra, variously comprised of tuned gongs, chimes, drums, flutes, chordophones, xylophones, and small cymbals.

Gavotte (Fr.). A Gavot; an old French dance in strongly marked duple time (*alla breve*), beginning on the upbeat.

Gigue (Fr.) (zhig), **giga** (It.) (jē′gäh). A jig.

Glissando (It.). A slide; a rapid scale. On bowed instruments, a flowing, unaccented execution of a passage. On the piano, a rapid scale effect obtained by sliding the thumb, or thumb and one finger, over the keys.

Glockenspiel (Ger.). A set of bells or steel bars, tuned diatonically and struck with a small hammer. Also, an organ stop having bells instead of pipes.

Grace note. A note of embellishment, usually written small.

Grandioso (It.). With grandeur; majestically, pompously, loftily.

Gregorian chant. A system of liturgical plainchant in the Christian Church, revised by Pope Gregory I for the Roman Catholic ritual.

Gruppetto or **gruppo** (It.). Formerly, a trill; now, a turn. Also, any "group" of grace notes.

Habanera (Sp.). A Cuban dance, in duple meter, characterized by dotted or syncopated rhythms.

Half note. A note one-half the value of a whole note.

Harmony. A musical combination of tones or chords; a composition's texture, as two-part or three-part harmony.

Heckelphone. A double-reed instrument somewhat misleadingly called the baritone oboe; gives out a rich, somewhat hollow sound.

Hocket, hoquet. Texture in which one voice stops and another comes in, sometimes in the middle of a word; a hiccup.

Improvisation. Offhand musical performance, extemporizing.

Interlude. An intermezzo; an instrumental strain or passage connecting the lines or stanzas of a hymn, etc.

Intermezzo (It.) (-med′zöh). A light musical entertainment alternating with the acts of the early Italian tragedies; incidental music; a short movement connecting the main divisions of a symphony.

Interval. The difference in pitch between two tones.

Inversion. The transposition of one of the notes of an interval by an octave; chord position with lowest note other than root.

Key. The series of tones forming any given major or minor scale.

Key signature. The sharps or flats at the head of the staff.

Konzertstück (Ger.). A concert piece, or a short concerto in one movement and free form.

Krebsgang (Ger.) (krĕps′gähng). Literally, "crab walk"; a retrograde motion of a given theme or passage.

Ländler (Ger.). A slow waltz of South Germany and the Tyrol (whence the French name "Tyrolienne") in 3/4 or 3/8 time.

Larghetto (It.) (lar-get′töh). The diminutive of largo, demanding a somewhat more rapid tempo.

Largo (It.) (lar′göh). Large, broad; a slow and stately movement.

Leitmotiv (Ger.) (līt′möh-tēf′). Leading motive; any striking musical motive (theme, phrase) characterizing one of the actors in a drama or an idea, emotion, or situation.

Lento (It.) (len′töh). Slow; calls for a tempo between andante and largo.

Libretto (It.) (lē-bret′töh). A "booklet"; the words of an opera, oratorio, etc.

Lydian mode. The church mode that corresponds to the scale from *F* to *F* on the white keys of the piano.

Madrigal. A vocal setting of a short lyric poem in three to eight parts.

Mediant. The third degree of the scale.

Melisma. A melodic ornament with more than one note to a syllable.

Melos (Gk.). The name bestowed by Wagner on the style of recitative employed in his later music dramas.

Meter, metre. In music, the symmetrical grouping of musical rhythms; in verse, the division into symmetrical lines.

Metronome. A double pendulum moved by clockwork and provided with a slider on a graduated scale marking beats per minute.

Minor. Latin word for "smaller," used in music in three different senses: 1. a *smaller* interval of a kind, as in minor second, minor third, minor sixth, minor seventh; 2. a key, as in *A* minor, or a scale, as in *A* minor scale; 3. a minor triad, consisting of a root, a minor third, and a perfect fifth above the root.

Minor ninth. A small interval between two notes.

Minor third. An interval of three half tones.

Minuetto (It.) (mē-noo-et′töh), **minuet**. An early French dance form.

Mode. A generic term applied to ancient Greek melodic progressions and to church scales established in the Middle Ages and codified in the system of Gregorian chant; any scalar pattern of intervals, either traditional to a culture or invented; the distinction between a major key (mode) and a minor key (mode).

Moderato (It.) (möh-dĕh-**r**ah-töh). At a moderate tempo or rate of speed.

Modulation. Passage from one key into another.

Monodrama. A dramatic or musical presentation with a single performer.

Motive, motif (Fr.). A short phrase or figure used in development or imitation.

Musette (Fr.). A small oboe; a kind of bagpipe; also, a short piece imitating this bagpipe, with a drone bass; a reed stop on the organ.

Music drama. The original description of opera as it evolved in Florence early in the seventeenth century (*dramma per musica*).

Neoclassicism. A revival, in twentieth-century compositions, of eighteenth-century (or earlier) musical precepts, exemplified by many of the post-WWI works of both Stravinsky and Schoenberg.

Neumes. Signs used in the early Middle Ages to represent tones.

Nocturne (Fr.). A piece of a dreamily romantic or sentimental character, without fixed form.

Notation. The art of representing musical tones, and their modifications, by means of written characters.

Obbligato (It.) (ŏhb-blē-gah'tŏh). A concerted (and therefore essential) instrumental part.

Oboe (Ger.) (oh-boh'ë). An orchestral instrument with very reedy and penetrating though mild tone.

Oboe d'amore (It.). Literally, "oboe of love"; an oboe that sounds a minor third below the written notation; used in many old scores, and also in some modern revivals.

Octave. A series of eight consecutive diatonic tones; the interval between the first and the eighth.

Octet. A composition for eight voices or instruments.

Opéra bouffe (Fr.), **opera buffa** (It.). Light comic opera.

Operetta (It.), **opérette** (Fr.). A "little opera"; the poem is in anything but a serious vein; music is light and lively, often interrupted by dialogue.

Oratorio (It.) (ŏh-**r**äh-tô'**r**ē-ŏh). An extended multi-movement composition for vocal solos and chorus accompanied by orchestra or organ.

Orchestration. The art of writing music for performance by an orchestra; the science of combining, in an effective manner, the instruments constituting the orchestra.

Ornament. A grace, embellishment.

Ostinato (It.). Obstinate; in music, the incessant repetition of a theme with a varying contrapuntal accompaniment.

Overtone. Harmonic tone.

Overture. A musical introduction to an opera, oratorio, etc.

Pandiatonicism. A modern term for a system of diatonic harmony making use of all seven degrees of the scale in dissonant combinations.

Partita (It.) (pa**r**-tē'tăh). A suite.

Passacaglia (It.) (păhs-säh-cahl'yah). An old Italian dance in stately movement on a ground bass of four measures.

Pastoral. A scenic cantata representing pastoral life; an instrumental piece imitating in style and instrumentation rural and idyllic scenes.

Pedal point. A tone sustained in one part to harmonies executed in the other parts.

Pentatonic scale. A five-tone scale, usually that which avoids semitonic steps by skipping the fourth and seventh degrees in major and the second and sixth in minor.

Phrase. Half of an eight-measure period. Also, any short figure or passage complete in itself and unbroken in continuity.

Phrygian mode. A church mode corresponding to the scale from *E* to *E* on the white keys of the piano.

Pianissimo (It.) (pē-äh-nēs′sē-mŏh). Very soft.

Piano (It.) (pē-ah′nŏh). Soft, softly.

Pianoforte (It.) (pē-ah′nŏh-fôr′tĕh). A stringed keyboard instrument with tones produced by hammers; a piano.

Pitch. The position of a tone in the musical scale.

Pizzicato (It.) (pit-sē-kah′tŏh). Pinched; plucked with the finger; a direction to play notes by plucking the strings.

Plagal mode. A church mode in which the final keynote is a fourth above the lowest tone of the mode.

Polka (Bohemian, *pulka*). A lively round dance in 2/4 time, originating about 1830 as a peasant dance in Bohemia.

Polonaise (Fr.) (pŏh-lŏh-näz′). A dance of Polish origin, in 3/4 time and moderate tempo.

Polyphonic. Consisting of two or more independently treated melodies; contrapuntal; capable of producing two or more tones at the same time, as the piano, harp, violin, xylophone.

Polyrhythm. The simultaneous occurrence of several different rhythms.

Polytonality. Simultaneous use of two or more different tonalities or keys.

Prelude. A musical introduction to a composition or drama.

Prestissimo (It.) (prĕh-stis′sē-mŏh). Very rapidly.

Presto (It.) (prâ′stŏh). Fast, rapid; faster than "allegro."

Program music. A class of instrumental compositions intended to represent distinct moods or phases of emotion, or to depict actual scenes or events; sometimes called "descriptive music," as opposed to "absolute music."

Progression. The advance from one tone to another (melodic) or one chord to another (harmonic).

Quarter note. One quarter of a whole note; equal to one beat in any time signature with a denominator of 4.

Quintet(te). A concerted instrumental composition for five performers; a composition, movement, or number, vocal or instrumental, in five parts; also, the performers as a group.

Range. The scale of all the tones a voice or instrument can produce, from the lowest to the highest; also called "compass."

Recapitulation. A return of the initial section of a movement in sonata form.

Recitative (res′ĭta-tēv′). Declamatory singing, free in tempo and rhythm.

Reprise (Fr.) (rŭ-prēz). A repeat; reentrance of a part or theme after a rest or pause.

Retrograde. Performing a melody backwards; a crab movement. Also, one of three standard techniques in twelve-note composition (retrograde, inversion, transposition) wherein all notes of a set are played in reverse (i.e., backward).

Retrograde inversion. A standard technique in twelve-note composition wherein all notes of a set are played in a reverse succession, which also mirrors the original set.

Rhapsody, rapsodie (Fr.) (rähp-sŏh-dē′). An instrumental fantasia on folk songs or on motives taken from primitive national music.

Ricercare (It.) (rē-châr-käh′rĕh). Instrumental composition of the sixteenth and seventeenth centuries generally characterized by imitative treatment of the theme.

Rigaudon (Fr.), **rigadoon.** A lively French dance, generally in 4/4 time, that consists of three or four reprises.

Ripieno (It.) (rēp′yä′nŏh). A part that reinforces the leading orchestral parts by doubling them or by filling in the harmony.

Ritornello (It.) (rē-to**r**-nel′lŏh), **ritornelle** (Fr.) (rē-too**r**-nel′). A repeat; in a concerto, the orchestral refrain.

Romanza (It.). A short romantic song or a solo instrumental piece.

Rondeau. A medieval French song with instrumental accompaniment, consisting of an aria and a choral refrain.

Rondo (It.) (**r**ohn′dŏh). An instrumental piece in which the leading theme is repeated, alternating with the others.

Roulade (Fr.) (roo-lähd′). A grace consisting of a run from one principal melody tone to another; a vocal or instrumental flourish.

Rubato (It.) (**r**oo-bäh′tŏh). Prolonging prominent melody tones or chords.

Saltarella, -o (It.) (sähl-täh-**r**el′häh,-lŏh). A second division in many sixteenth-century dance tunes, in triple time; an Italian dance in 3/4 or 6/8 time.

Salto (It.) (sähl′tŏh). Leap; skip or cut.

Sarabande (Fr. (säh-**r**äh′bahn′d), Ger. (säh-**r**äh-băh-n′dĕ). A dance of Spanish or Oriental origin; the slowest movement in the suite.

Scale. The series of tones that form (a) any major or minor key (*diatonic* scale) or (b) the *chromatic* scale of successive semitonic steps. Also, the compass of a voice or instrument.

Scherzando (It.) (skâr-tsähn′dŏh). In a playful, sportive, toying manner; lightly, jestingly.

Scherzo (It.) (skâr′tsŏh). A joke, jest; an instrumental piece of a light, piquant, humorous character. Also, a vivacious movement in the symphony, with strongly marked rhythm and sharp and unexpected contrasts in both rhythm and harmony; usually the third movement.

Score. A systematic arrangement of the vocal or instrumental parts of a composition on separate staves one above the other.

Semitone. A half tone; the smallest interval in the Western scale.

Serenade. An instrumental composition imitating in style an "evening song," sung by a lover before his lady's window.

Sforzando, sforzato (It.) (sfŏh**r**-tsähn′dŏh, sfŏh**r**-tsah′tŏh). A direction to perform the tone or chord with special stress, or marked and sudden emphasis.

Sinfonia (It.) (sin-fŏh-nē′äh). A symphony; an opera overture.

Singspiel (Ger.) (zing**k′**shpēl). A type of eighteenth century German opera; usually light, and characterized by spoken interludes.

Sonata (It.) (sŏh-nah′täh). An instrumental composition usually for a solo instrument or chamber ensemble, in three or four movements, contrasted in theme, tempo, meter, and mood.

Sonata form. Usually the procedure used for first movements of classical symphonies, sonatas, and chamber works; may be used for other movements as well.

Sonata-rondo form. A rondo-form movement in at least seven sections, where the central episode functions as a development section.

Sonatina (It.), **Sonatine** (Ger.). A short sonata in two or three (rarely four) movements, the first in the characteristic first-movement, i.e., sonata, form, abbreviated.

Soprano (It.). The highest class of the human voice; the female soprano, or treble, has a normal compass from c¹ to a².

Sostenuto (It.) (sŏh-stĕh-noo'tŏh). Sustained, prolonged; may also imply a tenuto, or a uniform rate of decreased speed.

Spinet (spin'et *or* spĭ-net'). An obsolete harpsichordlike instrument; a small modern piano.

Staccato (It.). Detached, separated; a style in which the notes played or sung are more or less abruptly disconnected.

Stop. That part of the organ mechanism that admits and "stops" the flow of wind into the pipes; on the violin, etc., the pressure of a finger on a string, to vary the latter's pitch; a *double stop* is when two or more strings are so pressed and sounded simultaneously; on the French horn, the partial closing of the bell by inserting the hand.

Stretto (It.) (stret'-tŏh, tăh). A division of a fugue in which subject and answer follow in such close succession as to overlap; a musical climax when thematic and rhythmic elements reach the saturation point.

String quartet. A composition for four stringed instruments, usually first and second violin, viola, and cello.

Subdominant. The tone below the dominant in a diatonic scale; the fourth degree.

Submediant. The third scale tone below the tonic; the sixth degree.

Suite (Fr.). A set or series of pieces in various (idealized) dance forms. The earlier suites have four chief divisions: the Allemande, Courante, Sarabande, and Gigue.

Supertonic. The second degree of a diatonic scale.

Symphonic poem. An extended orchestral composition which follows in its development the thread of a story or the ideas of a poem, repeating and interweaving its themes appropriately; it has no fixed form, nor has it set divisions like those of a symphony.

Symphony. An orchestral composition in from three to five distinct movements or divisions, each with its own theme(s) and development.

Syncopation. The shifting of accents from strong beat to weak beat or between beats.

Tam-tam. A large Eastern unpitched suspended gong struck with a felt-covered stick.

Tarantella (It.) (tăh-**r**ăhn-tel'lăh). A southern Italian dance in 6/8 time, the rate of speed gradually increasing; also, an instrumental piece in a very rapid tempo and bold and brilliant style.

Tema con variazioni (It.). Composition in which the principal theme is clearly and explicitly stated at the beginning and is then followed by a number of variations.

Tempo (It.) (tem'pŏh). Rate of speed, movement; time, measure.

Tempo primo (It.). At the original pace.

Ternary. Composed of, or progressing by, threes.

Ternary form. Rondo form; ABA form, such as the minuet and trio.

Tessitura (It.) (tes-sē-too'răh). The range covered by the main body of the tones of a given part, not including infrequent high or low tones.

Tetrachord. The interval of a perfect fourth; the four scale-tones contained in a perfect fourth.

Timbre (Fr.) (tă**n**'br). Tone color or quality.

Toccata (It.) (tŏhk-kah'tăh). A composition for organ or harpsichord (piano), free and bold in style.

Tonality. A cumulative concept that embraces all pertinent elements of tonal structure; a basic loyalty to tonal center.

Tone-color. Quality of tone; timbre.

Tone poem. Also called "symphonic poem"; an extended orchestral composition that follows the thread of a story or the ideas of a poem.

Tone row. The fundamental subject in a twelve-tone composition.

Tonic. The keynote of a scale; the triad on the keynote (tonic chord).

Treble. Soprano. *Treble clef:* the *G* clef.

Tremolo (It.) (trâ′mŏh-lŏh). A quivering, fluttering; in singing, an unsteady tone.

Triad. A three-note chord composed of a given tone (the root), with its third and fifth in ascending order in the scale.

Trill. The even and rapid alternation of two tones a major or minor second apart.

Triplet. A group of three equal notes performed in the time of two of like value in the established rhythm.

Tritone. The interval of three whole tones.

Tutti (It.) (too′tē). The indication in a score that the entire orchestra or chorus is to enter.

Upbeat. The raising of the hand in beating time; an unaccented part of a measure.

Variations. Transformations of a theme by means of harmonic, rhythmic, and melodic changes and embellishments.

Violoncello (It.) (vē-ŏh-lŏhn-chel′-lŏh). A four-stringed bowed instrument familiarly called the cello.

Vivace (It.) (vē-vah′chĕh). Lively, animated, brisk.

Vivacissimo (It.). Very lively, *presto.*

Vivo (It.). Lively, spiritedly, briskly.

Voice. The singing voice; used as synonym for "part."

Whole tone. A major second.

Whole-tone scale. Scale consisting only of whole tones, lacking dominant and either major or minor triads; popularized by Debussy.

Woodwind. Wind instruments that use reeds, and the flute.

INDEX

Page numbers in **boldface** indicate extensive treatments of the indexed entry (i.e., composer or composition).